THE

ENGLISHWOMAN IN RUSSIA.

Reception of the Impirial Family at a Review.

THE

ENGLISHWOMAN IN RUSSIA;

IMPRESSIONS OF THE SOCIETY AND MANNERS

OF THE

RUSSIANS AT HOME.

BY A LADY,

TEN YEARS RESIDENT IN THAT COUNTRY.

With Illustrations.

NEW YORK:
CHARLES SCRIBNER, 145 NASSAU STREET.
MDCCCLV.

W. H. TINSON, STEREOTYPER, 24 BEEKMAN STREET.
TAWS, RUSSELL & CO., PRINTERS, 26 BEEKMAN ST.

TO

HER BROTHER,

THESE PAGES ARE AFFECTIONATELY INSCRIBED BY

THE AUTHOR

PREFACE.

Without troubling the reader with any account of a sea voyage from England to Archangel, as all travels on the "vasty deep" present pretty much the same features which have been so frequently and so well described by others, I will only observe that circumstances induced me to reside for more than ten years in Russia, which I have only recently quitted.

The following pages contain a simple account of the manners, customs, and *genre de vie chez eux* of a people whose domestic habits are comparatively but little known to the English nation.

Of the truth of many of the anecdotes I can assure the reader; others I have had from good authority, and I have every reason to believe that they are veracious.

The names of persons that are inserted in the text are not those of Russian families: the Russians, like the ancient Greeks, have a termination denoting parentage; the syllables *vitch* for the masculine, and *ovna* for the feminine, are merely equivalent to the classic *ides*. Thus, Dmitri Ivanovitch, means Demetrius the son of Ivan; Cleopatra Ivanovna, Cleopatra the daughter of Ivan, &c. I have therefore betrayed none, because the surname is omitted; I have also taken the further precaution to change *one* of the names in every instance, lest my friends should incur any evil consequences from their government, which is at the present time so exceedingly suspicious, that, for the most harmless expression, the offender who made use of it would be liable to be banished to Siberia.

I trust that I have done full justice to all the amiable and *social* excellences of the Russians. Of their other qualities I beg the reader to form his own judgment. "Une nation de barbares polis," said a French gentleman, in speaking of them; but one cannot deny that they possess the *good* qualities of savages, as well as their *bad* ones. Perhaps the Muscovite character is the most difficult of any to understand; and after living for years in Russia, it is very possible not to know the Russians. They seem indeed to possess two characters, each distinguished by traits diametrically opposed to those of the other. One may be considered as their private, and the other as their public character; and I cannot pretend to the power of defining them. I have seen a Russian colonel, known for his excessive severity, who would witness unmoved the terrible infliction of the knout, perfectly unable to control his tears at the mimic sorrows of a French actress. He that is mean and dispicable in public life, is often kind, amiable, and liberal at home. He who would be merciless and oppressive to his inferiors, is frequently affectionate to his family and sincere to his friend. The lady who would be shocked to say a petulant word to an acquaintance, would not hesitate to strike her maid; and though she would be overwhelmed with grief at the distress she could *see*, she would, by her reckless extravagance, cause the severest sufferings to her serfs, and reduce them to the extremity of want, without feeling remorse.

This slight sketch of Muscovite manners having no pretension whatever to literary excellence, the writer trusts that its manner of delineation will escape criticism, and that its truthfulness will counterbalance the many faults it undoubtedly contains.

The interest at present excited by a nation with whom the English are at war has induced her to listen to several friends who have recommended her to present these written observations to the public.

CONTENTS.

CHAPTER I.

CHAPTER II.

CHAPTER III.

CHAPTER IV.

CHAPTER V.

CHAPTER VI.

CHAPTER VII.

CHAPTER VIII.

CHAPTER IX.

CHAPTER X.

CHAPTER XI.

CHAPTER XII.

CHAPTER XIII.

CHAPTER XIV.

CHAPTER XV.

CHAPTER XVI.

CHAPTER XVII.

CHAPTER XVIII.

CHAPTER XIX.

CHAPTER XX.

LIST OF ILLUSTRATIONS.

THE

ENGLISHWOMAN IN RUSSIA.

CHAPTER I.

Aspect of the Dwina—Crosses erected by the peasants—Sunset in the North—Russian boats and barks—Boatmen—Their cargoes—Solombol—Shallowness of the river—Archangel—Samoïdes—Their mode of living—A visit to their Tchume, or encampment—Reindeer and Sledges—Samoïde bridegroom—A wedding-feast—The Samoïde costume Their ideas of a Supreme Being—A keepsake—Catching a reindeer—Manner of eating—Strange custom.

"By the quarter seven" sang out the musical voice of the sailor who was engaged in heaving the lead. I hastened on deck, and found we were crossing the bar at the mouth of the Dwina. I looked around on the banks of the broad but shallow river; they were flat and marshy, abounding in brushwood and stunted firs, small birch-trees, with here and there an ash, the coral berries of which served to enliven the mass of green foliage. There were some cleared spaces, which, at a distance, with the setting sun shining full upon them, appeared like verdant lawns, but were, in fact, only sheets of morass, of which, indeed, the whole province of Archangel mainly consists. Here and there, amongst the sombre and interminable forests, I descried, far distant from every human habitation, a solitary Greek cross, erected by some pious peasant or grateful fisherman, on his escape from danger. Contrary as such are to our more spiritual creed, yet I confess that I never could gaze unmoved on the holy symbol of our faith, thus made an offering from a simple and devoted heart. Many and many a time, during my long journeys, through hundreds of versts* of the forest-land and sandy plains of Russia, have I felt cheered by this sign of a belief and church that we (because we are happily more enlightened) are too apt to condemn; yet our ancestors, to whom the Russians, in their present state, may be compared, did not find it an useless symbol to awaken sentiments of religion in their breasts.

The evening was beautiful, and the sunset magnificent! the sky and river, the forest, the distant ocean, and the whole landscape, seemed wrapped in a flood of crimson light; every object was as perfectly distinct as in broad day, the only difference being that there was no shadow. The native barks glided calmly past us, strange-looking things, gaudily painted with red, black, and yellow designs, on the rough wood. Their clumsy vanes resembled those on Chinese junks; some were in the form of a serpent, others in that of a fish, a griffin, or some fabulous creature or other, and decorated with streamers of scarlet, all fluttering in the slight breeze that swept down the stream. The heavy one-masted vessels, with their large square sails, reminded me of the old pictures of the Saxon boats some thousand years ago. The boatmen are fine-looking men, of the real and pure Russian race, uncontaminated by a mixture with the Tartar blood, of which there are so many traces in the middle provinces. Their dress is picturesque, and serves greatly to enliven the landscape; their gaily-coloured shirts show off to much advantage their sturdy forms; their costume, their manly beards, fair complexions, and

* A verst is about five furlongs. A verst and a half, with the addition of six yards makes a mile.

light flaxen hair, might cause us almost to imagine that we were gazing on the men of Hengist and Horsa, who lived years and years ago ; they were singing a monotonous and sad yet pleasing air, as they walked to and fro the whole length of their bark, propelling it with their long poles through the shallow part of the river. Their cargoes consist of articles of which the odour is not savoury, such as tallow, sheepskins, and hides in the raw state : evil awaits the nose of him who stands to leeward.

I landed at Solombol, which is the port of Archangel, as vessels of any considerable burthen cannot proceed so far up the river as the city, on account of the shallowness of the water.

Archangel, although the capital of the province, and the chief port in the north of Russia, by no means answers the expectations of a foreigner who has seen it only in the large letters printed on a map : it was (for it has since been burnt down) a long straggling street of dismal-looking wooden houses, mostly painted dark gray or black, with the window-frames and doors of a staring white ; the only buildings that were tolerable were (as is commonly the case in Russian provincial towns) the government offices, the gymnasium, and the churches. A more wretched place dignified by the name of *city* it is impossible to conceive ; but we comforted ourselves with the reflection that we should not remain long in it, a few months at the utmost, when we calculated upon bidding adieu to it for ever ; we therefore determined upon philosophically bearing all the *désagrémens* which we might be condemned to meet with. It contained, at the time of which I am writing, about twenty-five thousand inhabitants, including the foreigners (mostly Germans) and the government authorities, but it was a miserably dull place. In the winter, which lasts about eight months of the year, we lived almost entirely by candle-light, our monotonous existence only varied by a drive in the sledge, or a stiff formal ball at the governor's of the province, in which our sole amusement was staring at the uniforms, bowing to his excellency, and eating bonbons. I do not know how we should have got through the dreary winter, had we not been cheered by the consolation that summer would come some time or other, though it appeared distant enough in the prospect as we walked out during the short hour of daylight, or rather twilight, in the middle of the day; when we made ourselves still more miserable by continually conversing of the daisied meadows and shady lanes, the forest glades and pretty flowers of "merry England." Not only did we suffer terribly from *mal de pays*, that extreme longing for home that amounts to a malady, but the heaviness of the sky seemed to affect the mind, as if the excessive cold had frozen all one's energies. It appeared of no use struggling against our misfortunes, so we resigned ourselves to our fate, and made ourselves as miserable as possible. There was only one circumstance that afforded us amusement, and that was the visits that some savages, a tribe of Samoïdes, occasionally paid to the town; they came from their desolate country to avoid the rigour of their cold climate, by passing a few months in the *more genial south;* indeed, comparatively speaking, Archangel was a Naples for them, since here the mercury freezes *only sometimes.* These poor people, who belong to the Esquimaux race, as some suppose, are natives of a wild, inhospitable land, stretching far away to the north: little is known of their manners and customs *chez eux;* but when they descend from their high latitudes, and make the neighbourhood of the Russian towns their asylum for the winter, they seem to live in much the same way as the gipsies do, pitching their tents wherever they may find it most convenient to do so, and obtaining their subsistence either by the sale of reindeer, of coats made of their skins, and of curious dolls dressed in their own fashion, or by begging.

We determined to pay our uncivilized friends a visit. There were but 18° of Reaumur; the sky was beautifully blue; the sun was so kind as to cast a few odd rays upon the wide plains of snow, stretching like the waves of the ocean towards the utmost verge of the horizon ; there had been foggy weather during several preceding days, and the particles had frozen so thickly on the trees, that the branches, hanging pendant with the weight, had an indescribably beautiful effect, like gigantic white ostrich-feathers, or as if the forest had been transformed by sudden enchantment into glittering crystals ; in fact, it was the very beau idéal of an hyperborean landscape.

Above a dozen sledges, each drawn by four reindeer, with either a male or female Samoïde acting as coachman, were waiting in the yard. After making a good provision wherewith to treat our new friends, and taking every precaution against the severity of the cold, by wrapping ourselves well up in warm fur cloaks and skins, we each took possession of the particular equipage allotted to us. These little reindeer sledges are very slightly constructed to enable them to pass lightly and swiftly over the deep snow ; in form they are something like a small boat, supported by a frail-looking frame ; they are not meant apparently for a sociable people, for there is only sufficient space for one person in each, besides the driver, who sits sideways in front, and who guides his pretty-looking team by means of a long pole. The men and women are so much alike among this people, that we were obliged to ask which were masculine and which feminine. A lady-driver fell to my share, who beat the deer rather more than the others, and seemed in a particularly bad humour ; perhaps, as the Samoïde wives are really and truly subjected to their husbands in all things, being treated like slaves and drudges, her good man might have caused her to feel his power and physical strength before setting out, for, when he spoke to her, it seemed very much as if he were swearing ; so in turn SHE was unmerciful to the weaker creatures in *her* power. Our road lay across the river ; the "Tchume," or encampment, being at about eighteen versts on the further side; the country was covered with snow, so that nothing but an immense white plain, varied here and there by a dark stunted fir, formed the landscape in whichever direction we turned our eyes; to strangers the novelty of such a scene is agreeable, but one soon wearies of its monotony. The sun had not long risen, it being nearly noon; so we had the advantage of daylight, a rather scarce commodity in the dreary north; and as we were all inclined to be unusually gay, we made the desolate wilderness quite re-echo with our laughter, to which the clicking of the reindeer's hoofs formed a kind of castanet accompaniment. Nature has provided them with widely-spreading feet, which prevent them from sinking in the snow, and which open and shut with a smart snapping noise at every step they take. In about an hour and a half we reached the Tchume, to which we had been guided by the long wreaths of gray smoke ascending from the midst of the pine forest. Here we found a little colony encamped; there were four tents constructed in a very simple fashion, in form very like a sugar-loaf; the frame was composed of fir-poles joined by some means at the top, the whole being thickly covered and lined with reindeer-skins. We peeped into one of the tents: in a space of about eight feet in diameter were huddled together men, women, babies, and dogs, somewhat in the mode of herrings in a cask: at first the smoke was so thick that I could discern nothing distinctly; but I soon perceived that the inmates were well wrapped up in furs; their greatest enjoyment seemed to consist in getting as warm as circumstances permitted. In a small sledge filled with the softest skins was a diminutive baby; I should think it could not have been more than a few weeks old; its pretty face (for it *was* pretty although a Samoïde) was half covered with its fur wrappings; its bright black eyes and Lilliputian features made it look like an Indian doll. The rigour of their climate does not, it seems, congeal the tender sympathies of the human heart, for its mother fondled it with the greatest affection and pride ; she was much delighted with the notice her infant attracted, and, although she did not understand a word we uttered, yet she gathered from smiles and signs, the freemasonry of nature, that we admired her baby, and she was pleased and grateful. We made her a little present for its sake, and then went to visit the other tents ; we found them all constructed on the same plan.

There were a great many men and women belonging to the tribe ; their dress was curious ; the men's was composed of a long gown, called a militza, furnished with a hood lined with fur ; the whole consisted of prepared reindeer-skins sewed together with the tendons and sinews of the animal ; the leg-coverings were a kind of boot, which, being much lengthened, served for other garments as well ; they were striped white and brown, the former being the under fur of the deer, the latter the upper ; they were neatly stitched together, and formed, I should imagine, a very effective protection from the climate. The ladies' dress differed in many respects from that of their lords and masters, inasmuch as it was much finer, which may cause the malicious to remark that the same vanity reigns in the female heart in every race and clime alike : it consisted in a kind of gown very much ornamented ; across the shoulders there were alternate brown and white stripes ; from the waist downwards it was further decorated with pieces of black and red cloth, so arranged that at a distance it had in some measure the appearance of a plaid petticoat ; indeed, an odd idea struck me, that perhaps the tartan was derived from the originally savage dress of the ancient Scotch and other Celtic nations : the whole garment was finished by a deep fringe formed of the long hair of the reindeer's beard ; the hood was separate from the dress, and furnished with lappets to cover the poll of the neck. As for the rest of their attire, it was precisely similar to that of the men. In regard to their persons, the descriptions that have been given of the Esquimaux are equally applicable to the Samoïdes; indeed they are apparently of the same family. They have a language peculiar to themselves, but many speak Russian, and some of our party got up quite an agreeable conversation with them. They informed us, among other things, that they had been to a grand wedding some time previous: the bridegroom, it appears, was, according to their ideas, the richest man they had ever heard of; he had countless herds of reindeer, and militzas without number; but, as the most convincing proof of his boundless wealth, we were assured that he gave so much strong waters on the occasion, that everybody became so drunk that they could not move. I do not recollect this happy man's name, or whether the bride was young and beautiful; doubtless they will both be celebrated in the ballads of their native land, and be the theme of wonder and admiration to their countrymen for future generations.

Most of these nomads have been baptized into the Russian Church; but a gentleman assured me that they paid very little respect to its forms and ceremonies; and he mentioned a circumstance that would seem to indicate that they had a much higher sense of the Supreme Being than the besotted serfs of Russia possess. It appears that he and another gentleman had paid one of the tribes a visit, when one of the men asked him if he were a Russian? On being answered in the negative, he showed him some pictures of saints, hidden under some skins in the tent, and, pointing to them with disdain, he exclaimed, "See! these are Russian gods, but ours (raising his hand towards heaven) is greater; He lives up there."

These savages can also feel, and deeply too, much gratitude for kindness. I remember when I had the pleasure of meeting, in Petersburg, M. M——, of the Académie des Sciences, who was sent some years ago to explore the northern regions of Asia, he showed me some little figures carved out of a mammoth-bone ; they represented the chief of a tribe and his wife in their national dress, and had been given to him by the former as a token of his gratitude and esteem. He had heard that amongst other people it was frequently the custom to give your own portrait to a friend, and therefore he had begged M. M—— to accept his. M. M—— also related to us the extreme kindness he had experienced from some of those uncivilized races. He was attacked with a severe fever, owing to the great privations and fatigue he was obliged to undergo in his long and trackless journey across almost endless forests and morasses, sometimes floundering through stagnant water up to his horse's saddle-girths, at others pursuing his dreary path with dog-sledges in intensely cold weather, without provisions or places of shelter. At last he was so very ill that he did not expect to live, and begged to remain behind. His companions dug a kind of cave for him out of the snow, and left him to his fate ; he remained unconscious he knew not how long. When he recovered his senses, the fever had left him, but his hunger drove him almost mad ; there seemed nothing but death before him, and, after having in his extremity devoured his gloves and other articles of clothing, he gave up all hope, and resigned himself to the terrible fate of perishing of starvation in the wilderness ; but when all chance seemed lost, he suddenly heard a dog bark ; he crawled out of the cave ; a tribe of these Samoïdes was passing by, they caught sight of him and stopped ; some of them advanced and gazed on him with astonishment ; his famished state filled them with compassion ; they placed him in a sledge, and conveyed him to their tents, where they tended him with the greatest care and kindness until he was enabled to rejoin the "expedition," to which they conducted him. He rewarded them with various trinkets highly prized among these people ;

but such actions are above recompence. We had not come unprovided with refreshments suited to their taste, and we produced sundry bottles of strong brandy, at the sight of which their eyes sparkled with unwonted fires ; each of them was regaled with a tumblerful, which both ladies and gentlemen tossed off as if it were water, and which had no other effect than that of rendering them in infinite good humour with us and each other. Even my sulky driver and her husband felt its power, and drank a loving cup together, whilst they began to chatter much faster, and became very obliging. The daylight was disappearing, so we began to think of returning home. Being desirous of tasting what a haunch of reindeer was like (which, by the by, we afterwards found to be extremely tough), we resolved upon purchasing a fine young animal, which, "all unconscious of his fate," was quietly grazing amid the numerous herd scattered around. At our request the proprietor seized a lasso, and with unerring aim caught the poor little creature by the horns, and, gradually hauling in the rope, sailor's fashion, soon brought it near enough for another Samoïde to lay it dead at his feet with a blow on its forehead. This gave us an opportunity of witnessing a truly savage feast ; for, no sooner were they given to understand that we only required the haunches, than they tore out the heart and liver, and immediately devoured them warm and raw ! I remarked that they had a very peculiar manner of eating ; they held the meat with their teeth, and, like the Abyssinians, cut off each mouthful with their knife so close to their nose, that we were in constant fear lest its tip would be sliced off at the same time. I was assured that amongst these people, when the father becomes too old to follow his usual pursuits, it is the duty of the eldest son to kill and bury him ! Just before I quitted Russia I met a chief and chieftainess of the Samoïdes, wearing an ornamental head-dress of gold, and was told that they were staying at the winter-palace, but for what purpose I could not learn ; perhaps the government means to make use of them in the present war ; if so, it can only be in America against the Indians of the British territories.

The cold greatly increased ; before we reached home the snow fell so thickly that we could scarcely see ; indeed it seemed more like cutting particles of ice than aught else, so that we were glad to find ourselves again under a warm roof.

CHAPTER II.

Wedding of a Starosta's daughter—Politeness of the host—The guests—The bride—Bridal etiquette—Description of the bride's dress—The bridegroom—The hospitality shown—The amusements of the guests—Improvised songs—The bridegroom's riches—Demeanour of the company—Dance of the peasant women—Dance of the men—National songs.

There was but little to vary the monotony of our life in Archangel, as we had but few opportunities of seeing much of the Russians. In the spring we decided upon paying a visit to Vologda, having received an invitation to pass a few weeks at the house of the governor of the province. In the midst of our busy preparations for the journey, the Starosta, or head man of a neighbouring village came to beg the honour of our company at a festival which he proposed giving the next day to celebrate his daughter's marriage. We accepted the invitation, and the following morning hired a boat to take us across the Dwina, for the village was situated on the opposite bank at the distance of about eight versts. We had no sooner landed than the bride's father, the Starosta himself, came out to welcome us, and to conduct us to his house. A great number of people were assembled in front of it ; they all seemed very merry, and were gaily dressed in their best attire : we passed through the crowd and followed our host, who ushered us with many profound bows into the best apartment, where we found a numerous company already arrived. There were at the least thirty women, all in their national dress, seated in straight rows round the room ; most of them had their arms crossed, and remained almost motionless ; their gaily coloured silks and showy head-dresses had a very striking effect. The bride herself, a pretty-looking girl of about seventeen, was seated at the upper end of the room with the bridegroom at her right hand. A table, covered with a white cloth and tastefully ornamented with festoons of artificial flowers and bows of pink ribbon, was before them, on which was placed the wedding-cake made of flower and honey, with almonds on the top ; several dishes of sweetmeats, preserves, and dried fruits were arranged around it. It was, as I was told, the etiquette for the bride not to speak even to the bridegroom ; but we went up to her, and offered our congratulations, which they both acknowledged by a graceful inclination. The Starosta ordered chairs to be placed just opposite the table, and begged us to be seated, so we had a good opportunity of examining and admiring the bride's dress. It was composed of a coiffure nearly a foot high, somewhat resembling a brimless hat ; it was of gold, enriched with pearls and fastened on by a knot of gold tissue behind, which was edged with lace ; her ears were decorated with handsome rings, and round her neck were innumerable rows of pearls. I expressed a doubt as to whether they were real ; but I was assured they were so, only they were defective in form. Her casackan or jacket was of gold cloth, with a border of pearl embroidery, the sleeves of cambric, short and very full, tied up with blue ribbon and finished by a lace trimming ; the skirt of her dress was of crimson flowered silk, having a gold border nearly a foot deep, with gold buttons up the front. This is the national costume, but it varies in different provinces, and is not equally rich. But then the Starosta was well to do ; he was not only the head man of the village, but he had shops of his own in Moscow and in St. Petersburg. I noticed that the bride's fingers were loaded with rings ; indeed she seemed to have on all the finery the whole family could muster. As for the bridegroom, he was a good-looking young man of twenty-two or so, and very respectably dressed in the costume of a shopkeeper, which consists of a long blue coat called a caftan, closely buttoned up to the throat. We were presented with tea, coffee, wine, bonbons, cakes, fruit, &c., in succession, all of which we were expected to partake of, or the hosts would think themselves slighted, and their hospitality insulted. The spoons I remarked were of Tula work, and had the appearance of being of gold, but were in reality of silver-gilt, with arabesque flowers all over them, which they say are done with some kind of acid : I believe the secret is not known out of Russia.

All the Russian women assembled at this festival were of the upper class of petty shopkeepers or farmers, and they were dressed in the same costume as the bride, with perhaps fewer ornaments. During the whole time we were in the room their amusement consisted in singing, one after the other, in a low kind of chant, songs improvised in honour of the occasion, all the rest of the company sitting silent and motionless as statues. As soon as one had exhausted all her available talent on the subject, another took it up and gave us her ideas upon it. According to one, the bride was too young to be married : she wondered how her mother could part with her, and thought she should have kept her at home for a long time yet. Another seemed to think she was doing perfectly right to marry her daughter, after bringing her up so prudently, and making her so clever in household affairs. A third wished to settle the matter entirely by praising the bridegroom ; "he was so gay of heart, he loved his bride so well." His possessions, it appears, were worth having, and enough to tempt a village-maid ; for "he had plenty of cows, pigs, and horses ;" and as the climax to all these advantages of estates real and personal, she assured us, "that he could take his wife to church in a droshsky !" The whole of the guests remained quite silent, listening with a serious face to the songs ; there was no laughing or chatting ; each kept her seat and preserved such intense gravity all the time, that they evidently considered matrimony as no joke after all, and not in the least amusing. Were I malicious, I would remark that they had every one of them been married themselves. After we had remained a reasonable time in the company of the young couple, we went outside to see the guests assembled in front of the house ; there we found several women dancing a wearisome kind of dance, if such it might be called, which consisted in merely walking to and fro in pairs placed one behind the other in a long line. They moved forwards and then backwards to a monotonous singsong kind of air ; on advancing, the first two changed places with the last couple, and so on in succession. The amusement seemed to afford them intense delight, and so fond are they of it that they keep it up for hours together. On the opposite side of the yard the men were having a ball amongst themselves; their performance was more entertaining, and we laughed heartily at a comic pas de deux by a couple of young men, who capered about in a very diverting manner. Another peasant danced a solo in a very good style. After the dancing the men sang us some national airs ; each took the hand or leant on the shoulder of his neighbour, "in order to unite the tones," as they said. We thanked them for their entertainment, and re-entered the house to take our leave of the good Starosta and his family, when we again expressed our wishes for their happiness, but we were not allowed to depart until we had drunk their health in a glass of champagne, a wine which the Russians give upon all extraordinary occasions. As were stepping into the boat the peasants gave us a parting cheer, and far away, when the village was quite lost to our view in the distance, we heard their wild voices still singing in chorus their beautiful national airs in honour of the young Russian bride.

CHAPTER III.

Travellers in Russia—False impressions—Civilization in the Czar's dominions—Public roads—Morasses and forests—The Vologda road—Wretched horses—Rough roads—The crown peasants—Aspect of the villages—Civilization of the *people*—Vanity of the Russians—Provincial towns—The churches—The postmasters—The yemstchicks, or drivers—Personal appearance of the peasantry—Their costumes—Crossing the Dwina—Pleasing scene—Village burying-ground.

The generality of travellers in Russia, at least of those tourists who have obliged the world with 'Winters in St. Petersburg' and 'Journeys to Moscow,' containing the most flourishing accounts of the state of the roads, the high civilization, the rapid strides to excellence, &c., of the Czar's dominions, are unfortunately limited to a class who, having a few months' leisure, and being desirous of change, take the voyage to Russia as one promising more novelty than the hackneyed roads of France and Switzerland. Their ordinary plan is, to take the steamer to St. Petersburg, and after a stay of a short time take a "run" to Moscow, whence they return in time for the "boat," and hasten back at the rate of ten or twelve knots an hour, carrying away with them the most erroneous and false ideas of the real state of things, the mere surface of which they have scarcely had time to skim. Had they remained a few years among the Russians, not living, as the most part of the English do, in little colonies by themselves, but mixing with the people, and had they travelled a few thousand miles over the cross-country roads, they would soon have had "the gilding taken off the ginger-bread" of Muscovite civilization. In fact, the excessive exterior polish always reminded me of a woman with her face painted, who hopes by factitious bloom on her cheeks to hide her ugliness. Moscow and St. Petersburg are certainly fine cities; the former may be regarded as the true Russian capital, the latter is merely a handsome imitation of other European great towns. Having seen them, the stranger has seen all that is civilized in the empire. In illustration of what I have said, I may remark that, excepting the chaussée from the western to the inland capital, and from the former to Warsaw, there are really no roads; those fine macadamised highways so much lauded by travellers, and deservedly so, extend but a few miles beyond the towns: farther on the route lies through immense plains of sand, endless morasses, and interminable forests in the north, and steppes in the south, across which the post-road has been cut; but this post-road scarcely deserves the name, for, generally, it is merely a cleared space cut through the woods, with boughs of trees laid down here and there where there are spots that would be otherwise impassable. There is little enough to vary the monotony of the journey; the miserable villages with their wretched inhabitants scarcely serve to enliven the scene.

The whole of the distance between Archangel and Vologda, comprising several hundred miles, with the exception of the two pretty towns Vycavajai and Velsk, is composed of those desolate features which, indeed, characterise nearly all the north of Russia. Sometimes we had to be dragged through sand so deep that our carriage-wheels sank a foot or two, and the eight ragged-looking brutes—they were scarcely worthy of the name of horses—would suddenly stand stock still, and thus confess their utter inability to fulfil their engagement of taking us to the next post-station. Whenever this happened, there was nothing for it but to descend from the carriage in order to lighten the weight, and to stand patiently until some peasants had been procured from a neighbouring village, who, by the aid of poles inserted between the spokes of the wheels, and by loud barbarous cries, aroused the energies of our gallant team to make further efforts and extricate us from this dilemma. After the usual number of Slavo Bogens (thank God) had been uttered by the wild-looking, long-bearded boors, and after being again seated comfortably, with every reason for congratulating ourselves that we were progressing, although at a snail's pace, perhaps I would be tempted to take a little nap, being convinced that I should lose nothing of the prospect, for I might be pretty sure of seeing the same endless forests of fir if I were to awake the next day. With this assurance I begin to nod, and, perhaps, by some unaccountable delusion am dreaming of the smooth highways and green hedges of merry England, when bump we come against something, the shock giving me such a rap on the head that it effectually dispels all visions and fantasies. I look out and find we are splashing gaily through a morass which hides in its bosom sly stones and stocks, and which seems as interminable as the sandy plains from which we have just escaped, and of which we shall have many repetitions before the journey is over. Of course, as every one knows, there are no inns on the cross-roads, and places whereat to rest at night are altogether unknown. Even on the great chaussées it is better to travel day and night and remain in the carriage, for he must be a bold man who would be willing to face the vermin of all kinds, even for a single night, in a way-side hotel. The better class of Russian travellers know well how they are peopled, and avoid them accordingly. As for the lower class, they are too much accustomed to such company to care in the least. A Russian lady whom I know once spoke to her peasants on the subject of cleanliness, and especially concerning the vermin. Their reply would have done honour to a Gentoo: "Ah, Sudarina, it is a *sin to kill them, because God has given them to us!*"

The post-station is generally kept by a government official: a samovar or tea-urn can be obtained from him, for the use of which he expects a few copecks ; and this, with the addition of black bread and salt, is all that can be procured during the whole route : it is therefore absolutely necessary to provide oneself with everything that is needful, such as bread, meat, tea, &c., and in very long journeys a cooking apparatus. If the traveller does not take spoons, cups, and plates, let him be very careful to wash those he finds at the station, or he may swallow some little animal and transgress the Gentoo laws, besides which entire confidence cannot be placed in the mode of their being purified. I remember taking tea at a certain monastery. There were many ladies and gentlemen at the abbot's party ; and, to make it more pleasant, his reverence proposed our adjourning to a summer-house in the garden to eat ices. The young monks or novices were to act as servitors, and they stood behind some bushes near the place where we sat. I confess my relish for the refreshment was somewhat taken away when I saw them lick the spoons and wipe them : I could not warn my friends, but I took good care not to make use of them myself. But in regard to travelling in Russia, I am sure that those who have done so in the summer time will well remember the miserable nights passed *en route*, the myriads of mosquitoes, rising like a brown cloud from the marshy grounds, allowing no rest, to which the excessive heat formed no agreeable addition. In Archangel the English sailors suffered so dreadfully from the bites of these insects that they were frequently obliged to go to the hospital : they used to declare that "it was worse than in the West Indies." The winter journeys, notwithstanding the extreme cold, are infinitely more pleasant.

The people at the post-stations are generally civil, and are much obliged for a small gratuity. As for the poor yemstchicks or drivers, they are overcome with gratitude at a trifling present of a few copecks at the end of each post

I remarked that the inhabitants of the village belonging to the crown, through which we passed, appeared more comfortably lodged and far more at their ease than those who were the property of private landowners : perhaps their less degraded look was owing to their enjoying upon the whole more freedom than those who are ground down to the dust by the tyranny of the petty noblesse. The crown peasants pay a poll-tax to the Emperor.

Some of the villages were in a most wretched condition, the houses dirty and dilapidated, without windows, and having only a little trap-door just large enough for a man to peep through, which shuts at pleasure to exclude the cold. Indeed the log-huts of the Russian peasants are very little better than the wigwams of the Red Indians, although sometimes the exterior is more ornamented. The inhabitants live in much the same manner as they did centuries before Peter the Great's reign. The *people* have not made a single forward step in the march of intellect, of which the admirers of Russia so madly rave. Scores of the Russians of the upper classes, I have heard, say the same thing, notwithstanding their own vanity, which so blinds their eyes that they imagine that by imitating the exterior polish of the French—although omitting the solid enlightenments of that nation—they have really become civilized, and many, I verily believe, think that they have even surpassed them. Perhaps the Czar would have done more towards the advancement of his people, and have benefited the cause of civilization more, had he spent his money in forming roads throughout his empire, and made the means of communication easier between the various towns, instead of playing the game of chess in Turkey, and sinking such enormous sums in the marshes of the Danube.

A short time since the Grand-Duke Alexander, the heir apparent to the throne, was at a banquet, when some one was remarking on the great advantage it would be to the country when the railway was finished between St. Petersburg and Warsaw. His Imperial Highness replied that it would be so indeed, but that his Majesty, being engaged in war with the Turks, was obliged to employ the money intended for its construction in defraying the expenses of the army. When we were passing through Poland, I noticed that the works had been entirely suspended. *A propos* of this subject I may mention that, when the railway between St. Petersburg and Moscow was nearly finished, orders came that it was to be ready on a certain day, as the Imperial family were to visit the latter city, and proposed going thither by train. There were several miles of it entirely unconstructed, but, to obey orders, they patched them up in the best way they could, and laid the rails down so that the waggons might pass over them. The most wonderful thing was that some fatal accident did not happen. The Emperor, of course, knew nothing about it, or perhaps he would not exactly have liked to risk *his own* life, and those of his court, on the Moscow railroad. We were staying near the spot at the time. So badly arranged was this road at first, that, when we went to St. Petersburg by it, we were kept thirty-six hours in the midst of the Valdai hills, in twenty-eight degrees of cold (Réamur), without anything to eat or drink. Some of the third-class passengers were obliged to be brought into the first-class waggons, lest they should be frozen to death ; and a poor peasant-woman's child died in her arms from the dreadful severity of the weather. Some of the passengers (one of them an officer in the army) fainted ; and all this was through the negligence of the authorities. So many complaints were made that it is now well managed and the conductors are very civil.

The description of one provincial town in Russia is applicable to almost every other. The most remarkable buildings are the churches and monasteries, the domes and cupolas of which are painted green, gilt, or of dark blue, with golden stars sprinkled over them, each dome and minaret being surmounted by a glittering cross standing on a crescent; the gymnasium, or government school for young gentlemen; barracks (a *sine quâ non*), and a post-office: these, with a few good houses, and many mere wooden huts, similar to those in the villages, make the substance of a country town, up to the very barriers of which the interminable forests form the suburbs. We changed horses and driver at every station; the postmasters are bound to have horses in readiness for all travellers furnished with a padarosjnai or government *feuille de route.* They very often make a little money by suddenly losing their memory regarding the horses at their disposal, as they only recover it again at the sight of a small piece of silver, which serves wonderfully to recal to their mind's eye the vision of sundry rough nags in the fields at the back. It is but just to them to say that the apparition of a military uniform possesses the same magic influence.

The life the poor yemstchicks lead must be miserable in the extreme: any complaint lodged against them is pretty sure of procuring them a good beating; and I have seen the conductors or guards of the mail-coach thrash them unmercifully with the sword, or give them such blows on the ears with the post-horn as to make one feel sick at heart to think that any human being was obliged to endure so great an indignity, and that without the hope of redress. The mode in which they live I can compare to nothing but to that of dogs. Wherever we stopped at night on our summer's journeys we were almost in danger of stumbling over the bodies of these poor people; for all the space in front of the station was crowded with what at first sight I really thought were heaps of brown skins on the bare ground, but which I soon perceived were yemstchicks, all in readiness to be hired by the next travellers who might be passing. When a carriage arrived, they would suddenly start into life and draw lots amongst themselves as to who should take the turn: he on whom the lot fell immediately fetched the horses and mounted; the rest threw themselves on the ground and instantly returned to their slumber, so exactly like a number of animals that it was painful to see them. In the winter-time they sleep in cribs something like a horse's manger, with a little hay or straw. "Our peasants," said a Russian to me, "are nothing but brutes; the only argument with them is blows, for that is all they can understand." Is this, then, the land in which civilization has made her abode, and whose wonderful advance in the path of wisdom is to form an era in the records of the human race? Surely those who are under this delusion can have but very little idea how small an amount of civilization exists beyond Moscow and St. Petersburg, or they must have been too ready to believe the boastings of the Russians and the flourishing accounts of superficial travellers.

A Russian village is generally composed of a long row of wooden houses on each side of the post-road, with usually a line of birch-trees in front. Some of the well-to-do peasants, or those amongst them who are the most ingenious, have the eaves of their cottages ornamented in a very pretty manner with a kind of border of so light and elegant a description that it may be compared to wooden lace; the windows, where there are any, are decorated in the same manner. At the entrance of the villages we generally saw painted on the same board the number of men and cows contained in each; the fair sex were not thought *worth the trouble* of being enumerated.

As to the inhabitants, they are true children of the soil; the men have something fine in their appearance; they wear a loose shirt fastened around the waist. In some of the villages through which we passed a few of the men had boots on, but the greater part had only leggings bound round with thongs, sandal-fashion; their feet were furnished with shoes of a kind of basket-work, made of strips of the birch-tree. The women had on a kind of coarse chemise with full sleeves, and over that the national dress, the sarafane, which was generally of common blue or red cotton, having no boddice, but kept on the shoulder by a band of the same. The married ones wore a handkerchief tied round the head in a peculiar manner ; most of the girls had their hair formed into a long plait hanging down their back ; the children ran about at play almost in a state of nature, having on only a short shirt with open sleeves. Nearly every house in the villages was furnished with a kind of settee outside, where in the evening we frequently saw groups of the peasants sitting to have a chat or sing together the national airs, of which they are very fond. During our journey we had to pass several rivers on rafts, which were dragged to the opposite bank by means of ropes. We had to cross a very rapid branch of the northern Dwina, which had been much increased by the melting of the snow. Here we were very nearly drowned, for, the carriage being too heavy for the raft, it began to sink when in the middle of the stream ; but fortunately, through the great exertions used by the peasants, we at last reached the shore. We continued to follow the course of the Dwina for more than fifty miles. I do not know anything that gives a more dreary idea of a country than the sight of a broad and silent river, whose unbroken surface reflects no human habitation as far as the eye can reach, not a single bark to ruffle the mysterious stillness of the waters, nor any living thing to awaken the echoes of those dismal forests of pine, which stretch far away to the verge of the horizon, and seem an impenetrable bar to the advance of civilization.

Such is the aspect of the Dwina and its dark, untrodden shores ; yet, in coming to a very broad part of the river we were greatly delighted by a scene which, like many others—we know not why or wherefore—became indelibly impressed on the mind, a pleasing and vivid picture of the past. The scene of which I speak may seem in description not to be worthy of remark, nor perhaps would it have appeared remarkable to us had we not previously passed so many monotonous days. In a bend of the river, at the confluence of several smaller streams that empty themselves into the Dwina, we suddenly came to a considerable elevation rising abruptly from the water. The sun had just set, but his parting rays still illumined the beautiful gilt cross surmounting a small church which crowned the height above us ; the lamps were already lighted and gleamed through its long narrow windows, and borne on the calm summer breeze came the voices of the monks and choristers singing the magnificent responses of the Greco-Russian Church. It was a saints'-day, and the people from the neighbouring village, dressed in their gayest and best attire, were hastening up the paths in groups of twos and threes ; others were crossing the stream in boats ; but all were intent upon worshipping the heavenly Father of All in his holy place.

A little farther on we passed the burying-ground of the village. Most of the graves were marked by a rudely constructed cross in wood, but some of these were so old and broken that little of their original form remained.

CHAPER IV.

Vologda: its inhabitants—A Polish lady—Treatment of the Poles—Russian ladies: their politeness—Peter the Great's civilization—Slavery: its effects on the character—Conversation—Card-playing—A princess—Poverty—Filthy households—Equal division of property—Cause of poverty—An old gambler.

Vologda is a pretty town, but we did not prolong our stay in it beyond a few weeks, being desirous of returning to Archangel to make our preparations for proceeding to St. Petersburg. There is nothing very remarkable in the place. We made several acquaintances among the Germans, Russians, and Poles, of whom the inhabitants chiefly consist; among the latter was a most amiable Polish lady, who, together with her husband, had been banished thither for some political offence. I shall never forget the pride and exultation with which she presented her son, a lad of about ten years old, saying "that he could not speak a word of Russian," and that she took every care to prevent him from learning the hated accents of the Muscovite. It was then that I learnt that it was a general custom of the government to banish into the interior of Russia those Poles who were suspected or convicted of minor political faults, the more grave crimes being punished by an exile into Siberia. I have since met with those Polish offenders in many places, and I must say that, as far as it has been in my power to ascertain the fact, they have been well and kindly received even at the Governor's table, nor would any one imagine that their stay in the place was compulsory. It is now ten years since I first went to Russia, and I have resided there until the last three months, not living like a stranger in the land, but in the closest intimacy with Russian families, and I willingly bear witness to their general hospitality and kindness of heart, not towards the rich alone, for a well-educated person, let his circumstances be what they may, is always well received. The ladies are most amiable and polite; they are, however, often accused of want of sincerity, but, in my opinion, unjustly so. We are too apt to judge foreigners by ourselves, and think that they ought not to utter sentiments that they do not feel; but the fact is, what they mean only as expressions of every-day civility, we translate literally into those of regard, and hence our false estimate of their character. A Russian lady will say, on your being introduced, "that she is delighted at having the advantage of your acquaintance," "that she has much esteem for you," and so on; all of which is only very kindly meant to put you at your ease, and prevent you from being *gênée* in her house; but, in regard to real worth and goodness of heart, she is by no means deficient. In a thousand instances I have remarked acts of benevolence and charity that would do honour to the name of Russian, and serve to counterbalance grave faults and errors with which unfortunately they are mingled. Such must be expected in a nation on whom civilization was thrust at the sword's point; and perhaps Peter the Great did his country more harm than good by obliging them to adopt the similitude of a state that ought gradually to be acquired. No civilization can be truly solid unless it be reached step by step through the weary road of experience. Gilt frames have all the *appearance* of gold; but scrape off the exterior, and nothing but worthless wood is underneath. One does not build a house without first laying the foundation, nor does a child run before it learns to walk! The *people* of Russia would very likely have been more advanced in the real essentials of a civilized state if Peter had never obliged them to wear short-skirted coats, and their wives to appear in public unveiled. In the summer-gardens in St. Petersburg a walk is still shown, up and down which the half-savage Czar obliged the Russian ladies to promenade with their faces uncovered, whilst a regiment of soldiers was drawn up on each side. To do them justice, they soon learned to profit by the lesson, and have gone infinitely further than their instructor *could* have intended them to do. The immoral conduct and the inconceivable want of delicacy of many of the ladies of rank cannot fail to have a very unfavourable influence on others below them, especially as the court is regarded as the criterion of what is right. Were I to relate the almost incredible actions of many of the titled dames, I fear I should be accused of falsehood, but I am happy to say there are some noble exceptions ; indeed, I have had the pleasure of knowing many who are an ornament and a pattern to their sex. The state of slavery, which is so disgraceful to an European nation, must also greatly influence the domestic character of the ladies, for, being surrounded by so many menials always at hand, it must induce habits of indolence ; and "idleness," as is well known, "is the parent of many vices." Many of the ladies never do any work, and are almost ignorant of the use of the needle. "Why should I sew, when I have others to do it for me ?" is a common question. The absence of the necessity of being employed, and the want of mental resources, drive them to pass their existence in reclining on the sofa and reading some silly French romance when alone, or to the card-table when in company. There is really no conversation in Russia, unless the ridiculous compliments and inanities of a drawing-room be dignified as such ; the ladies generally discuss the price and quality of their acquaintances' dress. "Where did you get that charming mantle ?" "From France." "O, indeed ; ah ! now I see it could only be made in Paris." "How much did you give an arsheen for your dress ?" &c. Such are the efforts of the Russian ladies' ideas. The remainder of the evening is made up of flirting, eating bonbons, and *jouant aux petits jeux* for the unmarried. As for the married, they sit down to cards and play the coquette with some friend near, or make remarks on the personal appearance of their acquaintances :—"I saw Madame Vasiliwitch yesterday—how old she is looking!" "It is your turn to deal, madame." "How much the princess paints! she puts on so much white! I think an old lady *ought* to rouge, but really she uses too much." "You have made a miss-deal." "Madame Beck is separated from her husband; she is going to sue for a divorce." "Well, it is lucky she and her husband are Germans, for if he had been a Russian she would never get it." "How old is she?" "O, she must be forty at the least." Such is a sample of the conversation at a soirée; nor are the subjects on which the gentlemen converse one whit more intellectual. "Que voulez-vous?" said a nobleman one evening—"que voulez-vous? on ne peut parler la politique, et il n'y a rien à faire que de jouer aux cartes;" and it is certain that the dread of being everywhere within hearing of some government spy must be a disagreeable check on conversation. It is astonishing how much the absence of political discussion influences the amount of information current in society, or how much freedom of speech contributes to intelligence; any one who has lived in Russia can bear witness to this fact. When we were near the frontiers of Prussia, some French and German gentlemen got into the railway carriage, and began conversing on the present state of Europe. One of the latter remained quiet for a few minutes, and then said, "My friends, listen: we shall in less than an hour have quitted the territories of Russia: until we do so, let us be silent, for how do we know who may be within hearing?" The others acquiesced in the justice of the proposition, and not until we reached Myslowitz did they give any further expression to their thoughts.

But to return to the Russian ladies. I remember I once went to call on the Princess O——ff: she was of very good family, but extremely poor, yet of course she could not do without a carriage, horses, a footman, and maid-servants, but the state of dirt and misery in which she lived would disgust almost a beggar amongst us. A very filthy lacquey, in livery, the facings of which were scarcely visible, so discoloured were they with long use, ushered me through a room, quite as dirty as himself, to a second apartment, in which was seated the princess. She was at breakfast, it being twelve o'clock. The abominable filthy room, her equally disgusting attire, and the super-dirtiness of a miserable little maid who brought her some rusks, made me almost afraid to take a seat on the chair placed for me. She very politely requested me to partake of her refreshment, which I as politely declined : but imagine, gentle reader, how infinitely I was disgusted when she took up a piece of paper from the table, spat in it, and then replaced it near the bread she was eating ! She begged me to come and see her again, as she assured me she was very fond of the English : I need not say that I did not repeat my visit. Candidly speaking, this was the only instance I met of such an extremely filthy ménage ; therefore, I hope it formed a rare exception. I must, however, say that, in St. Petersburg, I once called at a house where the footman who opened the door presented so dirty an appearance that I would not enter it, and therefore cannot say whether it was his own fault or that of his master. In order to give an example of the state of moral feeling in the country, I will narrate a little incident that occurred one evening at the house of a lady of very high rank : a Madame ——, the wife of a governor of a large province, was present ; and Prince T——koi, who had been ordered to join his regiment, had come to take leave of his friends : to my astonishment, Madame —— burst into a violent flood of tears, and "refused to be comforted," when she bid him adieu. On my inquiring why she was so affected, the prince being no relation of hers, I was informed that, "poor thing ! she was so deeply in love with him that she was unable *maîtriser son émotion.*" I ventured to remark that it was rather disagreeable to her husband that she should make so public a display of her preference for another. For my pains I was told that I had no heart, and that, like all the English, I was quite destitute of feeling. I *do* believe that not a lady was there present who did not regard her as quite a martyr of sensibility.

Many of the noblesse are extremely poor ; indeed it is almost a wonder how they can exist. A great cause of their indigence is the equal division of the family estates among all the children. M. M——ff, a gentleman belonging to one of the most ancient houses in Russia—indeed, he used to boast of his descent from Rurick, the founder of the empire—often bitterly lamented the subdivision of the property. "My father," said he, "had eight children ; he was possessed of a fortune of four thousand slaves, a very handsome estate ; when he died, we each had five hundred as our share ; I have four sons and a daughter, among whom my patrimony must be again subdivided ; if they marry, they must be very poor, and if they have families, still more so ; by this means, my descendants will eventually become mere beggars." Another common cause of their poverty is their propensity for gambling, which ruins many. One day an old gentleman called on Madame P——ska, a lady with whom I was well acquainted in St. Petersburg ; he came to borrow a few rubles, which she kindly gave him. On his leaving the room, I begged to know what had thus reduced him. "Ah ! poor man," said my friend, "think how unfortunate he has been ; he once possessed fourteen thousand slaves, and he lost them all at cards." I said I was sorry that a man of his years should have rendered himself miserable by such a vice. "How old do you think him ?" asked my friend. "Oh, sixty at the least." "Sixty !" answered she, "he is past eighty, only he wears a wig, paints his eyebrows, and rouges to make himself look younger." Wretched old man! he died soon after I saw him, on his return from a card-party; he was found lifeless on his bed, and did not leave a single rûble to defray the expenses of his interment.

CHAPTER V.

Our journey—Kabitkas—Russian custom—Endless forests and morasses—Desolation of the country—Musical yemstchick—Scarcity of inhabitants—Criminals: their aspect—A bad mother—Monastery of Seea—Visit to the abbot—The church—A saint's shrine—Peasants—Change in the scenery—Accidents—The driver—A contented veteran—Love of country—Soldiers' songs—Russian melodies—Yemstchick's gratitude—Another driver: his prospects in life—Beautiful effect—Ladinapol—Schlusselberg—A village inn in Russia.

After our return to Archangel we had to wait there some weeks, until the winter roads had become sufficiently hard to render sledge travelling pleasant. We procured a kabitka—a kind of Russian vehicle much resembling a large cradle on slides—bought a mattress to fit into it, and provided ourselves with enough provisions for our long journey, such as frozen fowls, soups, &c., which we were to thaw at the different stations. As it was quite unsafe to traverse roads so unfrequented alone, we agreed to join a party of Russians and Germans who were going to visit the capital. It was arranged that our kabitka was to precede those of our acquaintances, as we were strangers to the country. On the morning of our departure we assembled at a house belonging to one of our acquaintances: a great many friends had met there in order to see us set out, and to bid us God speed on the journey. We seated ourselves, conformably to the Russian custom, a few moments in silence: champagne was handed round to drink to our success; the whole company then arose, and assembled at the gate to see us comfortably seated in our sledges; some of them even escorted us beyond the barriers of the town before they would bid us adieu; nor was it without regret on our side that we took leave of those kind-hearted people, whom in all probability we should never see again.

Once fairly on our journey, we found ourselves surrounded by those dreary forests and boundless morasses (now hidden by the deep snow) of which we had so recently had so much experience. I do not know whether this wild region is not more agreeable in the winter-season, as then its barrenness is concealed. It is not an exaggeration to say that four-fifths of the northern portions of Russia consist of the sandy plains and marshy forest-land I have already described, but, in the winter, it matters little what lies under the frozen snow.

From Archangel to St. Petersburg we passed hundreds of versts of this description of country. In these districts utter desolation reigns, scarcely a living thing is seen ; even the birds have deserted them, and have flown to the neighbourhood of the towns, to find there the food their native woods can no longer afford them. A solitary wolf or fox may occasionally be descried, either skulking among the bushes or sitting watchfully by the wayside, in faint hopes, perhaps, of some weary horse being left on the road to die and to become the victim of the hungry droves now lying perdus in the forest depths, and only scared from the traveller's path by the tinkling of the bell attached to the sledge. No other sound breaks the weary silence but the yell of the yemstchick inciting his team to greater speed, or his wild voice chanting forth the songs of the people, which echo far away through those melancholy forests, and only serve to awaken the heart to a still greater sense of the utter desolation around. Yet Nature is always grand, and perhaps never more so than in the wilderness.

No inhabitants dwell in these tracts, with the exception of the few poor peasants whose huts surround the government post-stations ; it is a rare occurrence indeed to meet a human being, and for hours one travels on, and the only sign of being in a civilized country is the wooden cross, gray with age, placed here and there by the wayside. Several times on the journey we met gangs of wretched criminals, heavily chained, and escorted by soldiers, whose duty it is to conduct them from station to station. Along the roads in Russia the traveller may remark small brick houses, placed at intervals of about twenty or twenty-five versts; these are the places at which these gangs rest on their way to Siberia. One of these miserable escorts was standing still as we were changing horses, which gave us the opportunity of examining their countenances. Features more debased or expressions more frightful it is impossible to conceive. Crime and every evil thought seemed to have deprived them almost of even the traces of human beings; I shuddered as I gazed on them. Among the convicts was a woman with a face, if possible, more horrible than that of the men; she had a child with her, a poor little thing of scarcely five years old, that was suffering dreadfully from the hooping-cough; instead of treating it with kindness and compassion, its wicked mother was treating it unmercifully, until even the men, her companions in crime, brutalized though they were, called out shame on her, and begged her to desist. I never felt so convinced that punishment was justly deserved as in the case of this wretched woman.

At the distance of about fifty-five or sixty versts from Archangel we came to a monastery at a place called Seea; it was surrounded by woods and lakes, which, in the summer-time, must have a very pretty effect. For a Russian building, it was quite an ancient one, and was erected before Peter the Great's reign: it was the sanctuary to which that monarch often retired to perform his devotions. Like most monasteries in the empire, it was surrounded by a wall, having a curiously dovetailed top with towers at each corner pierced with loopholes. One of the gentlemen, who was acquainted with the abbot, proposed to us to pay him a visit; we all of course willingly assented, and turned out of the post-road for the purpose. Half a verst brought us to the gates: on ringing a bell, one of the holy brothers appeared, who to our disappointment informed us that the Father (for such they designate their superior) was ill and asleep, but offered to awake him if he wished; we thanked him, but begged that the abbot's slumbers should not be disturbed on our account, and requested the monk to express our great regret at his superior's indisposition, with good wishes for his recovery. The monk, seeing us about to depart, entreated us to take some little refreshment in the refectory: on our declining, he asked us if we would not like to see the shrine of their patron, St. Anthony, whose body was interred in their church. We accepted his offer, and followed him into the cathedral, which, like all Greek places of worship, was filled with pictures of the innumerable saints of their calendar, and wretchedly-painted scripture-pieces. Having walked round the interior of the building, and examined the very curious lamps hung before several of the images, we were led to a shrine quite brilliant with lighted tapers and oil, and here our guide pointed with evident pride to a full-length likeness of the saint placed on the top of a long box that covered his mortal remains. Above it was a wretched daub of Virgin and a Child, which he triumphantly informed us was the holy man's own work. Although there was nothing to admire in it, we saw that it would give him pleasure to express our satisfaction, and therefore did not fail to do so: we also made the offering of a piece of silver to the church, which seemed to raise us immensely in the good monk's estimation. After thanking him for the trouble, we left the monastery of St. Anthony just as a party of the peasantry from a village close by, dressed in their best clothes, with smooth hair and well-combed beards, were reverently ascending the steps, bent on asking the prayers of the respected superior for the success of the ensuing harvest.

Having traversed about four hundred versts, we came to the

town of Kargapol; it contains nothing remarkable, and is composed of wooden houses, as usual. From this place the scenery began to show a little variety. We had no longer to complain of those monotonous plains of which we were so thoroughly weary: the country now became diversified by hills and valleys; sometimes we were rapidly galloping up a declivity (for the Russians drive at the top of the horse's speed up a hill), at others we were gliding along the edge of a precipice. One of the horses slipped aside, and by so doing broke his thigh bone; the poor yemstchick cried most bitterly, saying that his master would beat him almost to death. We were so grieved at his misfortune that we made up a little subscription for him, which afforded him some consolation, and, I dare say, served to comfort him under the correction. As for our unlucky steed, we were obliged to leave him behind on the snow; and doubtless, in a few hours, his carcase had furnished an unwonted feast to the prowling wolves with which the forests around were infested. During the next post, we were doomed to meet with more misfortunes, for our yemstchick drove us so near to the edge of the road that he turned us both out into the midst of an enormous snow-drift. I really thought we should be smothered, for the kabitka rolled right over upon us; being half-buried in the snow was disagreeable enough, but to have pillows, mattress, portmanteaux, and a whole shower of small etcetera, with which our sledge was filled, upon our backs, rendering it impossible for us to move, was even worse. The other kabitkas had by this time come up, and great inquiries were made for our yemstchick, who had unaccountably disappeared; presently a voice was heard, whose smothered tones seemed to come somewhere from under ground, and to our horror we found that he was just under us, and that the kabitka had jammed him deeply into the snow, so that he could not get out. To raise the sledge was the first thing to be done, and with the aid of the other yemstchicks, we were extricated from our dilemma: our coachman was pulled out of the snow. We expected to find him half dead, or at least with some bones broken; he, however, merely shook himself, just as a dog does on coming out of the water, and jumped upon his seat as if nothing had happened. Our friends, finding that we were neither of us hurt, enjoyed a hearty laugh at our expense: I make no doubt that we cut a sorry figure. As for our yemstchick, he was ready to go down on his knees to ask our forgiveness. He begged to know if we were bruised at all; being answered in the negative, he repeatedly crossed himself, and thanked God for our sakes, and perhaps for his own too. We were glad enough to get into the sledge and drive on, to escape the jokes with which our friends assailed us. Our yemstchick had been a soldier, he said, and boasted of having served the Czar in every government in his dominions; but now that his time was out, he had turned post-driver. He told us that the last province he had been in was Podolia, of which he gave the most flourishing accounts.

"But," said I, "why did you not remain, when, as you say, your prospects were so good, and the country so delightful?"

"Ah! Matutchka, how was it possible? I thought of my native village far away in the north. I was always longing to see the snow and pine-forests again, which made me so miserable that I asked for my discharge; and, as I had served the required term, here I am."

"But how did you return from so great a distance? Did the government send you back?"

"Not at all, Barishna! I walked all the way."

"What! fifteen hundred versts?"

"Yes, to be sure; that is nothing."

"But I suppose you live comfortably here. You have a little pension, I dare say?"

"Pension! no, only the officers ever get that, and they only when they are wounded. But as for being well off, slavo Bogen! we live as our neighbors do. I have a wife and two children; we get plenty of black bread and salt, and very often stchie. What else could we wish for?"

It was really something agreeable to hear that even this poor man could feel attachment for his miserable village of log-huts, situated, doubtless, in the midst of some dreary morass in this obscure corner of the earth. My reflections on the wonderful affections everywhere felt for the scenes in which childhood has been passed were interrupted by the driver asking if we would like to hear some of the songs the soldiers used to sing on the march. On our assenting, he began in a full, deep-toned tenor, awakening all the echoes of the surrounding forests. The burthen of his song was concerning some country belle who danced so elegantly that even the Czar himself came to see her performance. According to all accounts, the hearts of the village-swains were all sore with being so much in love with her; but she settled the matter by choosing a happy fellow named Ivan, whose felicity, we were assured, was inconceivable. This love does not appear to have been entirely disinterested, for there followed a long list of the bride's trousseau. She had a *crasnoi sarafane*, or red gown, and was further endowed with some pillows and a counterpane; added to which she was the richest bride in the whole village. The air was pretty, and, like most Russian melodies, in the minor key; the whole was terminated by the peculiar scream which finishes each cadence. We were so amused by our yemstchick that we were quite sorry when we arrived at the station. Notwithstanding his *mal-adresse* in overturning us, we made him a present, which was so much more than he expected, that he was overpowered with gratitude, and crossed himself many times in wishing us a prosperous journey.

He was succeeded by a merry little fellow, who entertained us by giving us a confidential tableau of his prospects in life.

He began by informing us that he was going to be married, and that he was so much in love he could get no rest night or day; that his intended bride's name was Katrina; she was seventeen and he was twenty-one, and "Please God, they should soon be as happy as they need be." He also volunteered a song, the subject of which was a soldier's daughter who had fallen in love with the major of the regiment; but, it appears, her case was a hopeless one, as he was going to wed another.

Night had now closed in, and for the first time during our journey the full moon shone in all her splendour upon the scene; during the previous days the sky had been much clouded, and occasional falls of snow had prevented our remarking a most beautiful effect produced by the shadow of the trees on the pure glittering plains beneath. I can compare it to nothing but a mezzo-tinto drawing, only infinitely more defined. There was not a breath of air to stir the branches of the lofty pines interlaced over our heads; a mysterious silence seemed to pervade the very atmosphere we breathed; it was excessively cold, and the moon lighted up the clear sky with such brilliancy, that we could easily read a moderately-sized print; the snow at the same time glittered and sparkled like millions of diamonds strewn in our path, and clung to the sombre foliage of the forest like gems of the purest water on sable plumes. Yes, truly, even this barren land possesses beauty and loveliness. One who has travelled through a night such as this will never forget the impression left on his mind by so splendid a scene, and will cease to wonder at the attachment of the barbarian serfs to their isolated villages.

The next day we reached Ladinapol, an insignificant place. The extensive lake of Ladoga not being sufficiently frozen to make it safe for us to cross it in our sledges, we continued our route by the post-road. We passed the small river Swere, and soon came to the town of Ladoga on the Volkof; from thence we proceeded to Schlusselberg, on the lake which formerly belonged to Sweden, and of which Peter the Great deprived her. It was in the castle of this place that his son was confined.

Once during our journey we were tempted to see what a village-inn was like, for after travelling eight days and nights we felt so thoroughly worn out by fatigue, that we thought any place in which we could rest a little would be welcome; we therefore asked our yemstchick if there were no house of entertainment at the neighbouring hamlet. "Ay, surely," replied he, "there is a very good tavern for travellers at the other end of the village."

"Then drive on, pray, my good fellow, and let us be there as quickly as possible."

"Horro sha Barishna !"

Crack went his whip, and our steeds, having a vision of hay near at hand, were tempted to stretch their legs into a real gallop; we, in the meanwhile, had the *douce illusion* of thinking that we should soon have a smoking samovar on the table and a few hours' repose. Alas! how our hopes were disappointed! Our kabitka suddenly drew up at a miserable-looking peasant's isba, half tumbling down, from the foundation having sunk a foot or two on one side. The yemstchick rapped at the door, which was opened by a dirty, long-bearded old fellow, who seemed to have had quite enough whisky to make him perfectly stupid. When we at last succeeded in making him understand what our wishes were, he said that he had a room in which we could very well pass the night. Our Russian acquaintance begged us to alight, which we did in the faint hope of finding the interior better than the exterior would lead us to suppose. Our host thereupon threw open the door of an apartment, on the floor of which, some dozen or two of peasants in their sheepskins, men, women, and children, were huddled promiscuously on the bare boards. The heat and stench were intolerable; one look was sufficient. I and my friend hastened back to the kabitka, nor did we heed the repeated assurance of the worthy landlord that we could sleep very well on the table! Our compagnons de voyage, however, had the courage to pass the night somewhere in the house; we ladies preferred the refuge of our kabitka, which was drawn under an open shed that served as a stable as well. Our slumbers were somewhat disturbed by the horses' noses sniffing at us several times during the night, attracted, I suppose, by the hay placed at the bottom of our sledge. According to the accounts our friends gave of the manner in which they had passed the time, we had, notwithstanding this annoyance, every reason to congratulate ourselves on having given the preference to the stable.

There is a chaussée from Schlusselberg to St. Petersburg; so the remainder of our journey was easily enough accomplished, nor did we observe anything more that was worthy of remark excepting the very wretched state of the villages belonging to the Count Sherrematief, in the neighbourhood of the capital, which we thought were a perfect disgrace to one who is considered the richest nobleman in the empire.

THE ALEXANDER COLUMN AND WAR OFFICE. PAGE 59.

CHAPTER VI.

Appearance of the capital—The public buildings—The statue of Peter—The quays—The lighting of the streets—The shops and shopmen—A bargain—The dwornicks: their wretched life—Tea-taverns: the company assembled—The itinerant merchants—Cossacks—Circassians: their fidelity—The soldiers of the line—Shameful treatment—The butitchnick—A sad occurrence—Winter aspect—The Nevsky perspective—Costumes—A drowning man—Police Regulations—Number of murders—A poor man's funeral—Funeral cortège of a prince—Effect of twilight—Convicts—The Metropolitan—The Emperor—Police regulations on salutations—The Kazane Church.

I WAS greatly disappointed with my first view of St. Petersburg. From the extraordinary accounts I had so often read of its magnificence, I was certainly led to expect something infinitely more grand. A drive of half an hour enables the stranger to pass through all the best parts of the city. It is true that in one tableau are assembled a number of splendid buildings, such as few capitals afford ; but if within the same space were collected all the finest public buildings in London, with all the advantages of the great extent of ground and clear atmosphere, enabling the visitor to obtain an unobstructed view of their various beauties, it would be easy to guess which would present the most imposing appearance ; added to which, it must be recollected that the edifices in St. Petersburg are for the most part only of brick and stucco. That this assemblage of all that is splendid in the city gives at first sight a magnificent *ensemble*, I do not deny ; but, like everything Russian, the showy façade only hides what is mean behind. In the same tableau we see the admiralty, on a line with which is the Winter Palace itself, facing the War-office ; in the intermediate space stands the Alexander Column, with the bronze angel on the top, whose head is bowed in adoration, and who bears a golden cross in his arms. In the large square of the Admiralty stands the celebrated statue of the Czar Peter, on the left hand of which is the ministerial and judicial department. Behind the statue is the Isaac Church, not yet finished, a heavy-looking building of dark granite, with gilt dome and crosses, and four ridiculous-looking little towers, one at each corner. Some affirm that the dome and cupolas are covered with thin sheets of pure gold, of the thickness of a ducat ; but this is quite a mistake ; they are only trebly gilt. The interior is in an unfinished state, but it will be much ornamented with rich mosaics ; and it is for this cathedral that the pictures and statues are intended which formed the cargo of the vessel that so cleverly escaped a few weeks ago being seized by the allied cruisers. On the bank of the Neva, opposite to this edifice, are the University and the Academy of Fine Arts, the latter a large and handsome square building. There is one really fine street in the city : it is called the Nevsky-Perspective, which as far as the Anitchkin bridge presents a splendid appearance, but at the other extremity degenerates into miserable dwellings, some of them of wood. The objects that attracted my attention the most were the granite quays with which the Neva and the canals are bordered, and which must have cost incalculable trouble, and an immense expenditure, both of treasure and human life, in their construction. The pavement in St. Petersburg is absolutely abominable, and only two or three streets are lighted with gas ; the remainder still retain the almost heathen obscurity of oil. *A propos* of these same oil-lamps : I was told by a Russian gentleman that the police authorities in the capital find them immensely to their advantage ; for by lighting two wicks instead of three, which greatly economizes the light and oil, and putting down the extra one to their own account, they manage to make a handsome profit by the end of the year ; and this will serve to show how, even in the merest trifles, the government is at the mercy of the *employés*.

All the *best* shops in St. Petersburg are kept by foreigners ; articles of clothing are very dear, especially those imported, which I was informed was mainly caused by the very great duty imposed on them, and by the unwise restrictions of the government. The *Russian* shops are almost all confined to the Gostinoi Dwor, a kind of bazaar, situated in the centre of the town. It is a square building, surrrounded by a piazza, and contains an immense number of warehouses. We never passed through it without being reminded of the London " 'prentices " in Walter Scott's 'Nigel,' who formerly in Cheapside saluted the passers by with "What do ye lack ?" Just the very same thing may be heard in Moscow and St. Petersburg ; for at the door of each shop either the master or a servant takes his station, and endeavours to draw the stranger's attention to his goods : "What do you wish, Sudarina ? beautiful ribbons, laces, collars, handkerchiefs ?"

Another calls out, "Warm boots, shoes, slippers !" A third assails one with "Fine bonnets of the newest fashion ; velvet, silk, satin, whatever you wish !" A fourth with "Brooches, rings, scissors, knives (real English), bracelets," &c., &c. All this is pronounced with inconceivable volubility, which, at the first hearing, seems to be some interminable word peculiarly Russian. The shops that strike a foreigner most forcibly are those filled with pictures of the saints, household gods, and crosses. Here a St. Anthony or St. Serge, a Virgin and Child, or a Catherine, as the purchaser may require, can be bought at any price, from sixpence to fifty guineas. These portraits are highly ornamented with an immense quantity of gold and pearls, or tinsel, according to the sum the buyer may wish to give for his patron and guardian angel, and make a glittering show in the warehouse.

Having arrived at the shop to which the stranger has been directed, the purchase is made somewhat in this fashion :—

Lady. "I wish, if you please, to look at some French ribbons."

Shopman. "Horro sha, Sudarina" (very well, lady). The shopman takes down a box, the contents of which are undeniably Russian manufacture.

L. "These are not French—I want *French* ribbons."

S. "These are *real* French : they are from Paris."

L. "No, I am sure they are not."

S. (After again most energetically repeating his assertion) "Well ! how much do you want ?"

L. "Show me the ribbons, and then I will tell you."

S. "How many arsheens did you say ?"

L. "Show me the French ribbons."

The shopman unblushingly puts back the box which he has so recently declared contained the real article, and takes down another, which is filled with ribbons really of French fabrication.

L. "How much is this an arsheen ?"

S. (With a most graceful inclination) "Seventy copecks."

L. "Seventy copecks ! Why the price is only fifty, and that is all I will give you."

S. (Quite indignant) "Fifty ! they cost us more than that ; you shall have it for sixty-five."

L. "Fifty."

S. "Bosja moia ! No ! I can't think of fifty—say sixty."

L. "Not a copeck more than fifty."

S. "By Heaven ! I can't sell it for that price ; you shall have it for fifty-five."

L. "Will you take fifty or not ?"

S. "I can't indeed." (He shuts up the box and puts it back into its place.) "You shall have it for fifty-three."

The purchaser refuses to be cheated of even three copecks an arsheen, and walks out of the shop ; she has perhaps gone half-a-dozen yards, when the shopkeeper's voice is heard calling out, "Barishna, Barishna ! come back, if you please !"

L. "Not a copeck more than fifty."

S. (Having persuaded her to re-enter the warehouse, says in a confidential manner) "You shall have it for fifty-one."

L. "I said fifty, and I will give you no more."

S. "Well ! say fifty and a half !"

L. "If you don't like to take what I said, I will go to the next shop."

S. (Finding that his customer will *not* be cheated) "Horro sha, Mosjna ! well, you may have it ; how much do you want ?"

L. "Six arsheens." He proceeds to measure the ribbon, and she takes out her purse, and gives him, perhaps, a five-rouble note to change. The shopkeeper's hopes of cheating begin to revive at the sight of the note, for he can't find the amount of the balance due to his customer by two or three copecks.

L. "You must give me three copecks more ; this is not right."

S. (With a very low bow), "Isvenete veno vat, I beg your pardon, I am in fault." The remaining three copecks are slowly produced, and the customer at last walks away with her ribbon. In this senseless manner do the Russian shopkeepers waste their own time and that of the purchaser. One would think that the minutes thus lost would be of more value than the consideration of the profit of a few copecks more.

Every house in Russia has a kind of out-of-door servant, called a Dwornick, who may be considered as the real police of the country, for it is he that guards the establishment from thieves, &c. His duties are of a very varied description ; he attends to the state of the yard, sees that the roof is free from snow, brings the water from the river, and is at every one's call night and day. Their place is no sinecure, poor fellows! and I never could find out when they had time to sleep; for in addition to all that they have to do during the day, they watch over the house at night, and from seven in the evening until the same hour the ensuing morning they are obliged by the law to sit outside of the gate, to keep a look-out for all comers. Theirs must be a very hard life; yet, to do them justice, they seemed gay enough in the long summer evenings; many a time have I heard them tinkling on their balaika, or triangular guitar, and humming the wild airs of their native village, hours after I have retired to rest. In the winter, however, it must be dreadful to be obliged to remain so many hours exposed to the intense cold of a northern climate. In all their sorrows tea and votku (a kind of Russian whisky made from rye) seem alternately to be the consolation of the lower classes. See that house at the corner; the upper part of it is devoted to the goddess Bohea, which is sufficiently indicated by the rude painting of a tea-urn, surrounded by a numerous progeny of white tea-cups on a dark-blue ground placed over the door. The windows are open, which enables us to see what is passing within. Long-bearded shopkeepers, in their blue caftans, well buttoned up, istvostchicks or droshsky-drivers, rough peasants from the country, in their loose shirts or sheep-skins, and with queerly-cut hair, are all seated in little groups, round small tables, placed in lines down the whole length of the room, as many as it will contain. Young boys, in loose shirts, and mostly without shoes or stockings, are running about attending the wants of the guests, bringing little loaves to one, rusks to another, and tea to all. Tea-cups do not seem to be the the fashion, for most of the guests are drinking out of glasses; some prefer cream, but the majority have a slice of lemon swimming on the top, and "a portion" of sugar in a small saucer, all ready to be used, is near at hand; they do not put it into the glass, but hold it between their teeth, and suck the beverage through it. They seem happy and contented enough as we see them now, but doubtless each could tell of some act of oppression and violence which weighs heavily on his heart, and which will inevitably be avenged some day or other by him or his children's children!

Let us cast a look into the cellars below. If the first floor be dedicated to a Chinese deity, these are under the protection of a classic god that indeed ought to be the tutular deity of the Russian people. The gigantic bunches of purple and white grapes on a gold field plainly indicate that "Votku is sold here," and that Bacchus holds his reign in this subterraneous temple, even if we did not perceive the state of those reeling mujiks (peasants) and young boys continually going in and out, in danger of stumbling down the steps of the drinking-shop, the doors of which are happily closed, and thus prevent our being disgusted with what is passing within: we will therefore stand aside for a few minutes and remark the passers-by. If it be summer, we shall see the lemonade-boys with their large glass jugs and one glass for universal use. Sometimes, instead of this beverage, they vend a kind of drink made of cranberries. I dare say what they sell is very refreshing, but its purity cannot be depended on. The bread-merchants with their portable tray supported by a strap round their shoulders; the fruit-venders, whose treasures are crude enough and never ripen in this northern clime; the flower-girls with well-arranged nosegays; the begging monks and nuns, with their board covered with cloth, on which is embroidered a cross, and on which the pious are expected to place a trifle, which they pretend go to their religious house—their disagreeable whine is the true tone of a hypocrite. All these are mixed up with an indefinite number of peasants and *employés*, of whom, with the exception of the military, the population at this season seems composed, for the "families" are all out of town, enjoying the short summer on their estates, or at the "Islands" in the environs of St. Petersburg. There seems no lack of uniforms, notwithstanding that the soldiers are "aux camps" some forty versts from the city: but this is the capital of a nation kept down by the knout and the sword. Yonder are four horsemen abreast: they are Cossacks. Remark their black sheepskin caps, their blue frock-coats tightly fastened by a narrow belt round the waist. By-the-bye, it must be a great misfortune if they grow stout, for the belt is only allowed to be of a certain length, as if even flesh and blood must obey military regulations. Their immensely long spears with red shafts are supported by a leathern strap; the hay is curiously twisted up into a kind of gigantic ring and fastened to the saddle-bow. They have good features, but are too small in size to be handsome figures. Those two soldiers that you see coming on horseback, looking round with ineffable disdain upon the people, are Circassians: their proud and stately bearing, their magnificent dress and ancient arms, recall to our remembrance the days of chivalry, when in the olden time the warriors of merry England went forth to fight Saladin on the plains of Syria. Their closely-fitting burnished helmets, with little scarlet ornament at the top, their steel veil falling over their necks, their shirt of linked mail, the plate-armour on their legs, and their barbed steeds, make us imagine them to be some ancient knights of high renown ready caparisoned for the tournament. Their piercing black eyes and noble features do not belie what we have heard of the beauty of the Circassian race. These are probably some of the tribe that have been induced to swear fealty to the Czar, or perhaps are two of the hostages from Circassia. I remember a gentleman telling me that the Circassians were among the most faithful of the Emperor's soldiers: perhaps the time may be near at hand in which their fidelity will be put to the test. You see those other soldiers opposite; they cut but a poor figure by the side of the Circassians. They are some of the infantry of the line; their downcast, inanimate look, their thin and miserable forms, tell of the many kicks and blows, the scanty rations of black bread and salt, the life of drudgery, and the shameful ill-treatment to which, poor wretches, they are too much accustomed. "It is no wonder our soldiers are brave," said a Russian official to me; "they have so little worth living for, that, as Grinion the author says, 'they lose nothing when they lose their life:' the only way to make a good trooper is to make him care nothing at all about his existence." What abominable policy!

That little house at the corner of the street is inhabited by a butitchnick or stationary policeman; he is placed there to keep the streets in order: I am sorry to say he has not the reputation of being very honest himself. So many stories are told and known to be true concerning the police in Russia, that they really may be regarded as the wolves instead of the watch-dogs of the community. Among the many examples of what is here asserted, I remember two. The first was that of a servant-girl who was the slave of a lady with whom I was slightly acquainted, and who was one evening sent out to purchase something. The girl, like the generality of domestics in this country, was not of good character, and she stopped to talk with the butitchnick, who invited her into his house. She was never seen again alive, and several weeks passed before any trace of her was discovered. By chance, as the police-officer was going his rounds, he entered the man's cabin, and looking round he caught sight of a very small portion of a cotton dress that was jammed between the boards of the floor. He instantly had them taken up, and beneath them was found the body of the wretched servant-girl: the butitchnick confessed that the silver rouble intrusted to her had tempted him to commit the murder. The second case was that of a lady who went to take a walk in the Strogonoff gardens, at a few versts' distance from St. Petersburg. She was seen to enter them, but she never left them again. Nothing was heard of her during nine months, notwithstanding the untiring efforts of her friends and the large sum offered by them for some information concerning her fate. Many of her acquaintances were therefore reluctantly obliged to conclude that in some sudden fit of insanity, she must have committed suicide by throwing herself into the water. The mystery was, however, at length cleared up. It so happened that a gentleman, a friend of this lady's, while taking a ride, was accosted by a butitchnick, who asked him if he would like to buy a parasol. It immediately struck him that it was very similar to the one which the unfortunate lady had in her hand when she so suddenly disappeared. He therefore told the man to keep it until his return, which would be soon, as he had only to call on an acquaintance. The policeman, suspecting nothing, promised to do as he was requested, and the gentleman rode on. The butitchnick's surprise may be well imagined when he saw him come back with the police-master and two or three of his men to take him into custody. He soon met with the punishment he so well deserved : he was knouted, and, if he survived, was afterwards to be sent to the mines. No man in Russia can be punished unless he confess his crime, but means are resorted to for making him do so. This man's reason for committing the murder was his being unable to withstand the temptation offered by the lady's handsome dress, and he unconcernedly lifted up a part of the floor of his house and showed where he had buried her.

In winter the aspect of the streets of St. Petersburg is very different from what it is in summer. Instead of the venders of lemonade, &c., we see the itinerant tea-sellers furnished with a kettle well wrapped up in towels to preserve the heat, and a whole row of glasses in a kind of leathern rack in front of them, slung round their neck in some way or other : their tea finds a ready sale among the groups of red-faced, sheepskin-clad boys and men whom they meet in the street, and the shopmen in the Gostinoi Dwor. Instead of droshskies, the sledges filled with ladies, smartly dressed in gaily-coloured bonnets and fur-lined velvet or satin cloaks, glide swiftly along the streets. The Nevsky Perspective is crowded with belles and beaux, all anxious to display the newest fashions from Paris. The innumerable officers saunter along equally desirous of admiration. Here and there may be seen a nurse in the full splendour of the national costume—gold embroidered head-dress, the resplendent pavoinik and crasnoi sarafane, kasackan, and immense amber necklace, which they wear "pour guerir les humeurs froides," as they say. The coachmen are conspicuous from their red velvet caps stuffed with wadding and trimmed with gold lace, and their long caftan with red scarf tied round their waist; their strangely cropped hair* and bushy beard, all covered with frozen breath, appear as if they were thickly powdered with snow; their horses' backs are like fleece from the same cause, and icicles hang round their mouths and from their eyelids. The canals and river are frozen three feet deep, yet that does not prevent the washerwomen from still following their occupation of rinsing the linen in the holes made in the ice. One would think that their fingers would freeze, but the fact is, the water is so much warmer than the air, that they have no fear of that, yet they must surely suffer from standing so many hours on the ice: their loud laughter and rude jokes, however, seem to contradict this opinion. There is a crowd standing further down—what has happened? Let us ask this shopman.

"It is only a man in the water, Madam: he has slipped down through the hole in the ice, that is all."

"But why do they not pull him out?"

* I was informed that they tie a string round the head and then cut the hair in a straight line: the poll of the neck is shaved quite bare.

"No one must touch him until the police arrive; it is their business."

"Good heavens! the poor man will be drowned meanwhile."

"Tchto delat?" (what is to be done?) answers the shopman, shrugging his shoulders. And there *is* nothing done, at least to the purpose; for, of course, in the quarter of an hour or twenty minutes expended in fetching the police, the poor creature has had ample time to be drowned, and his body, when at last fished up from the water by the accredited authorities, is set up on a droshsky with a butitchnick to hold it on, and so is driven, a horrid spectacle, through the streets to the station. This is one of the senseless regulations of the Russian police, that everything must be done by their agency; surely it ought to be lawful to save a fellow-creature's life under any circumstances. When I was staying at Twer, one of the men-servants, in a fit of jealousy, thought proper to hang himself in an outhouse. One of his companions happened to enter and saw him struggling; he did not dare to cut the cord, but ran to fetch the authorities. They came, and poor Ivan was nearly cold. I recollect, on the road to Nova Derevna, seeing a carriage tear along the stones as if the horses were wild, and the coachman was lashing them like a madman. It appears that he had accidentally run over a drunken man, and was so afraid of the consequences of stopping a moment out of humanity to raise the poor wretch, whose leg was broken, that he thus frantically drove on. If the man had been killed he would have been punished as if for a murder, and the carriage and horses confiscated; but in any case, had he been caught, the latter part of the sentence would have been carried into effect, and he himself would have been severely beaten.

Another stupid regulation also exists. If one man should happen to see another lying murdered on the ground, and should be so unwary as to give information of the fact to the authorities, he is in danger of being himself detained until some trace of the real assassin be discovered. An English person informed me that he was one day crossing the river, on foot, at an early hour in the morning, and, to his horror, he saw the body of a murdered man lying close to a hole in the ice. Apparently, those who had committed the dreadful crime had been alarmed just as they were on the point of sinking their victim in the Neva, and had fled and left him. As for the Englishman, he did not dare to give information of it, as he knew too well the penalty. Who can tell how many wicked deeds are done in this gaudy capital, between the setting and rising of the sun, on a long winter's night, or how many of the murdered have floated beneath the ponderous ice, silently pursuing their frightful voyage towards the gulf! Alas! many, very many, I have been repeatedly assured by those who had every means of knowing the truth.

Yonder is a poor man's funeral—how sad! There is not a single mourner to follow him to his final place of rest; perhaps he was a common soldier or a convict, for here one is almost as much respected as the other. The coffin is nothing but a long, roughly-made deal box, stuffed with straw (a few pieces of which escape from under the lid), and is dragged along on a peasant's sledge, with as much unconcern as if it contained the body of a dog. How different from the magnificent funeral cortège I saw only yesterday! it was that of the Prince L. The road was strewn with branches of fir; numbers of men preceded the procession with flaming torches in their hands; the bishop in his mitre, the priests in their silver-bordered robes; the choristers chanting the funeral service in solemn tones; the splendid coffin with its rich and beautiful mountings; the glittering pall of cloth of gold; the magnificent canopy of crimson velvet with white ostrich feathers waving in the wind, as if they mocked the lifeless corse beneath them; the footmen in their white-bordered coats, cocked hats, and long streamers of red, blue, and white ribbons. The innumerable carriages and sledges, marshalled in a long line by the gensdarmes, closed the procession; the soldiers presented arms to the dead. Yet all his riches and nobility could not free the proud Prince L. from Nature's heavy debt, nor prevent him from treading the same dreary path as yon poor friendless wretch.

St. Petersburg never looks so beautiful as on a summer's night; the buildings are then seen to a great advantage. The peculiar twilight of these latitudes casts a softness, yet a clearness, over them, of which those who have not seen it can have no idea: the utter silence of a great city, in what seems broad daylight, gives a mysterious feeling to the heart, and subdues the thoughts. I was never more struck with the beauty of St. Petersburg than once, when, on returning from a party at a late hour, I was crossing the upper bridge from Kemanoi Oustroff: the long line of palaces fading away in the distance, the magnificent quays, the calm river, the unbroken stillness, all produced the effect of a fairy-scene, as if they were fabrics of a vision too lovely to be real, erected on the enchanting shores of a lake of liquid silver.

But, see! yonder is a strange group. They are prisoners being escorted out of the town by soldiers. There is a Cossack of the Back Sea among them. What a savage look he casts around! The long hairs of his shaggy white cap almost fall into his eyes, and make him look even more ferocious than he otherwise would; his legs are heavily chained, so are those of his companions. The man next to him is a Cossack of the Ural; his rough sheepskin cap, like those of the soldiers, and wild-looking dress, mark him as a complete barbarian. It would be difficult to decide which has the more villanous countenance of the two. We need scarcely ask what their crimes are. That young girl cannot be more than sixteen, yet she has been knouted, and is now sufficiently recovered to be able to accompany the gang to Siberia ; her crime was that of striking her mistress : she will not be reclaimed by the wicked wretches with whom she is marching. The charitable are bestowing alms on them, kindly wishing to alleviate their sufferings as much as possible, and the money will enable them to buy some trifling comforts on their journey. One of the convicts seems to be the treasurer of the party, for everything is handed over to him. There is kindness in that poor peasant who is running after them to give them the little he can afford. The Russians are, generally speaking, a good-hearted people, and would eventually become a noble nation under a freer and better government. Many of their vices and crimes proceed from ignorance and *fear*.

That fine carriage with six horses, the two first bearing postilions in long frock-coats and prodigious cocked hats, putting us in mind of our respected friend Punch on horseback, the two footmen behind in the same becoming costume, and the coachman holding the reins, *à la Russe*, with outstretched arms, contains the Metropolitan of St. Petersburg. He is a venerable-looking old man, with a long snowy beard and straight head-dress, like a brimless hat, covered with white cashmere falling down behind: his forehead surmounted by a diamond cross ; his long loose robe hanging in rich folds ; his breast covered with crosses and stars, for every profession has a military rank in Russia, give him a most imposing appearance ; if not exactly like that of an apostle, he may remind us of the high-priest of Rome, when Rome was mistress of the world. The people salute him, and uncover their heads with much reverence ; he raises his hand, and seems as if he were bestowing his benediction on them. But let us stand on one side, for the Emperor's sledge is coming ; he is dressed in a gray military cloak and leather helmet, ornamented with gold, precisely similar to that of any other officer. He has a fine face ; his fair complexion, and the general cast of his features show his German descent, but there is something peculiarly disagreeable about his eyes. His noble figure amply fills the sledge, which drives at a rapid rate past us. His majesty looks much older than he did a few months ago; his hair is grayer and his shoulders rounder, yet he is a fine man still. He acknowledges the low bows of his people by a military salute, and leaves behind him as he advances many open mouths and wide-stairing eyes among the sheepskin gentry, who perhaps have but just come into St. Petersburg with the "winter-loads," and can scarcely gaze their fill at the Czar, who, in their ignorance, they imagine a kind of God upon the earth. Look! the Emperor is giving a military salute to some ladies in a blue carriage, with two Cossacks in scarlet behind; it is her Majesty the Empress and her daughter. The red uniform of the Cossacks is the distinctive mark between her livery and that of the wife of the heir-apparent, which is blue.

It must not be imagined that all the respect with which the Czar is greeted is quite spontaneous. A Polish gentleman told me once an anecdote of an acquaintance of his. He had recently arrived in the capital from some out-of-the-way place in Poland, and, as the Emperor does not wear his crown in the street, he of course did not know him from Adam; he therefore committed the crime of not taking off his hat when the Emperor passed. On his return home he had a notification that he must uncover on meeting his Majesty. He did not fail to do it the next time, and saluted him with two or three low bows quite down to the ground. He soon had another visit from the authorities, ordering him out of the city, which made him practically to understand that the Czar could have too much respect paid him as well as too little. I need scarcely add that the Pole did not delay his departure, and thought himself fortunate in being able to return in safety to his obscure village in his own country.

Mais allons! Let us continue our walk down the Nevsky

Perspective. The carriages with scarlet liveries and lined with wolfskin are those of families belonging to the court, of which there are plenty in St. Petersburg. The shops or magazines as they are called here to distinguish them from the common Russian warehouses in the Gostinoi Dwor, all have signboards with the articles their proprietors sell painted thereon—a proof of the general ignorance, for, if the people could read, such signs would not be necessary. Opposite, you see is a hairdresser's ; he himself is represented on his signboard as exercising his skill on the head of a very sentimental young gentleman dressed for a ball ; he unites phlebotomy with his other accomplishments, for vis-à-vis is represented a very fine lady in a blue dress and pink bows looking very so-so, whose arm is at the mercy of the operator, while a boy in a white shirt is holding the basin.

Next door to the hairdresser lives a milliner, whose gay caps and bonnets are duly delineated on her board. Yonder is a toy-shop, with a fine painting containing the most artistic grouping of rocking-horses with happy little boys on them for ever smiling, and Punch reclining wearily on a drum, mixed up with swords and guns that will never kill Turks, and helmets, shakoes, Cossack-caps, &c., destined to raise ambitious hopes in many a childish breast. But we have reached the Anitchkin bridge, which crosses the Fontanka. These four equestrian statues in bronze have a fine effect ; the human figures endeavouring to restrain the fiery steeds are full of life and animation. There are some fine buildings near ; that large handsome mansion on the right hand belongs to Prince Wasiliwitch ; the long range that you see yonder to the left is the Catherine Institution ; it contains some hundreds of young ladies belonging to noble families, and like most establishments of education here, is a government one. It is of no use going further than the Anitchkin bridge, because there is absolutely nothing to see ; the houses beyond it degenerate greatly, so we will return. That large white mansion is the palace of the Archduchess Olga, which she inhabits when she visits the capital. Leaving the Gostinoi Dwor on the left, we look down a street, facing which we see at a distance the Michael Palace, a handsome edifice. Soon afterwards we reach the Kazàne church; it is built on the model of St. Peter's in Rome, only on a diminutive scale. We will finish our morning's ramble by entering it for a few minutes and examining the interior. It is large, and the space, unobstructed by pews, appears even greater than it is; the fine marble pillars supporting the roof are surmounted by gilt capitals; the pavement is tesselated; the walls are covered with pictures, before which silver lamps are suspended, and stands are placed, in which are stuck innumerable thin wax tapers, reminding us of the joss-sticks of the Chinese. That portrait, before which the ignorant lower class are performing their devotions, and bowing so low that their foreheads touch the ground, is the likeness of the Emperor's daughter Alexandrine, who died some years ago. Alas! and are the days of heathen apotheosis not yet passed away? Must we, in the nineteenth century of the Christian era, see anything so shocking as this? What difference is there between the adoration of Romulus by the ancient Romans and this idolatry? Before that shrine opposite are kneeling two nuns; one of them is only a novice, as shown by her black velvet cone-shaped head-dress and gauze veil hanging down behind; the other has a straight head-dress covered with black cloth; they are both habited in gowns of black serge, and carry rosaries. A face, however beautiful, could never look so in this unbecoming costume. Near them is a poor woman decently clad, whose repeated prostrations, and the tears coursing each other rapidly down her cheeks, show that true devotion, and perhaps repentance for sin, can be felt even by one so humble and ignorant as a Russian peasant-girl. The massive balustrade round the altar, the gate of the Holy of Holies, and the candelabra are of real silver, made, as they say, from the spoils of the "grande armeé," when the French invaded the country ; but who can believe all the Russians say ? We have often heard them boast, among other incredible triumphs of their arms, that they took Paris in 1814, and they even had the assurance to deny that any one else had aught to do with their entry into that city. The large filagree silver doors that enclose the Holy of Holies are shown to advantage by the crimson velvet curtains behind them. We ladies are not allowed to enter the "sanctum," so we must content ourselves with the knowledge that there is nothing worth seeing inside, and with admiring the portraits of the saints inserted in the gates ; they are really well executed, but "saint-painting" is a *profession* in Russia, something like that of the artificers of brass who worked for the great temple of Ephesus. This royal-looking lady is St. Olga, whose only claim to merit was that of introducing the Greek religion into Muscovy. Her horrid cruelty and detestable immorality would lead us to think that she deserved any other abode than that of heaven. These people, just coming up the steps as we are leaving, are a party of pilgrims come on a devotional journey to St. Petersburg ; they have no cockle-shells or gourds, no staves nor sandal shoon, as we generally see on the stage. They have all the appearance of common mendicants, with a stout stick in their hands and a wallet on their back ; and such indeed they generally are, for under the pretence of a pilgrimage they manage to make a very profitable begging tour through the country.

CHAPTER VII.

Places worth visiting—Peter's Museum—The Czar's works—Curious effigy—The war-horse—The Nevsky monastery—The saint's shrine—Magnificent tomb—Superstition—The cemetery—Catherine—Imperial mausoleum—Description of the sarcophagi—Prisoners—Political offenders—Spy system—Bombardment of Odessa—Dumb spy—A spy of rank—Assemblée de la noblesse—Masked balls—Russian civilization—Love of money—Inebriety—Society in St. Petersburg.

THERE are many places well worth visiting in St. Petersburg: such as Peter's Museum at the Academy of Sciences, the Palace of the Hermitage, the Monastery of Alexander Nevsky, &c. &c. The first of these (Peter's Museum) contains a great many relics of the Czar after whom it is named; many of them are the work of his own hands—models of ships, a chandelier, some iron articles, shoes, and little ivory figures. There are also his tools and instruments, carefully preserved under a glass case. In another apartment is the effigy of the great Peter himself, modelled in wax, habited in one of his own court-dresses, having shoes on that he himself made, and the head is decorated with his own natural hair made into a wig. Unlike the Russians generally, he had dark eyes and hair, and his features had more of the southern cast than of the northern. He must have been of immense stature, for a rod was shown us which we were assured was exactly his height, and its length was some inches more than six feet. Another room contains the horse on which he rode at the battle of Poltava, when the royal Swede "was taught to fly;" it is a wiry little animal, of a light brown, much resembling in size and appearance one of the small species ridden by the Cossacks, but quite out of pro-

A.W. ORR, Sc.

PETER THE GREAT'S STATUE AND THE OFFICE OF THE SENATE. PAGE 78.

portion to the gigantic Czar, whose feet must have nearly reached the ground. I believe there is another museum also called after Peter the Great, but we did not go to see it.

At the very end of the Nevsky Perspective, after passing a vast number of miserable dwellings, we reach the Nevsky Monastery, from which the street is named. Alexander Nevsky is an imperial and warrior saint, and was Czar of Muscovy. After his death he was canonized for some reason or other ; and, of course, with all his imperial and religious advantages, his shrine is greatly visited and much reverenced by the people. It seems a general rule, not only among the heathen nations of antiquity, but with the Russians as well, that, when thoroughly tired of the "fantastic tricks" played by their monarchs "before high Heaven," they are content to worship them as gods, though they might themselves have forwarded them on the road to Paradise. The late Emperor Alexander, though not yet dignified with the title of *saint*, has obtained the first step towards it by being surnamed the "*Blessed*," but why and wherefore no one could ever tell us.

The Nevsky Monastery is a large pile of buildings painted white, with a green roof ; the road to it leads through an avenue of birch-trees, as is generally the case in Russian monasteries. A large cathedral forms the principal attraction, for in it is contained the saint's shrine, which is very magnificent and consists of an immense silver monument, several yards in height, and placed against the wall : in the front is a sarcophagus of the same metal on a raised dias ; on its cover is a full-length likeness of the dead, crowned by one of those circles of radiant glory in pure gold which distinguish the Greek images,* and further decorated with a wreath of artificial

* The Greek Church forbids any carved images, although it allows painted ones : they say "graven images" are expressly forbidden ; how they get over the ensuing "nor the likeness," &c., they could never satisfactorily explain.

flowers. At the head of the tomb a beautiful silver lamp is always kept burning, which casts down on the features a soft light, and gives them a peculiarly pleasing effect. At the foot of the shrine are seated two large figures of angels in silver, and at each side of it is a military trophy consisting of shields, spears, battle-axes, &c. &c., all of the same precious metal ; over the sarcophagus was thrown a magnificent pall of cloth of gold most richly ornamented. I was assured by the Russian lady who accompanied me that the body of the saint lay uncorrupted beneath.

"And do you really believe that Alexander Nevsky's corpse is exempted from the decay of other mortals?"

"Undoubtedly I do," was the reply : "I have as little doubt of it as that I see you now before my eyes."

"But have you ever seen it?"

"No! that of course is not allowed, but the priests have done so, and they tell us that he lies there just as if he were asleep ; even his limbs are not become rigid, and that is one of the great proofs that he is worthy of being numbered among our patron saints." Seeing me still incredulous, she added, "I assure you that at Kiev there are numbers of the uncorrupted bodies of our holy men and martyrs, which, if you went thither, you could see yourself and be convinced."

"But perhaps the monks have the secret of thus preserving them ; I have heard so."

"I will not talk to you any more," replied my friend ; "you English heretics will not believe any of our miracles."

She quitted me, and went up the steps leading to the sarcophagus ; and devoutly kissing the hands and feet of the image, she repeatedly crossed herself, while she muttered a few words in prayer ; and having made the offering of a piece of money, by slipping it through the top of a well-secured box, she turned to accompany me out of the church. We lingered a few moments longer to admire the rich canopy, supported by massive silver pillars, that overshadows the tomb, and to read the name of "Souvarof" on a small mural slab, and then proceeded to the cemetery attached to the establishment. It was much crowded with monuments ; broken pillars, surmounted by a gilt cross, weeping female figures of the purest white marble, and simple white crosses, were among the most common and interesting of these offerings to the memory of the dead, made by affection, ostentation, or hypocrisy. It was here that Peter III., the husband of the too famous Catherine, was interred, for she would not even allow him to repose with his ancestors. Perhaps the idea of herself being placed side by side with him of whose dreadful death she stands arraigned, might not have been a very pleasant one. After Catherine's decease, Paul had his father's body removed to the fortress, which has been the mausoleum of the imperial family since Peter the Great's reign. I was told that he caused the nobleman who had actually done the murderous deed to stand as guard the whole of the first night alone in the church, between the tomb of the woman whose wicked orders he had obeyed in the hopes of sharing the crown (of which reward she cheated him), and that of the unhappy monarch whom he had murdered : the fearful feelings of that night's dreadful ordeal rendered him a maniac during the remainder of his life.

We visited the chapel in which the members of the Romanof family are deposited. Their resting-place is extremely simple, and is an ordinary church. The tombs or sarcophagi are merely long boxes, standing in rows before the altar, each covered with a crimson velvet pall, on which the arms of Russia are embroidered. I was told that they were precisely similar to the tombs of the Sultans in Constantinople, with the exception of the turban.

Among other things we were shown the cushion on which

Souvarof, the half-barbarian general, reposed when in his tent ; it was of leather, stuffed with straw ; but as I have no respect for the man, I was not much interested in seeing it. On the other side of the river, opposite the fortress, is a statue of him "*en héros*," as our friend said ; *en barbare* would have been more appropriate.

On leaving the place we perceived several of the criminals (it being the state prison) peeping through the gratings of their cells ; the whole of one side of their heads was shaved, beginning with the line of the nose, and finishing at the nape of the neck, presenting a most strange appearance ; the object of this is, that they may be recognised if they should effect an escape. Beneath the fortress are the dungeons in which the state prisoners are confined ; I was assured that the dungeons extend to a considerable distance under the Neva. How inconceivably wretched such an existence must be !—in darkness, silence, and solitude, it seems wonderful how they can survive, even for a few days. The church clock chimes every quarter of an hour, which must be wearisome enough to the unhappy creatures within hearing. At one time I was residing just opposite to this place, on the other side of the river. One morning, at about nine o'clock, I perceived a long line of sledges crossing the ice, preceded and followed by a party of mounted *gensdarmes:* each equipage contained a gentleman and one of the police. I found out afterwards that these poor fellows, most of them quite youths, had been incarcerated for some silly nonsense they had uttered about politics ; they were then being taken before the authorities to hear their final sentence. I do not think that any of them escaped ; they were hurried off to Siberia, in the prisoner's kabitkas that stood ready to receive them in the yard. It appears that they had been to a supper-party, and had taken more wine than needful, when they had talked pretty freely, of course. When three meet together in Russia, you may safely count one of them as a spy ; it proved to be so in this instance, for information was quickly given that some horrible conspiracy was being formed. The result we have seen. A young *gendarme* officer used to visit at the house of one of our acquaintances ; his presence always produced restraint, as they are obliged by their duty to report whatever they may hear. *A propos* of the spy system : I was informed that, besides the secret police, there are eighty thousand paid agents in the country, among whom, to their shame be it spoken, are many Poles and foreigners. I am happy to say that I never heard an instance of an Englishman being so employed. A great many women belong to this hateful profession ; even some of the French milliners in St. Petersburg have the reputation of being agents of police. One would wonder how politics could be brought on the *tapis* while a lady is engaged in trying on a new cap or bonnet ; but these *marchandes de modes* have free admission to the masquerades, theatres, &c. &c., where they can exercise their detective talents. It is no exaggeration to say that a Russian subject scarcely dares to utter his true sentiments, even to his own brother or familiar friend. I am sure that I have often been present at conversations in which perhaps four or five would be taking part, each knowing that his neighbour was telling a lie, and avowing sentiments exactly contrary to those he felt ; yet the subject under consideration would be discussed with all the gravity and seriousness of entire conviction. Take for example the recent bombardment of Odessa : I was present in St. Petersburg at the time, and read the proclamation of the Emperor announcing to his faithful people the astounding fact that the allied fleets, mounting three hundred and fifty cannon, had fired for twelve consecutive hours upon the town, killing only *four* men, and that the people were so well behaved, they did not let even the tremendous cannonading interrupt their peaceful devotions ! Added to which, they were assured, after a few remarks on our fleet firing at too great a distance to be within range of the battery guns, that the English ships retired with great loss and damage. How this was caused when the Russian balls could not reach them, the Emperor forgot to explain. I had an invitation to dine with a family the very day on which the news came, and I would not be absent, lest it should be ascribed to some feeling of annoyance among the English. During the whole dinner (at which were some generals, other officers, and ladies of rank), nothing was talked of but this wonderful triumph of the Russian arms. I am convinced that there was not one single person there present who believed it ; but who could venture to doubt the imperial words ? Evil would have befallen him who had dared to do so.

I remember, when in the province of Archangel, a deaf and dumb gentlemen paid the town a visit ; he was furnished with letters of introduction to some families there, and was well received at the governor's table ; his agreeable manners and accomplishments, joined to his misfortune, made him a general favorite, and caused much interest ; he could read French, German, Russian, and Polish ; was a connoisseur of art, and showed us several pretty drawings of his own execution. Two or three times I was struck with an expression of more intelligence in his face than one would expect when any conversation was going on behind his back. It was not until three years after that I accidentally heard this very man spoken of in St. Petersburg. He was one of the government spies. It was no doubt for a very large sum that he had been induced to put so great a constraint upon himself, and it must have required long training to enable him to perform so difficult a part. This vile system must have a dreadful effect in demoralizing all ranks of society, producing hypocrisy, falsehood, meanness, and cunning, which are felt in the minutest relations of life. On one occasion I was conversing with a Polish lady and gentleman upon Count Custine's work on Russia, which is rigidly prohibited by the censor ;

in the midst of our conversation a gentleman called, and by some *à propos* accident asked if we had read the book in question. I, being English, immediately replied in the affirmative; but my Polish friends pretended that they had scarcely ever heard even its title; and although only a few minutes previously they had acquiesced in the justice of many of the Count's remarks, they said "of course they would not read a work condemned and prohibited."

I will add another instance. A general officer visited the province in which I was for some time residing; his rank gave him easy access to all the best houses, and he was sure to be met with at any grand dinner. Alas! he also was a spy. It was not until he had quitted the place that this began to be whispered, and it was afterwards confirmed. I have heard that professions learned and sacred, as well as honorable, all have members who act as spies upon the rest.

Among the places worth visiting in the capital is the "nobility's assemblée," at the corner of St. Michael-street and the square. When I first went to reside in St. Petersburg, these rooms were considered quite the *mode*, but now they are no longer so, for public places soon degenerate in Russia from the *comme il faut* to the *mauvais genre;* there were given balls and masquerades, at which the imperial family were frequently present; the ladies wore dominoes after midnight, but the gentlemen went unmasked. Any *lady* could intrigue the Emperor (no gentleman was allowed to do so), who frequently was surrounded by a gay little crowd of *beaux masques*, entertaining him with all the chit-chat and *conversations légerès* peculiar to the style of such amusements. I was informed that a great many Frenchwomen, even milliners, were furnished with tickets gratis, their gay badinage and cheerful manners serving so much to enliven the company. Among the tales of scandal which, in the absence of politics, share with actors and actresses the honor of being made the subject of conversation in Russian society, was one which I make no doubt whatever was a positive fact, and, as it is *à propos* to these *bals masqués*, I will relate it. A lady, the daughter of an old general named B——, was one evening at the masquerade; she intrigued a *personage* of very high rank, and while doing so, was imprudent enough to touch upon some forbidden subject; shortly after she left the assemblée and returned home, perfectly unconscious that orders had been given not to let her out of sight until her name and place of residence had been ascertained. The next morning she was disagreeably surprised by a visit from an officer of the secret police, who politely requested her to accompany him to Count Orloff's office. Such an invitation was, of course, not to be refused—she went immediately. The gentleman who received her was *aimabilité* itself; he kindly pointed to a seat that stood near, and blandly proceeded to ask her a few questions concerning the previous evening's amusement, to all of which the terrified lady tremblingly replied "the truth, the whole truth, and nothing but the truth," for no equivocation would have availed her in that place. When the interrogation was finished, the chair suddenly sank through the floor, and I am ashamed to say that from the hand of some unseen person below she received a correction such as little boys used formerly to be subjected to from the birch of the old-fashioned schoolmasters. I met this lady frequently in company, and knew her sister well. I had the anecdote from an intimate friend of the family, and have not the slightest doubt of its being true.

The same misfortune is said to have occurred about four months ago to a certain noble princess from the south, who expressed some sympathy with the cause of the Western Powers. I have often asked Russians, when they were boasting of their great civilization, if this were a proof of it. Once the reply was that "a great many of the Russian ladies deserved to be beaten, and that it would do them a great deal of good." At another time, in speaking of the peasant-women being so treated, a certain Prince A—— replied that "they were not worthy of the title of women, they were no better than cattle!" Once, on complaining of the impertinence of a servant, I was recommended to "box her ears well;" on my remarking that such an action would be a greater disgrace to me than to the girl herself, the lady, whose maid she was, answered, "If you do not do it, I will;" she rang the bell, the footman was told to send Marousha, and the instant she came, notwithstanding my entreaties, the lady administered with her own hand a sound blow on each side of the poor girl's head!

When abroad, the Russians invariably deny that such a state of things exists; they will even sometimes attempt to hide it in their own country, which shows that at the least they have the grace to be ashamed of it.

A stranger in walking through the streets in St. Petersburg, if he understands anything of the language spoken, cannot fail to remark that the general theme of conversation among the lower classes is *money*; scarcely one of the men or women passes by without our catching the words tchitvertack, grebinick, roup, &c. In no country is more avidity displayed in the pursuit of gain; only speak of a piece of silver, and a Russian's eyes sparkle at the sound, and he is ready to do anything in order to obtain it. Copecks and whisky are the two greatest temptations of his heart. M. P——ski, a gentleman of education, assured me, only the morning I left St. Petersburg, that they were in much more danger from the pillage of the lower classes than from any exterior enemy, and he expressed the greatest fears for the consequences of bringing so many thousands of wild savages of soldiers into the town, for, if they rose, it would be *en masse*, and he was fearful that the great temptation offered by the sight of a civilized capital for the first time would shortly prove an irresistible one ; if they did have an outbreak, it would sweep the upper classes away like a torrent.

In regard to the love of whisky to be remarked at every step, how can we wonder that the Russian boor is addicted to drinking when there is every inducement held out to him to do so ? he is more to be pitied than condemned. The government revenues are in great part acquired by the sale of votku ; there are people called brandy-farmers, who contract with the authorities for the monopoly ; they generally make great fortunes, and the poor *people* pay for all. The charge of inebriety among those of superior rank is entirely false ; a Russian gentleman seldom takes much wine, and the ladies *never ;* they have faults grave enough, but this is not one of them.

The society of St. Petersburg is, of course, as varied and as much divided into cliques as that of any other great city, and it entirely depends upon which circle the stranger has the fortune to be introduced into whether he be favourably impressed with what he sees, or the contrary ; from my own experience I should say that it is rare to meet with more agreeable people. I do not speak of their knowledge, or what is denominated mind, for there are not many lovers of deep study or profound erudition among the Russians, either gentlemen or ladies ; but of their kindness, good-nature, and desire to afford pleasure to others, the foreigner will have no reason to complain. It must, however, be confessed that their feeling towards strangers has much changed since the present state of affairs has commenced.

CHAPTER VIII.

Winter amusements—The opera and French theatre—Hamlet—A true Russian play—Corruption of the police—Anecdotes—The hermitage—The museum—Dinner-parties—Russian hospitality—Want of information—The censor's office: its restrictions.

THE winter amusements in St. Petersburg are the same as those of other capitals during the season—the opera, French theatre, balls, concerts, *bals masqués*, &c. The opera is of course an Italian one, and the same artistes perform there as in London. I was once at the opera when the Emperor thought proper to applaud the cantatrice (Castellan, I believe) by clapping his hands; he had no sooner done so than somebody hissed; he again showed his approbation—the unknown hissed a second time; his Majesty stood up and looked around on the assembled multitude, and the third time gave his applause; he was answered in the same manner as before. I soon after heard a terrible scuffle overhead; the police had discovered the hardy offender, and quickly dragged him out of the house: I never learnt what became of him; doubtless he was made to repent that he had dared to have an opinion different from that of the Czar.

A gentleman in our box suggested that it *must* be a foreigner, for no *Russian subject* would have dared to act so.

The French theatre is extremely good; all the best artistes from Paris are engaged for the season at enormous salaries. We were informed that his Majesty once said to the Director that "he was one of his best friends, because he amused society." A great deal more was perhaps *sous entendu* than the mere words expressed. It is certain that, as long as the government can get the people (that is, the upper classes—there are no "gods" in Russia) to wrangle and quarrel about the merits of an actress or a singer, instead of thinking upon what great events are passing around them, it is safe enough ; and security is worth purchasing at any rate. This last winter, as *very* extraordinary affairs were being transacted, Madlle. Rachel was imported : I forget the exact amount she received, but the diamonds and jewels with which she was presented were of enormous value, and her performance, the Czar's generosity, and her *conduct* furnished all the nobility and gentry with a fruitful theme of conversation. As the climax to all the compliments paid this actress, the Emperor did the *Empress* the *honour* of presenting Madlle. Rachel to her, and gracefully led her to his consort's presence. Madlle. Rachel, in return, wrote a flourishing letter to the Emperor (a copy of which was shown me), containing innumerable highflown compliments on his might and power, and she spoke of the tears of gratitude she shed on return to her lodgings, &c. : it was handed round with about as much reverence as we should do an autograph epistle of Shakspere or of Alfred the Great. Doubtless, the great tragedian laughed heartily at it all, and thought the Russians a set of dupes. As politics are dangerous subjects to talk about, and as people must have something to converse on, the actors and actresses take the place of "whigs and tories ;" their performance, of some "new measure ;" their manners and conduct, of "new bills and reforms ;" and the news of a fresh play, of "a change in the ministry." English people can only wonder how a society such as that in St. Petersburg can employ all their energies about such absurdities.

There are translations of *some* of Shakspere's plays performed ; the two most frequently witnessed are Hamlet and King Lear ; the class of shopkeepers, who may be called the *people* in Russia, for the others are mere serfs, are those by whom they are chiefly appreciated, and Shakspere is reverenced by most of them nearly as much as in England, although they have read his works only in a translation ; perhaps at some future time his lofty thoughts will have a good effect upon their opinions and conduct. When I was at Twer, I saw the part of Hamlet exceedingly well performed by a young actor, and the audience, even in this small provincial town, seemed thoroughly to appreciate it. I once went to a shop in St. Petersburg, when I remarked to a lady who was with me, "that the proprietor much resembled the portraits of Shakspere ;" although the remark was made in French, the shopkeeper understood it, and, to my astonishment, made me a low bow and thanked me. It was only a small fruit-shop, and we neither of us had the least idea that he had ever heard the poet's name.

Such of Shakspere's plays as Julius Cæsar, and others containing sentiments of freedom, are not permitted to be performed, and are not even translated.

The Russian stage is very destitute of good pieces, but I saw one which, being truly national, may serve to give an idea of their plays. It was the best I ever witnessed on the Russian stage, and it gives too true a picture of the unjust extortion and bribery which are also truly national, for they pervade all ranks in an equal degree. I was in perfect astonishment that the piece was allowed to be played at all ; one would think that pride alone would have prevented such an exposure of their prevailing vice to the foreigners with whom the capital is crowded.

It was called the "*Reviseur*," that being the title of an officer sent from time to time into the provinces to examine into the state of the government, and to report concerning the manner in which it is carried on.

The play opened by a domestic scene, in which the police-master, his wife and daughter, are all eagerly conversing on the shortly-expected visit of the *Reviseur*, and we are let into the secret of various amiable weaknesses and domestic plans to keep up an appearance of propriety; in the midst of which the elder lady suddenly sees a carriage pass, which she is sure can be no other than that of the great man himself. An extraordinary bustle ensues: the police-master, in all haste, gives various absurd orders to the *employés* under him, one of which is that "the soldiers should not, on any account, be seen without their coats, as it would be then discovered that they had no shirts on,"—the money furnished by the crown for providing them has of course been pocketed by himself and the colonel. After taking all the precautions he can think of, he hastens to inform the other principal men of the arrival of the Reviseur.

The next scene introduces us to the servant of the supposed functionary, who is no Reviseur at all, but a poor gentleman who is running away from St. Petersburg, on account of certain bills which he has not the means of paying. The miserable lodging, and the hungry lamentations of the unlucky servant, give us to understand the state of his master's finances, that he has actually expended the very last of his cherished rubles, nor does there appear to be any probability of his purse being replenished: how they will be enabled to continue the journey is a *casse-tête*. Thereupon the master himself enters, and, being quite as famished as his man, orders him to go and get something for dinner, for it appears he has been to the eating-house, and they refused to give him credit. The servant refuses to go without the money. At last, with the help of a great deal of blustering, he is persuaded to "try his luck:" he soon returns; he has been successful in some measure, for he is accompanied by the boy from the cook-shop, who has brought two dishes and—*the bill.* The savoury smell of the soup and beef drives the hungry pair almost mad, but the purse, unlike that of Fortunatus, is as empty as their stomachs, and, unless the boy gets the money, he is ordered by no means to leave the dinner. Now, here was a dreadful dilemma; but, in the midst of it, the police-master arrives: the distressed traveller is in fearful trouble, for he is convinced that the dreaded officer is come to arrest him; "he has, doubtless, heard of his flight from St. Petersburg, and has received orders to take him prisoner." The police-master, on his side, is equally sure that he is in the presence of the real Reviseur, but that he travels thus in disguise that he may take them unawares, and so detect their numerous acts of dishonesty and corruption: consequently, a most laughable dialogue ensues—the official trembles as he addresses the supposed great man, and is ready to cringe in the dust at his feet. At last the latter begins to see "which way the wind blows," and, perceiving to what profit he may turn the mistake, informs the other, as a very great secret, that he is really the Reviseur, and compliments him on his extreme penetration, which alone could have discovered him under such a disguise. No sooner has he done so than the police-master slips an excessively heavy purse into his hand, the contents of which have been furnished by himself and the other chief government officers, to blind his eyes, and to act as golden spectacles. Here the boy from the cook-shop re-enters to be paid for the dinner; the traveller takes out his newly-acquired riches, and is on the point of paying for it, when the police-master politely interferes, and orders the boy to put it down "to his account;" the latter casts a terrified look at the two, and, seeing what a powerful friend his customer has acquired, rushes off in extreme dismay. The official, then turning to the traveller, expresses the hope that they shall have the honour of his company at his house, and respectfully begs permission to write a few words to his wife to inform her of the intended visit; on its being graciously accorded, he sits down and indites a note, in which he bids her strain every nerve for the reception of the distinguished guest, for that she was quite right, it was really the Reviseur that she had seen.

In the following scene the wife and daughter are gravely consulting concerning the toilet proper for the occasion, as they have some sly matrimonial designs on the stranger's heart. The police-master returns home accompanied by all the chief officials in the place ; they have been all "oppressors and unjust judges alike," and every scheme is canvassed to ensure concealment. The soi-disant Reviseur arrives, and is received with all the slavish obsequiousness of which only *Russians* are capable. The poor shopkeepers, who come, according to the national custom, to present the bread and salt, and who have been fleeced by the authorities, are summarily dismissed, and can obtain no hearing for their complaints. As for the supposed Reviseur, he knows well the character of his countrymen, and takes care to profit by it by receiving bribes from every one. The inferior officers, whose turn to be introduced is not yet arrived, are all assembled outside the door, determined to listen to what is going on, and to see as much as the keyhole will permit them. Their anxiety is so great that they push the door down and roll over each other on the floor, to the great damage of their noses. Order being restored, the Reviseur gives audience to one at a time : they have received such severe contusions in the fall that most of them have patches on, and one has a black one covering the whole of his nose. Each gives a bribe to the great man, according to his rank : a great deal of laughter is produced by the one with the black nose not being able to find more than eightpence ; but the Reviseur takes it, being resolved to take all he can. After all these people are dismissed there is a grand flirtation with the police-master's daughter, whose visions of a splendid match can only be equalled by the exultation of the mother.

Having obtained as much as he can, our traveller thinks it "high time to be off," lest by any untoward chance his deception should be discovered. He pockets the money, in all eight hundred roubles, protests his entire satisfaction of everything, his eternal devotion to the daughter, and his fixed intention of shortly returning to marry her, in the midst of which the kabitka drives up to the door ; he takes his leave, and the traveller's bell is soon heard ; everybody runs to the window to take a last look at the retreating sledge ; the tinkling of the bell becomes fainter, and the act is finished.

The last act opens with a scene between the police-master and the shopkeepers, whom he most bitterly upbraids for daring to complain of his oppression, and refuses to be pacified until they have promised to send him various valuable offerings, so many arsheens of cloth, and so on, to act as peace-makers. At last, on this consideration, he consents to " think no more of it," and the poor people take their leave. They are replaced by the numerous friends of the family, who have heard of the intended marriage, and have come to congratulate them upon it. A shower, or rather a deluge, of compliments greets them on all sides, in the midst of which the police-master sneezes. When such an accident occurs, the Russians always exclaim, " *I wish you well*." It may therefore be imagined what a chorus of voices, each desirous to be remarked above the other, is heard simultaneously. Various grand plans are discussed for the future couple, and the whole family seem ready to die with triumphant exultation, when in comes the postmaster so much out of breath that he cannot speak. On recovering his voice he informs them that he has opened the letter that the traveller had forwarded to St. Petersburg, that he is no Reviseur, and that he had turned them all into ridicule, calling them asses, dupes, and fools, and had given a detailed account of everything that had passed. The distress of the whole company is inconceivable ; the police-master is frantic with despair, the daughter and mother faint, the ladies scream, the confusion becomes greater and greater the more they have time to reflect on their position. In the midst of all this terror, consternation, recrimination, and misfortune, enters a chasseur, who announces that the *real Reviseur* had just arrived. Their despair is now excessive ; it becomes deeper and deeper, whereupon the curtain drops and leaves them to their fate.

The acting was admirable throughout. I forget the name of the artiste who performed the first character, but he did it in a manner beyond praise. The comic actors in Russia are excellent ; there are not many first-rate actresses ; Mdlle. Samoiloff was the best—she has since quitted the stage.

Perhaps it may be thought that the preceding play is but a burlesque, an extremely exaggerated picture of what really passes in Russia. Far from it. The Count Z. was sitting next to me, and we were conversing upon the excessive truth of the whole, when Madame P. turned and entreated us, "pour l'amour de Dieu," not to pass such remarks, for if we were heard we might have a visit from the police before the next morning ; so we waited until we returned home, when every one acknowledged that the picture was by no means overdrawn.

We were once staying at the house of a provincial governor, and had many opportunities of hearing and knowing what was going on. The police-master was a colonel in rank ; the pay that he received from the government was not *forty pounds per annum*, yet he kept a carriage, four horses, two footmen, and a coachman ; his wife was always extravagantly dressed ; she had two or three children, and of course a maid and a cook, added to which she paid a visit every season to the capital. On my expressing wonder as to what miracle enabled him to support his family in such luxury, when it was well known to everybody that he had no estates, and nothing besides his pay, I was told a little anecdote of him that deserves to be recorded, if it be only to show to British tradesmen that their brethren in Russia have a worse incubus than that of *taxes* weighing on their hearts.

On one occasion the Colonel was going to St. Petersburg, but he had not a ruble in his purse, and how to find the money to defray the expenses of the journey was a question. He was not long in solving it, for he hit upon the following plan. There happened to be a rich iron-merchant in the town ; he called on him and ordered an immense number of poods of iron to be supplied for the use of the government. To what earthly use could a police-master put all this iron ? The poor merchant knew very well that iron was not the metal he wanted, and was glad to compromise the affair by begging his acceptance of a good round sum of silver roubles instead. As for the poods of iron, they peaceably continued to repose in the store, and our "*brave homme*" went and enjoyed himself very much in the capital.

Scores of similar anecdotes have fallen under my knowledge in every province in which I have resided. It was no longer an enigma to me in what way a police-master's carriage and horses were paid for. I remember going with a friend to the Persian shop in the Galitzin Gallery in Moscow. Whilst we were there a servant came in and ordered several silk dresses of the kind called canaouse to be sent to the house of the police-master. Never shall I forget the rueful look of the poor Persian as he gave them into the man's hand, for he well knew that payment was out of the question : he might send in the bill, which would be laid on the table and postponed *sine die*, but he could not refuse to send the dresses for fear of the consequences, as very likely some pretext would soon be found for ordering his shop to be shut up.

The Palace of the Hermitage is a place of great interest, and contains various beautiful vases in malachite, lapis lazuli, jasper, &c., of great value. There is one enormous vase, I forget of what stone : it is of an oval shape, and measures twenty feet in diameter. These objects are the work of criminals, and are brought from the Ural Mountains and Siberia. The apartments are very fine ; the floors are particularly worthy of attention, being curiously and most elaborately inlaid. The gallery of paintings is good ; those by Sneyder are excellent. I saw here Brulof's "Last Days of Pompeii," but it certainly did not answer the expectations I had formed of it from the immense praise previously bestowed upon it by my friends. The Russians used to boast that he was the first artist in Europe, but everything in Russia is "the first," according to their own account. Among the pictures here shown, the English stranger will see with regret the splendid collection once at Strawberry Hill, which were unhappily allowed to leave the shores of Britain : there are also some good statues and a few antiquities that are interesting.

The Museum in St. Petersburg is very small ; it contains some badly-stuffed birds and animals, and very little besides, nor would it be worth the trouble of visiting were it not for the celebrated remains of the mammoth which are preserved in it. Some portions of the skin and hair are shown ; the former is like discoloured board, the latter resembles enormous bristles.

A dinner-party in Russia differs little from our own, excepting that *all the dishes* are handed round, which is much more pleasant than the stiff formality of the joints being placed on the table : the lady and gentleman of the house are thus at leisure to enter into conversation with the guests, and can attend to the minor *politenesses* requisite. I was once at a large dinner-party in Moscow, and was surprised to remark that the host and hostess did not take their seat at all at the table, but walked about chatting first to one, then to another, recommending this wine or that dish to the attention of their assembled friends. I found that it was formerly a very general custom, but has now much fallen into disuse ; it had its origin doubtless in the anxious wish to perform thoroughly the duties of hospitality, for which the

Russians are justly celebrated. There is one custom tnat might well be entirely abolished. Each person washes his mouth out after dinner, and, after having well rinsed it, empties its contents into the finger-glass : it certainly is not pleasant to see a whole party thus employed. Immediately after coffee the guests depart ; they do not, as with us, remain the whole evening. This is a good arrangement, as it gives the lady the opportunity of going to the opera, or to a friend's house, as she pleases. There is little conversation worth remembering at a Russian dinner ; efforts at making those antediluvian solecisms called puns, or endeavouring to say bons mots, repeating the last anecdote, real or invented, of the Emperor, the Empress, or some fortieth cousin of the imperial family, news as to who has obtained the cross of St. Anne, or that of Vladimir, or of some other order of knighthood which the Russians are ready to sell their souls to obtain, some great honour done to one of the party by his Majesty's having looked at him, &c., flirtation, and paying personal compliments, are the staple of their "feast of reason." We have often remarked with astonishment the excessive want of general information among the gentlemen ; many of them seemed to know nothing at all beyond the frontiers of the empire. Knowledge is decidedly at a discount. Their showy exterior, their brilliant accomplishments of music and dancing, their fluency in speaking so many foreign languages, are apt to strike foreigners with surprise, and they give them credit for knowing all those *solid* acquirements which with us are the *sine quâ non* of a good education. An attempt to converse on any scientific subject would astonish every one, for it would soon show how *very little* real knowledge they possess. There is also another peculiar trait in the national character. A Russian will frequently pretend an intimate acquaintance with a subject of which he is perfectly ignorant, yet so well will he conceal this fact, that he will keep up the deception for an incredible time, when all at once he will ask some extraordinarily stupid question which shows you that he has not understood a single syllable of all that you have been saying. To this general rule there are of course many exceptions, but in speaking of a nation we take the majority. I do not know how it can be otherwise in a country where so absurd a department exists as that of the censor's, through which all books and papers must pass before they reach the hands of the community. The extreme fear of the government lest the nation should become too enlightened will some time or other meet with its reward, for they may as well attempt to curb the waves of the Atlantic as to stem the tide of civilization in its course round the world. It seems the rule with the censor's office to let all the books pass that are likely to increase the demoralization of the nation, such as the detestable novels of Eugène Sue and Georges Sand, the vicious works of Paul de Koch, and so on, and to exclude all those that would tend to its enlightenment, or would contribute to forward true and solid civilization. The overstrained sentiments, the caricatures of affection, the degrading views of society, and the familiarity with vice exhibited in these works, find their most ardent admirers in Russia, and will undoubtedly have a fearful influence at some future time when the "siècle de Louis XVI." shall arrive: then they will perform in action what they have learned in theory, and a terrible retribution will fall upon the heads of their rulers for their sin and wickedness in thus aiding their country's degradation.

I remember well the lamentations of one of the best living authors in Russia in speaking of his works, and his bitter regrets that the very parts he had most valued were not allowed to be published. Among others he mentioned a play, which really contained some most admirable speeches, but when it returned from the censor's office he showed us that they had all been erased, leaving nothing but the light conversations and "parties légères," which alone were thought suitable for public amusement; of course the play was never performed, for, as he said, "c'était parfaitement ridicule." How can a nation possess great poets, historians, or other literary men, when such an embargo is laid on mind and thought? "Our cleverest men are in Siberia," said a Russian one day: perhaps the remembrance of its snows serves to chill many a rising genius that would make his country greater than their vaunted army of a million of warriors. We were told that Karamsin, the modern historian, was obliged first to read over his pages in the presence of the Emperor before they were allowed to go forth to the world; it may, therefore, easily be conceived to what extent the truth of his statements may be relied on. So exceedingly strict are the regulations of the censor's office, that I used jestingly to say that the introduction of foreign literature would be, at last, restricted to the alphabet! A short time ago a gentleman of literary pursuits, being anxious to write a play, the subject of which was to be taken from English history, was making some notes on the different events, but every one of them was either too expressive of the love of liberty, or some equally well-founded objection was discovered. "But why not, then, take the story of Elfrida, the daughter of the Earl of Devonshire?" proposed I; "it is a thousand years ago nearly, and cannot much influence the present century."

"Impossible!" was the reply; "it would never be allowed to pass the censor's office, or be permitted to be performed on the stage here."

"But what is the objection?"

"Why, they would never let a play be represented in which Elfrida's husband deceives the king."

"But he was not the Czar of Muscovy."

"That does not signify; the *act* is still the same, and the possibility of a crowned head's being deceived would on no account be allowed."

By this it may be seen how impossible it is for a Russian author to write anything better than the silly farces and absurd comedies which are nightly performed to amuse the public in St. Petersburg.

CHAPTER IX.

Russian courtship—State of household servants—Anecdotes—Trousseaux—The matrimonial candidate — Matchmakers — Serfs' weddings — Rich dowry — Matchmakings — Curious custom—Russian marriages—Blessing the threshold—Bridal parties—Statute-fair for wives in St. Petersburg—Habit of painting—Lottery of marriage, &c.

IN Russia, especially among the lower classes, courtship and love-making, as we understand the terms, are little known. Marriages, for the serfs, are not "made in heaven," but by the proprietors of the estates and the land-stewards—the reason is obvious. As for the domestic servants, they cannot marry at all without the consent of their master or mistress (which is seldom given), or by purchasing their freedom at a price fixed by their owners; for if a girl wed a serf belonging to another proprietor, she must become the property of *his* master.

"Do you think I am going to let Zouboff marry Ivan?" was the speech of a lady one day: "why, I should never get another maid to suit me so well; besides which, I apprenticed her, for which I paid good money to Solavieff, one of the best dressmakers in St. Petersburg: and if I were to let her marry I should loose her services entirely." The fearful immorality to which such a state of things gives rise may be imagined, but not described: in fact, the vice of the lower classes can only be equalled by that of the upper: in the former it proceeds from their unhappy position and ignorance in the latter from idleness and corruption.

When staying, on one occasion, at the house of a lady of high rank in Russia, I was present at a scene that would scarcely be credited in England. The establishment was on a very grand scale; as many as sixty men-servants were residing at the house, and in the lapse of time the numerous boys, sons of these servants, had grown up into young men. The nobleman, on looking over his list, seemed to think that so many were not needed—at least, that they were wasting their time in town when they ought, for his advantage, to be down at the villages and getting married: he therefore ordered them into his presence—there were about twenty altogether. He began by telling them that it was quite time they should think of becoming settled in life, that it was their duty to be married, and for that purpose he would give them a fortnight, at the expiration of which he expected every one of them would have found a wife, and that they must go down to their village to do so.

The young men stood for a few moments in silence with downcast eyes and serious aspect; a little whispering took place among them, and then one of them stepped forward and respectfully intimated that the shortness of the time was such "that they were afraid they could not find so many marriageable women in the village, and it would take them longer to look about them, as they must make inquiries in the neighbourhood." Their master, therefore, granted them a week longer, with which they appeared satisfied, and withdrew. I had the curiosity to inquire as to whether they had succeeded in finding the requisite number of wives, and was assured they had all got married, and within the time specified.

At Moscow we became acquainted with a lady whose husband was one of the richest men in that city. She had the misfortune to lose her daughter, an amiable young person, in her twentieth year. According to the custom in Russia, her dowry had been prepared for her settlement in life :* it was on a magnificent scale, and consisted in enormous quantities of the finest linen, table-cloths, bed furniture, silks, jewels, plate, everything that a rich bride is expected to possess. It is the custom for the bride to furnish the sleeping apartment, the drawing-rooms, and the kitchen, to find the linen, &c., beside her trousseau ; and even a dozen new shirts of the finest quality for her husband. Everything is marked with the lady's name, as in case of a separation she may reclaim her dowry. The bridegroom has to fit up his own apartment and the dining-room, in addition to which he purchases the carriages and horses. This shows how very advantageous it is for the gentleman to enter the state of matrimony, especially as in Russia he generally depends upon his bride to find the *fortune* as well ; but, as a Muscovite once said in my hearing, "On doit être payé pour les épouser, car elles sont si ennuyantes !" It was on the anniversary of the young lady's death that her parents resolved to dispose of her trousseau, and with the proceeds to find dowries for six young portionless girls, whose prayers they hoped thus to secure for the repose of their beloved Marie's soul. I was staying in the house at the time, and I believe I saw all the candidates for marriage in Moscow. It was announced that *any* young person of noble birth (that is, of respectable station—the offspring neither of slaves nor of tradespeople) who wished to present herself would be eligible. I need scarcely say there was no lack of candidates for the promised dowry. I found that the lady's consideration was infinitely greater concerning the beauty of the six girls than their worthiness or their good conduct. All the virtues under heaven could not, in her eyes, counterbalance the want of personal attractions. She ran into my room one day, exclaiming,

* The Russians begin preparing a dowry for their daughters almost as soon as they are born, and they accumulate an immense quantity of things by the time they are marriageable.

"There are four more young persons arrived; pray come into the hall, for I wish you would give me your opinion as to whether you think them pretty." I accompanied her: there were, as she had said, four girls, decently dressed, the eldest of whom might have been twenty-two: one of them was really good-looking; she was perhaps eighteen. I was astonished to see the cringing baseness to which two of them stooped to obtain the dowry. They prostrated themselves to the ground, and kissed the feet of the lady. I was very glad that neither of them was chosen.

As soon as we had an examination of the different faces we adjourned to the next room, when my friend asked me what I thought of them. I scarely knew what to reply, but I decidedly gave my opinion against the two that had so disgusted me. She herself made an objection to one of them, by saying "that, as she had a handkerchief round her face, she had, she supposed, the tooth-ache, and she would not have one that had bad teeth." However, she settled the matter by sending for the best-looking girl, and dismissing the others. On her entering the room the following dialogue took place:—

Lady. "How old are you, young lady?"

Girl (with a low inclination). "Just eighteen, Madame."

L. "Have you any father, and what is he?'

G. "My father is dead, he was an *employé;* but my mother is still alive, she lives near the Kousmitski most (Smith's bridge)."

L. "Very well: what is your intended's name?"

G. "I have none, Madame."

L. "You have none! and yet you ask me for a dowry? How is that?"

G. (with a very low bow). "If you will promise me a trousseau, Madame, *I shall be able to find one before to-morrow morning.*"

Incredible as it may appear, she actually *did find* one, for the next day she presented herself, accompanied by a tall, fine-looking young man of about five-and-twenty, who came and examined the various articles of which the dowry consisted : he carefully counted each dozen of linen, had a strict survey of the six gowns and three bonnets, tested their quality, and, having been thoroughly convinced that there was no cheating in the case, consented to accept her "for better and for worse," and *her* marriage took place on the same day as that of the other five ; when my friend exultingly said, "that she was quite delighted at having found six *pretty* brides, for she should have been sorry to see such good wedding clothes thrown away upon ugly people."

In Russia many marriages, even of people of rank, are made up by professed matchmakers. In the villages an old woman is generally employed by a young man to find him a suitable partner ; he gives a correct account of the prospect his wife may expect, both of the agreeable and disagreeable ; how much work she will have to do, whether his mother be alive (for that is a great consideration, as the daughter-in-law is entirely under her rule during her life), how great a marriage portion he expects &c. ; even the number of gowns and shoes is specified. A girl being found that will accept the terms, the courtship does not last long, for the church ceremony takes place immediately, or as soon as possible. When a general order arrives in a village from the proprietor, desiring all the young men and women to get married, the priest makes very short work of the religious ceremony, and marries a dozen couples or so at once. A lady told me she was present when twenty-five couples were united by *one* perusal of the mass appointed by the Greek Church for the occasion.

Very frequently old women will go about begging from house to house for the ladies' left-off dresses, with which to make their daughter's trousseau, as they say, "unless she has a certain number, no one will have her." I have frequently myself thus contributed to a bride's dowry, for a Russian husband will take nothing by hearsay alone; he must be convinced by ocular demonstration that he is not going to be cheated.

Among the upper classes the "trousseau" is always shown for several days before the wedding takes place. I once saw one which was worth many thousands of pounds: there were dozens of everything, all tied up with narrow pink satin ribbon, quantities of table and bed linen, countless dresses, mantles, and all the etcetera of a a lady's toilette, beautiful jewelry and magnificent furs, everything that money could purchase, and in such abundance, that in the longest life-time it would be impossible to wear them out.

I knew a lady of very high rank in Russia, at whose house I frequently met some old ladies well known in St. Petersburg as a kind of "matrimonial attorneys." I was surprised that such persons should be so intimate with her, but my astonishment ceased when it was announced that "the Princess L. was going to be married." I guessed how matters had been arranged, and my conjectures were afterwards confirmed by the parties themselves, and I found it was a very common occurrence among the aristocracy.

As soon as the conditions are agreed on between a Russian and his bride, they go together to call at the houses of their friends and acquaintances to receive their congratulations: the same is done the day after the marriage ceremony has been performed.

The general rule in Russia that the lady's friends should find the money, which is of *rather more* consequence than *the bride*, and that the gentleman's friends should find the man to accept it, may partly account for the unhappy marriages and immoral consequences of them, by which one half of the inhabitants are enabled to amuse themselves with the scandal of the other half. I have frequently been told by the Russian ladies themselves, that, if a young person has money, it needs only to become known *for a certainty*, and suitors will present themselves even from remote provinces : it matters little whether she be good, handsome, or amiable ; they make an offer after having seen her but once, and they are married. It must, indeed, be a chance if they are happy.

One of the great reasons why the ladies in Russia are so extremely desirous of being married is, that they really enjoy no freedom until they are so : before marriage they are under so strict a surveillance, that they can scarcely go from one room to another without being watched. This excessive restraint only makes them abuse their liberty when they get it, and doubtless much of their légèreté may be ascribed to it. As soon as they are *Madame* instead of *Mademoiselle*, they frequently commence a life of dissipation that only ends when they are too old to enjoy it : they then devote the remainder of their existence to Heaven, hoping by the prayers of their age to efface the sins of their youth. Yet it is but just to say that illustrious examples of excellent and affectionate mothers, as well as amiable and devoted wives, are very often met with among the Russian ladies ; their natural kindness of heart and charming dispositions cause them to centre their affections on their families, and prevent them from falling into errors of which the highest classes are guilty. "Le nôtre est le siècle de Louis Quinze," said a gentleman one day, in speaking of the society in St. Petersburg. Alas ! with too much truth. Yet if we take his as a true comparison, we should find that *all classes* in France, even under the reign of such a a king at the head of such a court, were not equally corrupted.

I will add one more example of the manner in which alliances are formed in Russia. A lady, who had adopted her nephew, being desirous of seeing him settled, mentioned her wish one day to him. "Very well, *chère tante*, and whom would you wish me to marry!"

"*Eh bien!* there is Catherine ——; she is rich, of family, and would, I dare say, make you a suitable wife; I saw her some weeks since, when we were down on our estate."

"Is she handsome?"

"She is not bad-looking, and she is twenty-six."

"If you wish it, certainly, my dear aunt, I will go down to Tcheringoff and make her an offer."

He did so, and they were married.

In the northern provinces there is a curious custom. When a young woman is going to be married, she invites all her companions to an evening-party the night preceding the intended ceremony. When all the company are assembled, the bride begins to weep and lament, expressing the utmost sorrow at the change about to take place, and at her now being obliged to bid adieu to the pleasures and friends of her girlhood. In all her distress she is joined by her acquaintances, who each shed tears and mourn with her. During all the time the bridegroom is probably in the next room, and very likely catches a glimpse of his bride through the open door for the first or second time that he has ever seen her. An old woman always acts as the prompter on these occasions; her duty consists in warning the young person as to the proper time to weep, what she ought to say, &c., as until *she* begins it is not etiquette for the others to do so. I imagine that this custom is confined to some of the northern provinces, as I have frequently inquired about it elsewhere, and found it was quite unknown.

The marriage ceremony in the Greco-Russian Church is full of form, as, indeed, are most of its acts of worship.

The first Russian wedding I saw struck me as curious. A servant-girl of the family was married to the gardener; they both belonged to the same proprietor, therefore there was no possible objection to the match. As the Russians are very anxious to have as many witnesses as may be at the ceremony, the bride begged the honour of her mistress's company, as well as that of all those on a visit at the house. The lady herself assisted in dressing the bride, and made her a present of a great deal of finery for the occasion, among which was a white silk dress and a wreath of orange blossoms : she was present when the ceremony of parting the hair into two plaits* was performed, and appeared to take great interest in the whole affair. We all dressed *en grande tenue*, to do honor to the occasion, and repaired to the cathedral in which the marriage was to take place. On entering we found the happy couple already arrived ; the bride was standing on the left hand of the bridegroom ; she had two bridesmaids besides the two *garçons de nôces* necessary for the Greek ceremony. A moveable reading-desk stood in the body of the church, at which the priest took his place, assisted by the deacon or clerk. The bridal party advanced towards it, the bridegroom presenting the two rings (for among the Russians husband and wife each wear one) to the clergyman, who, having blessed and changed them, held them above the head of the kneeling couple, and made the sign of the cross ; he then addressed a few words to each, asking them if they had no greater love for another, and if any objection existed against the marriage. On their replying in the negative, he placed the hand of the bride in that of the bridegroom, and led them thrice round the reading-desk, the two *garçons de nôces* holding above their heads two silver-gilt crowns, ornamented with the miniatures of saints. A piece of rose-coloured satin was laid down at one part of the ceremony for the pair to stand on, and

* The unmarried girls have their hair done in one long thick plait hanging straight down the back; the married have two, which are twisted under the head-dress.

it is considered a very unlucky omen if the bride step on it before the bridegroom. The newly-married couple received the communion, and the priest, having read to them the portions of Scripture addressed to those who take upon them the holy state of matrimony, gave them his benediction, and the ceremony was concluded. If a widow marry the use of the crown is dispensed with.

After leaving the church we proceeded to the house of the bridegroom, to witness the ceremony of the blessing on the threshold. The bride bowed thrice, her brow touching the ground, and each time she was raised by the husband's friends; *his* mother then, holding a loaf of black bread above the head of her daughter-in-law, made the sign of the cross three times, and bestowed her blessing on the union, whilst others went to the image of the Virgin and Child, and lighted the lamp suspended before it.

A wedding in Russia is a general feast for all the friends and acquaintances of both bride and bridegroom, and only differs in the profusion and wealth displayed according to the means of the parties. Among the rich a splendid supper and ball are given, because among them the ceremony is performed in the evening; and when the newly-married couple wish to retire, their desire is intimated to the guests by the presentation of bonbonnières to each of them, when they immediately take their leave.

I often met bridal parties in the villages. I remember near Twer encountering a curious cavalcade, consisting of the wedding-guests of a yemstchick. He and his male companions were on horseback, carrying flags of different colours, or handkerchiefs tied to sticks; their hats were decorated with peacocks' feathers and faded artificial flowers, and their crimson shirts fluttered in the wind; they had no saddles, and with difficulty could keep their seats on the rough-coated wild-looking cattle they bestrode: altogether they presented a rather picturesque appearance. They seemed very merry, for they were singing with all their might some of their national airs, which we heard at the distance of a verst before we saw the party. As for the ladies, they followed behind, sitting *à califourchon,* two on each droshsky, and appeared too much occupied in eating gingerbread and cracking nuts to care much about the very ridiculous figure they made. The whole of the company seemed to have had quite enough whisky to make them not only gay but boisterous, and they appeared determined to forget all grief and sorrow, and to spend at least *one* day of their life in complete enjoyment.

Even the imperial sledge makes way for a bridal party, so of course we turned our horses aside to let all these gay people pass, which complaisance on our part seemed to give extreme satisfaction, if I may judge from the shouts of laughter on the occasion.

I once met a bridal party in a village in the province of Jaroslaf, which struck me as being very interesting; they had just quitted the church, and were apparently repairing to the young husband's isba or cottage. The bride was a girl of about seventeen, pretty and modest; she was slowly walking with downcast eyes by the side of her husband, who was a youth of twenty or so; their hands were clasped together, and the look of real affection he cast on his companion proved that, in their case at least, the marriage made at the command of their proprietor was not felt as an act of despotism.

Among the various modes of matchmaking in Russia I ought not to omit to mention that of Whit Monday. On that day a general meeting of lads and lasses takes place, at least of all those who are desirous of taking upon them the duties of a married life.

I went several times on such occasions to the summer gardens of St. Petersburg to see "the brides." Along the principal walk were two rows of candidates : on one side were the young men, on the opposite side the young women : they appeared to consist for the most part of shopkeepers and servants, and were of course all of the inferior ranks in society. They were dressed in a great deal of finery badly put on, and a great many colours ill-assorted. The young men were, upon the whole, rather good looking, but an uglier assemblage of young women it would be difficult to meet with anywhere, notwithstanding their painted faces and silk gowns.

Speaking of paint reminds me of a curious custom in Russia, which may serve to show how very common its use is among the people : when a young man is paying his court to a girl he generally presents her with a box of both red and white paint, as a necessary addition to her beauty. Among the upper classes this habit is also very general, and I have often been present when ladies have most unceremoniously rouged their face before going into the drawing-room. The lower class use a great deal of white paint, which gives them an extremely ghastly appearance, and must be very injurious to the health, as it turns the teeth quite black ; I was told that it consists of a preparation of mercury.

But to return to the "brides" in the summer garden. There seemed to be very little laughing or merriment among them ; there they stood, silent and almost motionless, with their arms hanging straight by their sides ; they had evidently come upon a serious business, and were heroically intent on carrying it through. I noticed that behind the young people were the elders of the family, to whom now and then they addressed a few words.

Being anxious to know in what manner matches were made at this "statue fair," I applied to an old lady of our party.

"Do you not see," replied she, "that the parents and friends of the candidates are behind them? Well, when a young man has fixed his choice on one of the girls, he informs his mother or father of it, who immediately proceeds to make all sorts of inquiries concerning her, as to the amount of her marriage-portion, quantity of wedding-clothes, what her household accomplishments are, &c.: having received the necessary replies, and given information in return, if it meet with the approbation of the parties the affair does not take long to be arranged to the satisfaction of all."

"But do you think they can be happy?"

"And why not?" replied my friend: "having once determined upon taking a ticket in the matrimonial lottery, the chances are they enjoy as much felicity as generally falls to the share of other couples. Marriages, you know, the proverb says, are made in heaven."

Those married in the Greek Church cannot be divorced, but I believe the union can be dissolved by the Emperor for some particular reasons. I have been told that, if the husband be banished for life to Siberia, the wife is perfectly at liberty to wed again, as in the eye of the law the former is to all intents and purposes considered as defunct, and has neither a name nor family, being only designated according to the number by which he may be classed, such as one, two, three, and so on. No one can be married more than *thrice* in Russia.

CHAPTER X.

The abbess—The inmates of the convent—The wardrobe—A young Russian priest and his bride—The archbishop—Ancient manuscripts—Alexis, son of Peter the Great—description of a monastery—Prisoners—The church, cemetery, and garden—Monastic serfs—The archimandrite—Superior and inferior class of Russian clergy—Peter the Great's policy—Political use of religion—A modern miracle—General estimate of monastic institutions—Proscribed sects—Russian hermits—Hermitage at Kastroma.

AMONG my acquaintances was the abbess of a nunnery in the province of Twer. Her reason for having embraced the sacred profession was one which we found common enough in Russia: "Je n'avais pas de succès dans le monde, ainsi je me suis faite religieuse," was her candid confession. She was of high family, but the generality of those who thus devote themselves to a convent life are not of a noble birth; indeed, we were told that by so doing those who are of gentle blood lose their rank. We frequently went to pay her a visit, and were always received kindly and with true Russian hospitality; but as the monks and nuns of the Greek Church are forbidden to eat any kind of meat, they can only furnish their table with fish cooked in different ways, generally in oil, and with pastry, sweetmeats, and so on; and, to confess the truth, I was not very fond of dining at the convent. The abbess was a lady well accustomed to the *politesse* of the world; it made no difference to her that I was a busermanca or heretic; she very politely took me over her establishment, and explained their mode of life: most of the nuns were either the daughters or widows of priests.

"Those young girls," said the superior, throwing open the door of a large apartment, "are the orphan children of priests;

they are being brought up in the convent as the proper asylum for such. They are, as you perceive, very busy in embroidering the church vestments."

"But what becomes of them in after life, ma mère?"

"Oh," replied the abbess, "some of them are married off to young priests, for, of course, you are aware that no pope* can have a cure unless he be married. Those who have not a chance of becoming so settled remain in the convent, and when they are of the proper age they take the veil; but as no one can do so until she is forty, they hold the position of novices until then."

The young girls were all occupied in embroidery. One was making a chalice-cover; it was about three-quarters of a yard square, of crimson velvet and pearls; in the middle was a resplendent cross, and the figure of a cherub with its wings spread, painted on some peculiar substance, was inserted at each corner. Another was engaged in ornamenting the collar of a robe with spangles and gold lace, with here and there the imitation of some precious stone. They seemed pleased at my admiration of their skill, and the abbess kindly offered to show me the wardrobe belonging to the church, which she assured me had been made entirely by the inmates of the convent. On my expressing a great wish to see it, she led the way through a long corridor; we descended some stone steps, at the foot of which was a door, which my friend opened. Here I was shown into several rooms surrounded by immense clothes-presses and chests of drawers. Each was unlocked in succession, and innumerable suits of vestments were displayed to view. Some were of silver tissue with flowers of silk woven on it, others of silk with gold flowers, or of cloth of gold enriched with pearl embroidery. Each seemed to be more magnificent than the last, and the dresses were in such quantities that I thought the holy sister

*The priests are so called in Russia.

who accompanied us would never have finished opening and shutting the drawers. I inquired whether the splendid materials had been presented to the establishment. "Yes," answered the superior; "all these vestments are made out of the palls thrown over the coffin at rich funerals. After the interment they become the property of the church in which the deceased is buried, and are put to the use you see. Many of the dresses," continued she, "are, as you may perceive, very ancient; some were embroidered in the reign of Peter the Great, and others in the time of Anne and Elizabeth. But you have seen enough of these; would you not like to visit our infant-school?" So saying she opened a door on the opposite side and led the way through the church. There was an old nun standing before an image as motionless as a statue; she was rapidly repeating in a low tone some prayers in Sclavonic, and then prostrated herself several times and kissed the pavement. The superior smiled approvingly as we passed, and then informed me that it was sister Marie, "one of the most truly devout women in the convent, for no illness nor any other reason ever prevents her from performing her religious duties either night or day." By this time we had reached a moderately-sized apartment, in which about twenty children were being taught to read by some of the nuns. They seemed happy and contented, and, to all appearance, were well treated: these were also children of priests. We afterwards visited some of the cells, which were very poorly furnished with a small mattress, a deal table, and one chair: we then proceeded to the refectory. It was their supper-time, being five o'clock, for the nuns retire to rest at six, in order to be enabled to perform mass at two o'clock A.M. The sisters were all seated at long tables, partaking of the mushroom-soup of which the Russians are very fond, but which is very distasteful to foreigners. We did not stay in the apartment, as we would not interrupt their repast. My friend the abbess often expressed the most enlightened sentiments regarding religious sects, and I always ascribed great liberality to her on those points, but I was assured that they were not her real sentiments, but that she very frequently uttered them merely out of politeness when persons of another creed were present. Whether that was the case or not I had, of course, no means of ascertaining, but it must, I think, be allowed that the members of the Russian Church are very liberal in their sentiments and conduct towards those of a different religion. They never display the bigotry and narrowness of mind too frequent among the Roman Catholics: they certainly prefer their own road to heaven, but their doing so is no reason why they should deem that *none other* leads to it. No one who has lived among them can really believe that the fanatical agitation so general at present in the country can be ascribed to any other cause than to the unwise policy of a government that thus influences the minds of the people.

One day, when I was at the convent, a young priest begged to speak with the superior. He was of an interesting appearance, apparently about twenty-four or twenty-five years of age; his beautiful hair was parted in the middle and hung down in wavy curls a foot long over his shoulders; his nose and mouth were well formed, but what gave extreme intelligence to his countenance was a pair of bright black eyes with dark eyebrows: altogether I had rarely seen a more prepossessing young man. He was dressed in the long purple silk robe with loose sleeves, the extremely becoming costume of the Greek clergy, and suspended round his neck was a thick gold chain, to which was attached a crucifix of the same precious metal. The abbess received him with much kindness, and after remaining a few minutes in the drawing-room they retired together into another apartment. A short time elapsed ere the superior returned: when she did so, she informed me that her visitor was a young priest to whom a cure had been offered, and, as no one can accept a cure unless he be married, he had called to inquire of her if, among the orphan daughters of the clergy in her convent, she could recommend him a suitable wife, "which is very fortunate," added she, "for there is a young girl named Annushca, whom I have been wishing to get married for the last year; she is just nineteen, and he could not find a better partner."

"But is she likely to be agreeable to the match?"

"I think so," replied the abbess; "but he is to come to-morrow morning to see her."

About a month afterwards, we saw the abbess's carriage pass our house. There were three young persons in it; one we had no difficulty in perceiving was a bride, by her orange-flower wreath and long white veil—the two others were bridesmaids. In another carriage was the young priest himself, looking as happy as possible, for on that evening he was to wed Annushca, the convent bride.

Among the Greek clergy, it is absolutely necessary that the priest should be married, but, if his wife die, he cannot wed a second, because they interpret the phrase "having one wife" in its entirely literal sense: should he have the misfortune to become a widower, he generally enters a monastery, as he can no longer have the care of a parish.

The priesthood in Russia form a class almost entirely distinct from the rest of the community: they mostly intermarry among their own families, and the circle of their acquaintance is limited to those of their profession. If a clergyman have no sons, an alliance with his daughter, if there be one, is much sought after by the young unbeneficed priests, as, on her father's death, his living becomes her dowry: it may therefore be readily imagined how many suitors are desirous of espousing a girl so portioned.

Our friend the abbess frequently came to pay us a visit. She was always accompanied by one or two nuns, who treated her with extreme respect: they waited on her with great attention, and supported her as she walked to and from the carriage, as if they were servants. I was told that she was a very strict disciplinarian in her convent, but, with two hundred women to govern and to keep on the road to heaven, some severity was, perhaps, necessary. If all the stories that I used to hear told of their backslidings were true, she had no sinecure of it, poor old lady!

I had many acquaintances among the clergy in the provinces, especially in Twer. I remember once I went to a fête given by the archbishop, and a very pleasant evening I passed. There was no dancing, of course, but we were entertained with singing and agreeable conversation. The young choristers and monks possessed beautiful voices; they stood among the thick shrubs and sang at intervals their charming national airs like so many nightingales, whilst the brothers of the monastery handed round refreshments of all kinds. Among the company were our friend the abbess and the superior of another convent at some versts distance: they were really very pleasant people. Our entertainer was a very reverend personage: his appearance well befitted his sacred position; his long snowy hair and beard, his benevolent countenance, and his stately figure, habited in the flowing robes of his order, gave him a true apostolic look, and made us almost wish that the English clergy would adopt so becoming a costume. His conversation was lively and interesting; he spoke several modern languages, including Greek and Turkish, and amused us greatly with anecdotes of his travels through different countries. I remember that, in speaking of the monasteries near the Black Sea, and in other distant provinces, he informed us that many of them contained valuable ancient manuscripts in Greek, Chaldaic, &c., which are most jealously guarded by the monks under whose care they are, although the holy men are ordinarily so ignorant that they cannot read them. He seemed to think that many works, now supposed to be lost, may at some future time be discovered in those unknown collections. On my inquiring in what way the monks had obtained possession of them, he told us that at the siege of Byzantium, and at the destruction of the library of Alexandria, many persons fled into the remoter districts for safety, and carried with them the manuscripts of valuable ancient writings, which, in the dark ages, gradually became lost to the learned men of the West. Whether the venerable archbishop was right in his conjectures, still, I believe, remains to be proved.

On our taking leave, he bestowed his benediction on us all, but not before he had made us partake of some excellent champagne, and I really quitted the palace with much greater respect for the Greek clergy than I had entertained before.

Among other estimable members of the priesthood may be mentioned the archimandrite of a very large monastery in the same province, to whom I frequently paid a visit. In this monastery, Alexis, Peter the Great's son, was confined for a considerable time. I saw the apartments that were appropriated to him: they had thickly-barred windows and strong doors, well suited to a prison; the furniture was in the same state as when he resided there, and consisted of a few tables and chairs clumsily made of deal, ornamented with green and red streaks on the unpainted wood. I could not help feeling compassion for the unfortunate prince, who, whatever his faults might have been, was certainly unnaturally treated and cruelly deceived by his father. I thought, as I stood in those small, close rooms, how many weary hours he must have passed, and how bitter must his reflections have been as, day after day, he gazed from those grated windows on the never-changing scene outside.

A description of this monastery will serve to give an idea of those buildings in general.

In form it was nearly square, and was surrounded by a high whitewashed wall, deeply dovetailed, having at each corner a small circular tower with a pointed roof, furnished with numerous loopholes. A gallery ran along the whole length inside, from which, in the time of the Tartar wars, the men could shoot their arrows on the besiegers. The gateway was surmounted by portraits of the Virgin and Child and those of other saints, before which a lamp was always kept burning. On entering, I found a well-kept grass-plot, on two sides of which were buildings three stories high, containing the cells of the monks, the superior's apartments, and the domestic offices. The lower range was partly devoted to a kind of monastic prison, in which disobedient monks and those convicted of bigamy were confined ; for, in Russia, the punishment for men guilty of that crime is imprisonment for life in some religious establishment ; the female convicts are, of course, sent to the nunneries. At the time of my first visit, there were *three* criminals confined in the monastery : one for having had three wives ; another who had killed a man in self-defence, and who, according to the law, was sent there for one year, to atone by repentance and prayer for the blood he had shed. One of the monks informed me that the prisoner in question was quite a youth, being only nineteen ; that he was crossing the river very late one night on a hired sledge, when, on arriving at a very solitary spot, the driver suddenly turned and attempted to strangle him. He found means to draw his sword, with which he gave a mortal wound to his assailant, who fell dead instantly. He remained for a few minutes horror-stricken at what he had done, and uncertain as to the measures he ought to take. At last, he lifted the lifeless body on the sledge, drove back to the town, and presented himself at the police-station. He was arrested, but, as there was every probability that he committed the act in self-defence, his punishment was the being sent to the monastery. The third prisoner was a monk accused of great immorality, who was shortly to be exiled to Siberia, but, as the final decision of the superior courts had not arrived, he was detained here in the mean time.

On the other sides of the square were the church, the cemetery, and the garden. The church was ancient, and contained various extraordinary old paintings of saints. Several monks were at their devotions when we entered ; their long black garments and silent demeanour, their frequent prostrations, and the burning lamps, almost led me to imagine them disciples of Zoroaster offering their adoration to the sacred fire, whilst the darkness of the building gave an air of sombre mystery to the scene.

The burying-ground was extensive, and I remarked some curious sarcophagi of great antiquity.

After we had examined all that we thought interesting, we were shown into the garden ; it contained a great many fruit-trees and shrubs suitable to the climate, such as apples, pears, currants, gooseberries, and raspberries, a large bed of sun-flowers, and about twenty beehives, for whose benefit the sun-flowers had, I imagine, been planted. On our return to the superior's apartments we passed through the large room in which all the servants of the establishment, as well as the peasants from the neighbouring village belonging to the monastic estate, were at dinner. Their repast consisted of large bowls of buckwheat, with oil, black bread, and salt, the whole washed down with quass, a kind of sour drink made of fermented meal—a dinner not according to our taste, perhaps, but nevertheless well relished by these poor people, who had acquired a good appetite by making hay in the fields outside of the walls.

But to return from this long digression. The archimandrite was a dignified-looking man of about fifty, and had lost his wife six years previously, when, according to the custom, he had embraced the monastic life. He had two sons, government *employés*, who resided with him in the establishment. He was a man of great erudition, and had views on religious points much too enlightened for his nation, as I was informed that he had been imprisoned some time before on account of opinions he had expressed concerning modern miracles, &c., but, in consideration of his high character for learning and moral excellence, extreme severity had not been resorted to. He always seemed much pleased at our visits, and received us with kindness and hospitality. My Russian friends had known him for many years, and respected him greatly. I was fortunate, certainly, in being acquainted with so many worthy people belonging to the Greek priesthood, and am glad to be able to speak well of a class of men of whom favourable opinions are not generally entertained by foreigners ; but I believe that many speak ill of them upon false reports, and judge lightly of the merits of the many from the disgraceful conduct of a few, or from those ignorant, debased members of the profession who are to be found in the remote villages and almost barbarous districts of the interior. I remember accompanying a friend once on a visit to one of her estates at about seven hundred versts from St. Petersburg ; the peasants came as usual to pay their respects to their proprietor. I was not astonished at any display of *slavish servility* on *their* part, as a long residence in different parts of Russia had too much accustomed me to such conduct, but I was greatly shocked and disgusted to see the priest descend to such meanness as to prostrate himself to the earth, and kiss the lady's feet : in fact he seemed not a whit superior to the degraded boors among whom he lived. A Russo-French gentleman, who had travelled over nearly every part of the empire, even to the interior of Siberia, informed me that the state of the clergy in the remote country places was inconceivably bad ; that they were ignorant, slavish, vicious, and drunken in almost an equal degree with the debased peasantry ; that, although it is strictly forbidden for a priest to be seen to enter a whisky-shop, yet they are not ashamed to send one of their flock to fetch spirits, nor do they blush to be seen intoxicated in the miserable villages of which they are the pastors ; that their wives and children are ragged and filthy, and are scarcely as respectable as those of the serfs. In what state of morality can the peasants be whose teachers are thus degraded?

Notwithstanding the evil state of things in the retired parts of the country, I was assured that great improvements have taken place of late years in the clergy at large, owing to the seminaries established for the education of priests, which are under the direction and management of efficient superiors. In the neighbourhood of most large towns many estimable and worthy members of the sacred profession may be found. It is a pity that the priesthood do not occupy a higher position in Russia, for, as everything is valued according to rank in the country, one would imagine that more personal respect would increase their spiritual authority. Peter the Great deprived the Church of most of its privileges on account of the political use to which they were put, and perhaps his successors have been unwilling to give too much influence to a body of men forming so very numerous a portion of the population, and possessing a great deal of power over an ignorant and superstitious people. Of this power the government makes use to its own advantage as an instrument by which to support its domination over the nation in the present crisis, and by its means contributes to the fanaticism now so rife in Russia, by wickedly appealing to the weak points in the national character, in making the aggression on Turkey wear the semblance of a religious war. Not only are prayers now daily offered in the Russian churches against the "English heretics," but even pretended miracles are resorted to in order to make the people believe in the sympathy of Heaven. A gentleman told me a short time ago that he had that same morning been present in one of the gymnasiums in St. Petersburg, when the priest belonging to the institution, in giving his wonted lecture on religion, informed the young men and boys there assembled that God had vouchsafed, in a wonderful manner, to show his gracious approbation of the imperial cause by performing a miracle in the sight of men. He went on to say that a child had been born during the previous week, which, to the astonishment of all beholders, when only three days old arose and uttered prophecies concerning the present war! Of course, this extraordinary little monster only said what was favourable to the Muscovite arms, and to the glorification of the Emperor and members of the imperial family; but will it be believed that in the nineteenth century, the age of railroads and electric telegraphs, any one would dare to utter such absurd blasphemies? Think of the wickedness of thus lying in the face of Heaven to forward the ambition of a man! But this man, be it remembered, is the head of the Russo-Greek Church, and is considered as infallible in his spiritual functions by the Greek clergy as the Pope of Rome is by the Romanists.

I found the monkish institutions by no means liked among the upper classes in Russia. I have frequently heard them say, "Those lazy monks and nuns, who pass all their days in idleness, ought to be abolished; they are a burthen to the community, and only eat up the bread of the industrious!" Yet those very people in their old age would, most likely, be continually making rich presents to them for their prayers, by which they hope to render more smooth their own path to heaven.

There are some sects of the Greek Church severely restricted by the Russian government. When I was at Twer a whole religious society, with their superior at their head, were arrested and put under judgment. I could not make out what their peculiar tenets were; but they were accused of shocking crimes and gross ignorance, perverting the doctrines of Christianity as a pretence for vile actions more becoming Indian idolaters than the followers of Christ. Dresses of black stuff embroidered with hieroglyphics and mysterious symbols, veils something like those worn by the familiars of the Spanish Inquisition, which have two holes for the eyes, together with all the etcetera of their degraded superstition, were brought to the governor's house as so many proofs against them. I believe the sisterhood were dispersed, and placed in different convents belonging to the orthodox Church.

Notwithstanding the excessive severity of the climate, hermits still exist in the immense and almost untrodden forests of the interior, who are held in the same estimation as saints by the population. A Russian noble informed me that in the province of Kastromà a curious subterraneous chapel had been discovered on the estate next to his : it had been dug out by the hands of one of these fanatics, and his skeleton was found lying before the altar, as if he had expired in the midst of his prayers. None of the peasantry of the district had ever seen any person answering to his description, nor was there any tradition concerning him extant ; he must have lived and died unremarked and unknown. Probably he was some escaped criminal or deserter, or perhaps a monk who had become deranged with distorted ideas of devotion, and was ambitious of aspiring to the honour of canonization. But how these recluses can possibly exist during the intense severity of a northern winter, where they can find the food to support them, or how they escape becoming the prey of the numerous wolves and bears with which the country abounds, is incomprehensible to me.

The Greek Church permits the New Testament to be read by the laity, with the exception of the Revelation of St. John, but the Old Testament is withheld. Children are taught religion by the priests, who are engaged, just as the masters of languages are, to give a lesson once or twice a week, for which they are also paid.

CHAPTER XI.

Aspect of the country—Sketch of the peasants—Forebodings of evil—State of the serfs—Anecdotes of proprietors—The French waiting-maid—Shameful treatment of serfs—State of crime—Mutilations and murders—Revenge for a beating—Dreadful vengeance of the serfs—Pleasing anecdote—Wealthy serfs—Recklessness of the nobles—Selling slaves—The cook and his sorrows—Anecdotes—Serf apprentices—The old gourmand—A good bargain and a bad one—The gardener—A boorish audience—The peasants—Superstitions and ignorance—Anecdotes.

IN the summer-time the country in Russia is very agreeable; the unconstrained hospitality of the proprietors, the manner of living, *sans gêne*, is particularly pleasant. Of course where estates consist of some five hundred square versts, and comprise immense forests and lakes, with a very scanty population, it would be absurd to expect that cultivation and flourishing appearance which we so much prize in England; yet there is a great deal to like and admire, notwithstanding. The plains extending far and wide, unenclosed by hedges; the bright green fields of flax or waving corn in the midst of forests of sombre pine; the broad silvery lake swarming with fish; the numerous eagles careering aloft in the clear blue sky; the peasants in their gaily-coloured costumes, merrily singing their native airs while at their work, or sitting down under the shade of the birch-trees taking their frugal repast; whilst in the background is seen rising from among the woods the white church with its blue dome bespangled with gold stars, its tapering gilt spire and numerous glittering crosses, all rendered doubly brilliant by the rays of an unclouded sun—all this makes a scene peculiarly Russian, but not the less beautiful. When the peasants have finished their repast, they devoutly turn towards the church and make the

6*

sign of the cross as they bow in gratitude for their daily bread; they will then throw themselves down in the shade to take their midday nap of two hours during the excessive heat:* this is not laziness, for the poor men generally get up at three o'clock in the morning, and do not leave off labour until ten at night; the continual twilight of a Russian summer enabling them to continue thus long at their employment. Towards the evening, if it be the eve of some saint's day, or great national holiday, we shall see them lively and merry enough, all dressed in clean shirts of the brightest hues, and gay sarafanes, dancing in the space before their houses, singing their native airs to the tinkling of their triangular guitárs, as if slavery were but a name and its burthens feathers. Alas! this is the sunny side of their existence. Could we but see the oppression of the land-stewards and the ill-treatment they meet with, we should soon discover how many clouds cast a shadow on their daily course. Men and women in name, and children in their thoughts and ideas, they are now governed like so many infants; but when the day comes on which they will awaken to their true condition, how fearful will be the retribution on the heads of those who have thus oppressed them. "We all look forward to a revolution," said a gentleman of great talent one day; "we all look forward to a revolution; and when it does break out, the French tragedy will be but a game of play in comparison to it." I often thought of his words when I saw the peasantry with their axes stuck into their girdle, a national custom, and shuddered to imagine the horrid deeds they will commit with these weapons when their vengeance shall have been aroused for the many years of injustice and cruelty to which they have been subjected.

Under the large landowners the lot of the peasantry is often

* The heat is so great for some weeks in the summer that I have heard people who have just arrived from India declare it is more insupportable than anything which they had experienced in that country.

tolerably happy ; and as they do not know what freedom means, slavery is not greatly felt ; but it is under the petty proprietors that they suffer the most ; then indeed they are to be pitied. It is among these that we are continually hearing of such detestable actions as in any other country would cause them to be excluded from respectable society.

I remember, among dozens of other instances, some little anecdotes which illustrate this :—

A *lady* (?) who was in St. Petersburg for the winter, and whom I met two or three times at evening parties, was one day extremely unlucky at cards : she had some servants (slaves) who possessed very beautiful hair ; and as she had not enough ready money to pay the debt incurred by her losses, she actually sent to a barber and had all their long tresses cut off, the sale of which enabled her to discharge it *honourably!* As closely-cropped hair is a punishment for immoral conduct, and exposes a girl to the jeers and mockeries of her companions, it may readily be imagined what a bitter mortification such an act must have been to them. I must, however, add that the person in question was a *Pole;* and as far as I have been able to judge, the Poles are infinitely more unfeeling and tyrannical to their serfs than the Russians.

I was once going to the opera in company with a Polish lady ; she came and begged me to wait a few minutes, as she was not quite ready ; she was magnificently dressed in dark crimson velvet, a profusion of jewels, lace, and marabout feathers. I took a seat in the drawing-room, next to her *cabinet de toilette,* whilst she completed her head-dress. Suddenly I heard a tremendous noise in the adjoining apartment; mistress and maid seemed to be endeavouring to outscold each other ; but as they spoke Polish I did not understand what it was all about. Presently a loud crash, and the fall of a heavy body on the floor, announced that some catastrophe had happened.

Very soon after the lady made her appearance, smiling with all the politeness possible, and expressing her regret at having kept me waiting. I made no remark, of course, nor did she allude to the mysterious fracas that had just taken place ; but I afterwards learned the facts of the case : the maid had not pleased her in her coiffure ; the lady scolded ; the girl answered impertinently, which so enraged her amiable mistress, that with the chair on which she was sitting, she knocked her down with so much violence that two of *her front teeth* were broken off in her fall !

An amusing anecdote was told me by a French lady. One of her countrywomen was engaged as dressing-maid to a lady of rank in Russia : one day, while combing out her mistress's long black hair, she hurt her head ; the lady turned round and gave her a slap on the face. The Frenchwoman, who had hold of her hair, which she was on the point of tying, so that it was all gathered together in her hand, grasped it tightly, and then inflicted a sound correction on the lady's ears with the hairbrush. Perhaps it may be thought that she was immediately punished by being taken to the police, or at the least summarily dismissed from the household. Far from it ; the maid knew the character of the Russians well, and also what she was about : she was perfectly aware that her mistress would not dare expose her, on account of the disgrace to herself ; for it would be an indelible one for a noble lady to have been beaten (in any place *but Count Orloff's* office), and especially by a menial : she therefore not only took the whole quietly, but presented the Frenchwoman with thirty silver roubles and a new gown, to buy her silence ; she was ever after treated with much consideration, and at the time the anecdote was told to me was still in the same situation.

When we were in the province of Vologda, I was one day walking alone in the garden ; presently I heard a loud voice, accompanied by a heavy thump on somebody's back frequently repeated. I stepped on one side, behind the thick shrubs, for I recognised the accents of the lady at whose house we were on a visit, and I thought she would rather not be seen just at that moment ; but I could not resist gratifying my curiosity so far as to ascertain who the person was who had displeased her. I found that it was the gardener, a tall athletic young man, who with a basket in his hands, was slowly walking down a path, followed by his proprietress, who between every sentence struck him a smart blow on his back with her clenched fist. The man was going forward with a downcast look, like a great overgrown child, exclaiming at intervals, "Isvenete, matutchka, isvenete, veno vat" (Pardon, mother, pardon ; I am guilty). As for the lady, when I gazed on her face inflamed with anger, and saw her infuriated gestures, I could scarcely believe that she was the same person whom I had seen in the drawing-room not ten minutes before, whose graceful hospitality and amiable politeness had impressed us all with admiration.

During our stay in Jaroslaf a commission was sent from St. Petersburg to inquire into the manner in which the slaves of a neighbouring estate had been treated by their proprietress. Her shameful conduct had driven the unhappy serfs to such desperation, that some of them had found the means to escape, and had fled to the capital ; they threw themselves at the feet of the Emperor, and implored him in the name of God their common Father, to be their friend and protector, and to do them justice, as they had none other that would help them. His Majesty (who, if unbiassed by evil counsellors and interested landowners, is always ready to listen to the prayers of his poor peasants) promised that, if he found that they were guiltless, and had spoken truly, he would see that they received justice, and immediately gave orders that the strictest inquiries should be made concerning them. The result was that the estate was taken from the lady who had so ill-treated the peasants: she was allowed a small pension, enough to keep her from actual want, out of the rents, and the property was put under the care of trustees, that she should no longer have the power in her hands which she had so disgracefully abused. Even her daughters were removed from her guardianship, lest her example should have a bad influence on them.

Many other instances have been mentioned to me in which the Emperor has displayed as much humanity as justice; undoubtedly there would be fewer abuses were it possible that the knowledge of them could reach him; but thousands of vile and unjust actions are committed that are hushed up and escape the punishment they deserve. The Russians stand infinitely more in fear of the Emperor than they do of their Creator. The common saying, "The Czar is near, but God is far off," gives a good idea of their feeling on the subject. I was once staying with a friend whose husband had at that time a great deal to do with the judicial department; and the horrible tales of crimes and cruelties committed by some of the proprietors that came under his excellency's consideration would not be credited. It is true that there are badly-disposed people in every country, but happily they have not, as in Russia, such power in their hands. The very recital of such deeds was enough to make one shudder. It is difficult to know the exact extent of the evil existing, as no accounts really authentic are published. I may mention a few that came under my *personal knowledge.*

When we were at Nova Derevna, not far from St. Petersburg, two hands recently severed were found near our house in a wood: they were tied together, but it was never discovered to whom they belonged, or who had done the dreadful deed.

When we were on a visit on Count ——'s estate, the head servant found in the garden the corpse of a woman who had evidently been murdered ; the act had not long been perpetrated, for the body was yet warm. In this case also it was never discovered either who she was or who was the assassin.

One of the trials that took place before my friend's husband was that of a proprietress who had amused herself with shamefully cutting and maiming several children on her estates ; when asked what could have induced her to commit acts of such demoniacal cruelty, her reply was, " C'était pour me distraire !" She was exiled to Siberia.

It cannot be expected of human beings, although they be born bondsmen and serfs, that they will *always* quietly submit to a tyrannical master, or that they will forego *revenge* when they cannot obtain *justice*. Many examples of the most dreadful vengeance have come under my knowledge in different parts of Russia. The first anecdote I will give is rather laughable than serious, and I mention it *en passant*, as it was one that occurred in my presence.

I was once dining at the house of a provincial governor ; eighty people formed the party, including a vast number of officers, employés, and their ladies. The feast was given in honour of the anniversary of the Emperor's coronation, so all the company were in full dress : his excellency was in his general's uniform, resplendent with gold embroidery and stars. When the footman handed round the dish of roast meat as usual, he cleverly contrived to upset all the gravy over his master's back, and in such a manner that epaulettes, facings and all, were covered with immense spots of grease : it was evidently done on purpose. The general rose in a great passion, but the man put on so contrite an expression, and so humbly begged pardon, that there was nothing to be done but to change the coat. I shall never forget the sly look of triumph the servant cast on his master's back as he followed him officially from the dining-hall, and the grin with which he returned to it with his excellency, who was obliged to make his reappearance in a plain black coat and civilian's dress. I afterwards heard that the previous day the footman had been severely beaten, for which he had thus taken revenge.

The brother of a gentleman in a provincial town, with whom I was well acquainted, had caused a peasant belonging to his estate to be flogged ; the man took the punishment quietly, and uttered no threats ; but the next time he met with M. P——ski he raised his axe, and with one blow clave his skull from the forehead to the chin. It was not until two days after that the body was found. The man was taken into custody, and accused of the murder ; he confessed it immediately, and was consequently banished to the Siberian mines.

Some years ago I met a lady and her daughter in society : they were in deep mourning, and, as I had seen them a short time before otherwise dressed, I asked a friend what near relative of theirs had lately died. "O, do you not know ?" answered she ; "I thought everybody was talking of it. Marie Ivanovna is now a widow ; her husband met with his death in a shocking manner : he had ill treated the daughter of a peasant belonging to his estate, which so raised the anger of the girl's father that, when he met him in the wood near his château, he attacked him with his axe, and killed him on the spot. Marie Ivanovna, finding that her husband did not return home, went with her daughter into the wood to meet him, and catching sight of some strange-looking object at a distance, approached it in order to see what it was. Her horror may well be conceived when she discovered that it was the body of her husband placed in a sitting posture, with his back leaning against a tree, and his hands on his knees, on which was laid the head that the peasant had severed from the trunk with his axe." As it was well known that the man had just cause for vengeance, there was no difficulty in discovering the murderer, and he was banished to Siberia. An instance was also related to me of the slaves burning their proprietors in their beds in revenge for their excessive cruelty.

A Swiss lady with whom I was slightly acquainted resided as governess in the interior of Russia, with a family who had a large estate and several villages. The three children slept in an inner room adjoining hers ; they were all very young ; the eldest was a boy of eight, the two others were little girls. One morning she arose ; her young charge were dressed ; and as they generally breakfasted alone, they were not surprised that they saw nothing of their mamma and papa ; the servants attended to them as usual, and they had no reason for suspecting that anything extraordinary had occurred ; but as the day advanced, they began to wonder that everything was so quiet in their parents' room ; the servants expressed the same surprise, and at last the Swiss lady determined upon knocking at the door, for she began now to fear that something serious had happened ; obtaining no reply to her repeated knocks, she ventured upon looking in. To her inconceivable horror and dismay, she beheld the lady and gentleman lying in bed with their heads almost severed from their bodies. She had the admirable presence of mind to prevent the children, who had crowded to the door, from entering, and so mastered her emotion that she did not scream or utter any exclamation that would betray her agitation at the dreadful sight ; but closing the door, she told them not to make a noise, for their parents were ill, and led them back to their apartments. She then summoned the household, to whom she communicated what she had seen, and sent off to the neighbouring town for the authorities. On the affair being examined into, it appeared that the murdered couple, although tolerably kind towards their household servants, were extremely oppressive and unjust in regard to the serfs on their estates ; and these latter, in order to free themselves from such tyranny, had committed this fearful crime ; yet in their revenge they still had some sense of justice ; they would not slay the children for the evil their parents had done. So quietly had they executed their designs, that they had not disturbed any of the domestics. This may be the more easily understood when it is mentioned that all the rooms in the house were on the ground-floor ; and it being the summer time, the lady and her husband slept with the windows open.

I heard of many more examples, but these will show that even the serfs of Russia, ground down to the dust as they are, will not always writhe like a trodden worm but will turn and seek revenge.

I must not omit to relate an anecdote more pleasing than the foregoing, which will serve to illustrate another trait in the national character.

Count B——, a gentleman of very extensive landed property in the south of Russia, was left an orphan at about the age of seventeen, and, of course, until he was of age he was under the direction of his guardians. On his attaining his majority he determined upon visiting each of his estates in succession. It was night when he reached the largest one in Little Russia ; he drove quietly to the house, as he thought unremarked by the villagers, but not so ; early next morning he was awakened by great noise and tumult ; he looked out of the window, and to his dismay beheld the whole yard crowded with the peasantry. A momentary fear presented itself to his mind, that the serfs had risen and that they designed his destruction. He determined, however, to meet the danger boldly ; he dressed, and hastened down amongst them. He was received with shouts that did not re-assure him, and then a sudden silence succeeded. This was broken by two or three of the oldest peasants, who advanced towards him, and with great respect begged to know if it were true that he was, as they had heard, deeply involved in debt. "Because," said they, "we do not wish to be disgraced by having a proprietor who is in such embarrassment. We therefore hope that you will allow us to discharge your debts, that you may be freed from it ; for that purpose we have collected together a million of roubles (*assignats*), which we have brought with us, and which we entreat you to accept." Some of their companions then stepped forward, having in their hands heavy bags and rolls of bank-notes, showing that they had the means as well as the will to ensure the success of their plan. The Count was too much affected to answer them immediately, but when he had acquired sufficient composure he thanked them heartily, but assured them that they were mistaken. "It is true," he said, "that on my father's death some of the property was mortgaged, but my guardians, by a careful economy, have been enabled to free it from all liabilities ; and now not a single copeck is owing to any one."

The peasants hesitated ; they did not wish to doubt his word, but were fearful lest he should have told them so because he did not desire their money. It was only by repeated assurances that they were at last convinced that it was a fact. They then begged he would accept the money as a present ; on that being declined, they would only be satisfied with the promise that in case he should find himself in difficulties he would apply for assistance to them and not to strangers.

It may seem strange to English people that serfs should be possessed of so large a sum as a million of roubles (45,000*l.*) ; but it must be remembered that many of them are not mere field labourers, but rich shopkeepers and tradesmen with large fortunes. Some of the slaves belonging to Count S. (a nobleman who possesses one hundred and twenty thousand souls on his estates) are among the wealthiest shopkeepers in St. Petersburg, and have hundreds of thousands of pounds capital. The question naturally arises, "Why do they not, then, purchase their freedom?" They cannot do so without the consent of their proprietor; and as he is not willing to give it, having a kind of pride in possessing people of such enormous fortunes, they remain in the condition in which they were born. It is said that very lately they have lent Count S. above one hundred and fifty thousand pounds to pay off debts on his property. The shopkeepers and merchants in Russia are now the richest class in the country; the nobility every year are becoming poorer. The policy of Catherine has worked well in that respect; for, they say, it was she who began to lower their power, which has ever been dangerous to the imperial family, and her successors follow in her steps. It is astonishing how reckless the Russian nobles are of the consequences of their extravagance. I was well acquainted with a family whose daughter was to be presented at court; to my certain knowledge they pawned a part of their hereditary estates to enable them to make a brilliant figure for the season. As their estates are generally pawned to the crown, and their improvidence and love of show make it very improbable that either they or their children will ever be in a condition to reclaim them, the consequences are not difficult to foresee.

It is not lawful in Russia to sell the serfs without the land, or to separate individuals of a family unless the parents accompany them; it is nevertheless sometimes done, for two or three instances have come to my own knowledge in establishments in which I was residing; and although I was present on the occasions, and know the terms on which the sales took place, Russians have often contradicted me, and assured me that such a thing was impossible, as it was not allowed. It is true, indeed, that it is *not allowed* by the law, but, if the two proprietors consent to the bargain, who is to complain? It certainly would not be the servant so disposed of, as her existence would be wretched enough afterwards; and we have often heard both male and female domestics beg another owner to purchase them, if they dislike the family they are in. After twenty-five years' service in their master's household, they can have the choice of being free or not; but they do not often profit by it, for, after the best years of their life have been passed in working for their proprietor, they with reason think that their old age should be taken care of by him; and that, if permitted, they would prefer passing the evening of their days in the village in which they were born, and among the scenes endeared to them by their youthful associations, to dragging out a toilsome and precarious life among strangers or in a crowded city. Many of the household servants are hired; they are furnished by their owners with a passport; they can then go whither they please, and serve whom they like, upon the condition of their paying the yearly abrock, or poll-tax, to him; but as this sum is not fixed by law, and the amount is entirely dependent on the will of the proprietor, he often abuses the trust, and manages to exercise a tyrannical influence even on those of his serfs who are at a distance and removed from his immediate power. The chief *cuisinier* in Madame B.'s house at Twer belonged to a landowner who lived in Kalonga, and who had furnished him with a passport. The man was clever at his profession, and had served a seven years' apprenticeship in a French house in St. Petersburg; he was therefore a valuable acquisition to a large establishment; he had three other cooks under him, and was very much respected. Madame B. was generous: his wages were high, and in addition she kindly allowed him to superintend public suppers and private parties in the houses of the neighbouring gentry, for which he received so good a remuneration that he realized a handsome profit. So far so good. By economy he might have saved in a few years sufficient money to buy his freedom, and he would have done so, as he was extremely anxious to marry one of the upper servants that lived in the same family; but then there was *the abrock,* and his master was one who never seemed to have enough. As soon as he found that Vassili was making money, he raised the amount of the poll-tax, and, by adding every year a little more to it, contrived to squeeze out of the poor fellow's hands almost all his earnings. Many and many a time have I seen the tears rolling down his cheeks as he saw that his hopes for the future were daily getting more indistinct, and that he had no prospect of becoming free and wedding Grushia. One day we found him sobbing bitterly over an open letter; he had just received it from his proprietor: it was, as usual, demanding *more abrock,* but, worse than all, it was an answer to a proposition made by Madame regarding his purchase: she with her wonted kindness wished to render all her household as happy as it lay in her power to do, and had told Vassili to inquire what amount was necessary to make him a free man. The sum named was so exorbitant that it was beyond the lady's means. Apparently his master was determined not to part with a property that afforded him so great an annual profit and the hopes of increasing it in future.

The way the Russians treat their household servants is sometimes very amusing—exactly as if they were babies. One day the eight footmen, and the five other men-servants at Madame R.'s, all had new liveries. Being desirous to see how they looked, Madame ordered them all into her presence; they came, with the porter at their head: the lady bade them stand in a row, so that she might see the effect; and having had a good survey of the waistcoats, commanded them to turn about, which they did in true military order, and gave us a gratifying view of thirteen pairs of broad shoulders, all covered with light blue broadcloth of the best quality; they then marched out as if they had performed an exemplary duty. At another time the family was increased by a raw recruit of a lacquey, about six feet two high, who was endowed with the awkward habit of letting everything fall that he took in his fingers. After he had exhausted the patience of everybody in the house, he was told that the next time he gave us a specimen of his *maladresse*, he should be punished. The very next day, as he was handing the dish of fish to Madame, down went the elegant silver slice ; after having picked it up with a very red face, he cast a terrified look on his master, expecting some awful retribution on his head for the sin he had committed ; when the lady, turning to him, ordered him immediately to go and stand *in the corner* for the rest of the time we should be at dinner. He obeyed with a most contrite face, and stood there like one of Madame Tussaud's wax-work figures, without changing countenance or moving in the least. It was wonderful how the other servants could keep a serious expression. We were nearly choked with suppressed laughter, it was so perfectly ridiculous.

It is frequently, indeed generally, the case for the proprietors to place many of their serfs out as apprentices to different trades, some as carpenters, others as hairdressers, shoemakers, tailors, cooks, milliners, dressmakers, &c. After their time is out, if their service is not required in their master's house, they are furnished with a passport, and pay the poll-tax like Vassili, of whom I have spoken. In many of the châteaux the domestics are capable of doing all the work in the family : one makes the shoes and boots ; another his master's coat ; a third, brought up as a coiffeur, is the valet ; a fourth, the head cook ; a fifth, the confectioner, who attends to all the preserves, pickles, and bonbons used in the establishment ; his place is no sinecure, as the Russians eat a great quantity of these things, especially in the winter time. In very large households there are serfs who have been educated as musicians and singers. One family with whom I was acquainted in St. Petersburg, had a private theatre, in which their own people performed operas in very good style :

the orchestra and vocalists had all been trained at the owner's expense, expressly for his amusement.

There is an old *noble* (?), an acquaintance of my friends in Moscow, who was possessed of an enormous fortune, and who made it his boast that he was the greatest gourmand in Russia: his whole conversation was concerning savory dishes and delicious meats, to the concocting of which his entire mental energies (if he had any) were devoted. His dreams were nothing but visions of soups, fricassées, and pâtés, varied with ragoûts, jellies, and macédoines. Whenever he called, we were sure to hear that his genius had discovered some new combination of good things, which he seemed to think redounded as much to his honor as Napoleon's victory at Austerlitz did to his, or as Newton's discovery of the theory of gravitation. By excessively high living, he had attained so preposterous a size, that the door of his carriage had to be made the entire width of one side to allow of his getting in and out: his eyes were almost buried in the fat of his cheeks, and his thick lips and heavy looks showed to what an extent he pursued the gratification of his favourite vice.

This *estimable* old gentleman, in order to have the cookery of every nation in the highest perfection, hit upon the ingenious plan of sending one of his serfs to each of the great capitals of Europe, in order that they might be initiated in all the mysteries of the *cuisine* of the country. One was in Vienna, another in Paris, a third in London, and the fourth in Naples. The sum this cost him was enormous, not only for the journeys, but on account of the high premium demanded for their instruction. The man sent to Paris was bound for three years; he was the most intelligent of the four; his master built immense castles in the air about him; he was never tired of talking of the great progress the man was making in the culinary art, whilst the agreeable prospect of innumerable good dinners, rich soups, and magnificent *entremets*, solaced him and served to cheer him up whenever an attack of indigestion caused him a fit of the "blues." He did not know, poor man, that the dreams of his distant serf were widely different from his own; nor perhaps had it ever entered his mind, that, in learning "*la cuisine Française,*" he might possible learn the language, and imbibe French notions of liberty as well—but so it was. The three years were out, and the old gentleman was on the tiptoe of expectation; his delicious *rêves* were about to become realized; he had invited a host of acquaintances to dine with him on a certain day. But, alas! the very morning on which he made so sure of welcoming with open arms his *chef de cuisine* from abroad, there came a letter, in which the *ci-divant* slave politely and delicately informed him that, owing to a great change in his views, both social and political, he could not decide upon devoting the rest of his days to *his service;* that he was going to be married to a charming young grisette, and had resolved upon becoming a French subject, as he was already one at heart. He concluded by returning his sincere thanks for the protection and patronage his former master had afforded him; sent the receipted bills for the expenses which had been incurred on his account, which he assured him had been honourably paid in his name, out of the money forwarded to Paris for the purpose, and finished with the most amiable wishes for his health and prosperity.

The grief and dismay of the old gourmand were inconceivable, and such an effect did the mortification take on him that he remained in bed a whole fortnight to lament in solitude his irreparable loss.

As for the other three, I never heard what became of them; but it is to be hoped that they all followed the same laudable plan.

Most of the dressing maids have served their time, and are milliners and couturières by profession. I was present one day when a bargain was struck for a dressmaker; it was at Jaroslaf, and a gentleman from a neighbouring estate had just dropped in to dine. In the course of conversation the host had accidentally mentioned that his wife was in great want of a good dressing-maid.

"Oh," said the guest, "if that be all, my wife has an excellent one that she will part with; she has been several years with a French dressmaker in St. Petersburg to learn the trade, and I am sure my wife would be glad to let Madame D——f have her."

"Eh bien!" replied the other, "and her price?"

"Two hundred and fifty silver roubles."

"That," answered our host, "is much more than we should like to give for a servant; we had better hire one; Madame D. is going to Moscow, and she must engage one there."

"What do you say then to two hundred?"

"Still too much."

"Well, then, listen, mon ami: you were talking of buying a new instrument; will you give me one hundred roubles and *your old piano?*"

Both parties agreed to these terms, and it was arranged that the girl should be sent in the course of the following week, and that the rickety old piano should be duly forwarded in exchange. Madame D.'s dressmaker arrived at the stated time; she was about twenty-five years of age, and a good needlewoman. After having served a month or six weeks, her mistress told me in confidence "that she thought she had made a fair bargain," and even seemed to intimate that the proprietor had cheated himself in the affair. I ought to add that the girl herself was a consenting party to the transaction.

At another time when I was in St. Petersburg, a young servant-girl of sixteen came into the room and begged to know if her mistress would buy her, for her proprietress wanted some money, and would be glad to sell her.

"I really do not know what to say to it," was the reply. "How much does she ask for you, Marousha?"

Girl (with a low bow). "Eighty silver roubles, Madame."

"Well," said the lady, "I will consult my husband about it, and will give you the answer after dinner." The girl made a low inclination and retired. On the husband's return there was a serious consultation concerning the proposed purchase. His remark had better be expressed in French than in English. "Quatre-vingt roubles argent! c'est beaucoup trop; et outre cela la fille a tellement les humeurs froides qu'elle serait chère même à un prix moins grand!" I do not know whether the proprietress agreed to take less on this consideration, or how it was arranged; but some weeks afterwards I learnt that the girl had really changed owners, at which she showed much satisfaction.

It is not allowed by law for the masters and mistresses to beat their servants, unless they be their own slaves; but it is easy enough to get it done by sending them with a complaint to the police, and, if the leaven of a few roubles be added, they will have as fair a quantum of stripes as are displayed on the American flag, or were ever administered in that land of freedom. The ceremony of whipping takes place in the night, and is performed in a place at the station devoted to the purpose. The reason given us was, that "the culprits cried out so loudly that it was much better to do it at that time than when everybody was about." In Twer the head-gardener thought proper to get intoxicated three days together; he had often been in the same state before, and the patience of his master was quite exhausted: so when he met him in the yard, perfectly unable to stand, he ordered the police-master (who happened to be then in the office making his reports) to take him under his care and administer a sound flogging, so that he might in future know what he would have to expect.

The order was well attended to, and the gardener was led to the station-house, where he suffered the penalty of his offence. The next day I was surprised to see him in the entrance-hall, looking as sober and demure as possible. He waited quietly until his Excellency appeared; he then prostrated himself several times at his feet until his face touched the ground, begging in the most humble manner to return thanks for the great kindness he had been shown. I could not think why he was so grateful, and asked the General if he had pardoned his late offence.

"Pardoned! not a bit of it," answered he, laughing; "he is expressing his acknowledgments for the sound beating I caused him to receive."

I could not help expressing my aversion to such meanness.

"You judge wrongly," said his Excellency; "the man, I think, displays very good feeling on the occasion. He committed a fault, for which I have had him corrected, and he now thanks me for my judicious punishment. You see by this that our people bear no malice in their hearts." He forgot to add that fear might have had a great deal more to do with it than gratitude.

It will certainly take many years, ay, centuries, for such a people to be in a condition to appreciate the blessings of freedom, and perhaps they are too Asiatic ever properly to do so.*

It is almost dangerous to endeavour to ameliorate their state. The cousin of a lady with whom I was intimate, having just returned from abroad, where he had witnessed the good effects of civilization, determined to devote his life and fortune to the

* So absurdly anxious is the government to prevent even the faintest echo of the voice of freedom from being heard in Russia, that it is a positive fact that the librettos of the operas of Masaniello and William Tell were ordered to be changed lest the subject should be too exciting!

enlightenment of his peasantry. The ignorant priest, however, made them believe that his design was to destroy their ancient customs and to subvert the religion of their forefathers. The consequence was, that the slaves formed a conspiracy against him, and shot him one evening as he was reading a book in his own sitting-room.

Some years ago a party of ladies and gentlemen, while spending the summer in the country, determined upon getting up a succession of theatrical amusements, just to try their effect upon the minds of the lower class. They accordingly fitted up a hall with great care, took immense pains to learn their parts, and when all was ready they invited the serfs as their audience, and gave them a holiday for the purpose of attending. The ignorant boors stood with open eyes and mouths wondering what it was all about, and what the gentry could mean by coming in and going out, and chattering so much to each other. After the play was over, the gentlemen asked them how they liked it.

"O, very well, Barinia," was the reply, "but we hope you will pay us for the time we have lost in coming to see it!"

It need scarcely be said that the entertainment was not repeated, their plan being thus stifled at the commencement.

In the autumn the women belonging to the estates have a very busy time; they help to reap the corn, cut the flax, and pull up the hemp-stalks, and then prepare them for sale by beating them with flat pieces of wood, which is extremely fatiguing, but they enliven their work by singing their national ballads.

In the winter both men and women employ themselves in weaving the Russian linen and canvas; the girls also in some villages make a pretty kind of lace. The produce of their winter industry is either sent to the proprietor, who disposes of it to the shopkeepers, or the women carry it about and offer it for sale in the same manner as the hawkers of Irish cloth do in

England. In the dark days or evenings, having no candles, they make use of slips of pine-wood or the bark of the birch-tree, which are very inflammable and emit a strong light that enables them to continue their work. They make the thread in the ancient manner with the distaff, which has quite a classic appearance.

In some of the villages, all the females make lace ; in others there is nothing but linen manufactured. I saw some beautiful samples of the former, the work of the peasants belonging to the Princess L., which would be admired even in London or Paris ; and a woman once offered to sell me a scarf for sixty roubles (10*l.*), which she assured me took her three entire years to make.

Some of the serfs are trained as hunters on the estates ; their whole lives are devoted to killing and ensnaring game in the forests, which is sold, and becomes a part of the revenue of the property.

When a very fine bear is slain, his skin is generally presented to the proprietor, together with the head. The skin is made into a magnificent rug, the head into a foot-stool, forming a handsome ornament to the drawing-room.

The peasants one day sent us a young bear ; he was not full-grown, but he was so enraged at being made captive that he gnawed his paws to pieces, and they were obliged to kill him. It is no uncommon thing to see young wolf-cubs offered for sale even in St. Petersburg itself, but I do not know to what use they are put. In the most northern parts, in which lynxes and ermines, squirrels, and sables are found, the hunters go into the forests for weeks at a time. They are provided with a little sledge, which they draw after them, containing the necessary provisions, and which they fill with skins as the stock of provisions diminishes. I was told that their quickness of sight is wonderful, and that they can discern at an immense distance the little black tip of the ermine's tail on the wide plains of snow that it traverses.

Whoever has travelled in Russia cannot fail to have admired the great skill of the peasantry in using their axes: it is no exaggeration to say that a common boor can build and furnish his house with the help of that instrument alone. Nothing can be more interesting than to watch a number of these poor people engaged in constructing their dwellings, and very much good-will is also to be remarked among them in assisting each other. All who have ever seen them must have felt the greatest admiration and even respect for the serfs, who, with all their faults, are really good-hearted, and possessed of natural talents which it is a shame and a sin in the government to stifle or render useless by keeping them in ignorance; but until slavery disappears from the land, and they are taught the proper use of freedom, it is nonsense to hope that great men will rise from the people. There was a poor man in Twer, a slave belonging to M. M——ff, a land-proprietor, who was possessed of a genius for painting that, in any other country, would have acquired for him both fame and fortune. Better for him had he been born an idiot! To him his talents were a dire misfortune, for his master, on learning his love for drawing and his great natural gifts, perceived at once that some handsome profit, by the way of *abrock*, might be realized for himself in cultivating them. Accordingly, he placed him with an ordinary portrait-painter, where he was forced to learn a branch of the art which, although the most likely to serve his owner's views, was most distasteful to himself, as he had genius for better things. He had no sooner served his time than the amount of poll-tax was yearly demanded: as everybody does not have a likeness taken, especially in a provincial town, it was no small difficulty to pay it. When we last saw him, he had pined into a decline, and doubtless ere this the village grave has closed over his griefs and sorrows, and buried his genius in the shades of its eternal oblivion.

As superstition and ignorance generally go together, we need not be surprised to find that, as the Russian peasants possess the latter, so they have the former quality. Many of their ideas have changed but little since their forefathers' heathen state in days of yore. They have the greatest faith in ghost-stories, sorcery, the evil eye, and the tricks of a mischievous kind of Puck called the Domovoi or house-spirit, who is a very useful being in a household, as everything that nobody wishes to take upon himself is laid on this naughty sprite. If the horses become thin, it is not because the groom sells the corn and hay; if the wine diminish or the sugar vanish, it is of course not Grushia or Marousha, but it is the ne'er-do-weel Domovio; if the tray of china fall down and the best set is destroyed, of course it is all *his doing:* in fact, there is scarcely a wicked act that he *does not do.* One day some cottages caught fire in the village near our country-house. Being only of wood and very dry, the flames soon rose to a considerable height. Suddenly, I saw several men run out of the isbas opposite. At the first moment, I thought they were going to help in extinguishing the flames. I was soon undeceived, for, as fast as their legs could carry them, they rushed in exactly the contrary direction, but stopped when they had reached the middle of a field, when they began beckoning and making the most violent gestures with their hands.

"Are those men mad?" I asked of a gentleman who was standing near, "or what are they doing?"

"O, no; they are sane enough," replied he; "but they fancy that by acting so they will induce the wind to change, so that their own cottages may not be destroyed by the flames."

Another time we were passing through an immense village, every house of which was burning. The peasants were standing in a group watching the cracking walls and rafters, and the long crimson columns of fire, as if it were some raree-show got up expressly for their amusement: they made no effort to save anything; perhaps they had tried the wind-conjuring and did not find it answer; so they let things take their course, and philosophically resigned themselves to whatever might happen. The only words I heard them utter were "Vot tak posmaterite!" a common expression among them, which may be translated "So only look!" and then, with open mouths, they were again absorbed in watching the ascending flames.

The crown allows a certain sum to the people in the imperial villages, if their houses are burned, to help to rebuild them. I was staying some time in the house of a provincial governor, and frequently saw the peasants come for money to enable them to reconstruct their isbas.

One morning we were surprised to see the whole yard filled with the peasantry; young and old were eagerly and loudly demanding to see the governor: he soon appeared and asked them what they wanted. They said that they had come to complain of the cruel treatment they had received at the hands of their proprietor, and a most sad picture they drew of their ills and grievances; they added that, driven to desperation, they had all left the estate in a body to ask protection. The governor spoke kindly to them, and promised them to make every inquiry, and that they should be righted, but begged them meanwhile to return home to their village. Some of the men stooped down, and, taking up a handful of earth, placed it on their heads, swearing that they took Heaven itself to witness that they had spoken the truth, and that, if they worked again for their owner, they hoped that trouble and evil would descend upon them like the dust upon their heads. The kind-hearted governor at length succeeded in pacifying them, and they quitted the yard. The inquest was begun but not ended when I left the province; so I had no opportunity of knowing in what manner it was decided.

A fatal instance of the superstition of the lower classes took place five or six years ago. A balloon ascent was announced to take place in St. Petersburg, and a French gentleman was to go up in the car. Everything went off admirably amid the gratified expressions of the citizens and assembled company ; it was a fine day with a little wind, and the enormous ball sailed beautifully along until entirely lost to view. I believe it was the last time that such a sight was seen in St. Petersburg, and it certainly was *the last time* that *this* balloon was seen.

For a long time no one knew what had become of it and the unfortunate aëronaut ; every one concluded that it had descended into the lake either of Onega or Ladoga, and nothing more was said about it. At last it was discovered that it had come down in the midst of a field near a village at some fifty versts from the capital, and that the peasants, who had never seen such a thing before, had murdered the unhappy Frenchman, under the conviction that he was a supernatural being, especially as they could not understand a word he said.

The superstitions of the Russians are not wholly confined to the lower classes : many a time when approaching a card-table have I been requested "not to come too near, lest I should cast an *evil eye* on the cards, and so turn the luck ;" and innumerable stories have been gravely told me about children who have fallen ill or died from its effects. In very few houses will they allow the number thirteen at table, and they will either cause one of the party to sit apart, or call an upper servant to dine, so that there may be fourteen ; and they deem it unlucky to hand the salt to any one unless both parties smile at the time. They have lucky and unlucky days ; if anything were to be begun on a Saturday it would be attended with misfortune. No true Russian would ever think of commencing a journey on a

Monday, and on entering the court-yard of a house it is a bad omen if the coachman turn the horses' heads round.

Many also put the greatest faith in love-philtres and charms, talismans and crosses; the belief in witches and the existence of sorcery is universal. If a hare* run across the path, or if a person meet a priest, it is an unfortunate omen that can only be averted by thrice spitting over the right shoulder; indeed, in the latter case it is thought better to return home at once, if the person be going on very important business, unless he make a present to the priest and induce *him* to retrace his steps. "Alexis Ivanowitch," said a gentleman to me one day, "was going to see the emperor this morning, but just as he was turning the corner he came upon three popes abreast. As the affair on which he was to see his majesty was a very important one, he gave them each five silver roubles to turn back, so that the ill luck might be averted."

"Why does not Cleopatra Gregorovna eat anything?" asked I one day of an acquaintance at a dinner-party, concerning a lady who sat opposite to me; "she looks wretchedly pale and thin."

"Oh, she cannot eat anything, she is condemned to a perpetual fast" (i. e. to eat of lenten dishes only.)

"Why so?"

"Because once, immediately after taking the sacrament, when she was a child about nine years old, she had a violent attack of vomiting, and the priests ordered that she should fast for the rest of her life, as it could only be the Evil One, you know, that had possessed her and caused so great a misfortune."

At another time I was travelling with an old lady who was continually taking a little sip of something out of a small phial.

*In Russia there are many superstitions regarding this animal; the people never eat it, as they consider it unclean. Perhaps this might have arisen from their ancient Pagan creed, as one of their idols had the body of a woman and the head of a hare.

Of course I could not ask her what it was, and, to tell the truth, I began to suspect her very wrongfully. I was soon undeceived, for the next morning the maid came to my friends in great tribulation, saying that her mistress had a bottle of *holy water*, which she (the servant) had had the misfortune to break in the night, and she did not know what would be said or done to her if the old lady were told of it, for she had caused it to be blessed before setting out in order to avert *their being overturned*, so that, if any accident happened to us, she alone would be blamed for it all, because she had spilled the holy water. As it was merely a wine-bottle of the commonest description, we advised the distressed girl to obtain another from the postmaster of the station, and to fill it at the neighboring well, promising, at the same time, the greatest secrecy on our part. She followed our counsels, and her mistress, who had not the slightest suspicion of what had been done, consoled herself as before, with the little sips, to our infinite amusement. The next day we fortunately arrived in Moscow safe and sound, which she has undoubtedly ascribed to the virtues of the contents of her bottle.

During one of my visits to Moscow I went into the church of Ivan near the Kremlin. I was astonished to see a stout-looking woman lying flat on her face on the pavement before one of the shrines, and barking like a dog. The priest was singing a mass, but his voice was nearly drowned by the noise she made ; the more loudly *he* sang, the more loudly *she* barked, and she seemed determined, come what would, to have the best of the duet. A crowd of people surrounded the altar, who stood crossing themselves with the greatest devotion, and bowing continually, but they did not seem at all surprised at the strange scene they were witnessing. A priest or deacon stood by with a tray in his hand, to whom many of the devout gave offerings ; and every time the chink of the money was heard, I remarked that the din became greater. At last I asked a bystander what it all meant, and what particular service was being performed.

"It is a woman," answered he, "that is possessed of the devil. She has lately arrived in Moscow from a great distance on a pilgrimage, and is in hopes of being cured by the saint. *The priest is exorcising the evil spirit.*" I immediately left the church, and never learnt whether he succeeded or not in driving out the demon, who doubtless disappeared when no more contributions were made to the tray.

Among the superstitions of the country may be mentioned the blessing of the cattle by the priest before they are sent out in the spring to graze, and of the different kinds of fruit before they are allowed to be sold in the market. The latter may be a wise law in the state of ignorance in which the lower classes are at present, for they are just like children and cannot govern their appetites, so they would infallibly render themselves ill by eating unripe fruit, if their superstition did not act as a check upon them.

The common people really believe that the pictures of saints can see what they are doing. A lady told me an amusing anecdote of a servant belonging to one of her acquaintances. It was during one of the two long fasts ordered by the Greek Church. The poor girl was sorely tempted by a can of fresh milk that was brought into the kitchen; the temptation was too strong, she could no longer resist it; so she took off her apron and threw it over the portrait of the Virgin (for in every kitchen, and almost in every room, some picture is suspended), being very careful to look that there was no hole through which she could peep. She then turned her back and took a long draught of the delicious fluid, after which she removed the apron and quietly tied it round her waist as before, being perfectly convinced that Heaven had been blinded to her backsliding.

The four besetting sins of the Russian serfs are their propensity for lying, their deceitful cunning, their want of honesty, and their frequent intoxication. But undoubtedly their state of slavery, their half-civilized condition, and the demoralizing effects of their government have mainly contributed to these grave defects.

Lying is but the handmaid of cunning and deceit ; and the two latter being in every known land of despotism and slavery a distinctive mark of the people, it would be absurd to expect that the Russians would be exceptions. So deeply-rooted are these vices in the national character, that it is rare to hear the truth spoken at all : even children will continue stoutly to deny a most palpable fact, and persist so resolutely in their falsehood, that neither threats, persuasions, nor coaxings will induce them to tell the truth ; no doubt fear is the origin of this evil trait. When I was staying in the country at about twenty versts from Jaroslaf, a quantity of plate was one day missed after dinner. The domestics were all in consternation ; the strictest search was made, but no trace of it could be discovered, when all at once the housekeeper remembered having seen a little village girl near the house : the child used often to come in the kitchen to beg for small scraps of the good things left, but had never excited suspicion. However, as every other inquiry had been made, she was sent for and interrogated. She was only eight years old, and she had been quite a favourite with us all ; there was something in her manner that made us think that she knew more of the affair than she chose to tell, and it was decided that she should not return home to her parents, but remain with the servants until she had confessed it. The extreme obstinacy and firmness with which she withstood every temptation of reward, and her constant denial of the truth, were wonderful, and for four whole days she still persisted in it. At last, finding that everybody was convinced that she knew the thief, and seeing that we were determined not to let her go, she acknowledged that her parents had instructed her to take the missing articles, and mentioned where they were hidden. The starosta or headman of the neighbouring village was sent for, search was made in the cottage, and there were the spoons and forks under a plank in the floor, as the child had said.

We ought not to accuse the serfs in general of want of honesty. They are very honest among themselves and towards their proprietor, nor will they often steal what is *his* property, excepting in the way of eatables, to which they seem to think they have a right ; nor do they consider it a theft to take what they wish of tea, sugar, coffee, &c. In regard to strangers and foreigners they are not so particular ; from them they take whatever is not likely to be soon missed ; the laws of property are totally forgotten ; but they are ordinarily so wretchedly poor, that the temptation must be very great, and they have never been taught better or shown a good example. The system of continual beating has never yet succeeded in teaching any people.

In regard to their want of sobriety they must be judged with the greatest indulgence. I have referred before to the inducements held out to them : to these we must add their excessively cold climate, which renders some stimulant almost necessary, and the love of excitement prevalent in all ranks in Russia : in the upper classes that is gratified by public amusements ; but in the lower by the gaiety and forgetfulness induced by intoxication. We must pity the poor Russians rather than condemn them, and earnestly pray for the time when their rulers will see that true power consists in their enlightenment rather than in their demoralization.

I remember, when the last revolution took place in France, and Louis Philippe was obliged to fly the country, it became the topic of conversation in a large evening party ; the Russians there present exultingly exclaimed that the two greatest nations in the world, namely, Russia and England, in the midst of all the countries of Europe, were alone tranquil and unshaken, even by the agitation and throes of monarchies surrounding them on all sides.

"Yes," said a gentleman near me, in an under tone, "his excellency says truly, but he forgets to add that there is a slight difference in the two people : yours is the repose of the living, but ours is *the slumber of the dead.* Russia should have for its flag a death's head and the motto *Resurgam.*"

CHAPTER XII.

Landed proprietors—Sketch of the country—The wolves: dreadful occurrence—A child lost—Winter amusements—Wolf-hunt—A cunning animal—Summer sketch—Russian costumes—The national dance—The peasants—Avarice of the landowners—Serfs and their treatment—Cruel and unprincipled proprietors—Opinion of the upper classes.

Mr. Oliphant, in his interesting account of his voyage down the Volga, mentions having fallen in with a vulgar landowner, who was addicted to habits of intemperance, and who was the envy of all because he was rich enough to become intoxicated on English bottled porter. Undoubtedly there are such low characters to be met with, but I believe they form exceptions to the general rule, for I must say that, as far as it was possible for me to judge, the landed proprietors in Russia are for the most part a very different class of individuals; they are not perhaps very refined or well-informed—far from it; and it is not possible that in the existing state of things they could become so. Many of them live with their families on their estates, surrounded by their serfs; their mode of existence is monotonous enough, and only varied by an occasional visit to the capital, or to the neighbouring town; the friends with whom they are acquainted are similarly situated with themselves. When we consider the immense distance the cities are apart, the total want of good roads, and the wide extent of their estates, it would be ridiculous to expect the high polish and great information that can only be attained by constant intercourse in good society and in civilized capitals. Supposing that a century ago, in the times of our fox-hunting squires, a traveller had accidentally met one of them in an intoxicated state on board of a Yarmouth hoy; he certainly, if he had no other opportunity of judging of the state of civilization in the rural districts of England, would have entertained anything but an exalted idea of its excellence. As far as it has been possible for a lady to remark, I have every reason to feel respect for the country ladies and gentlemen of the interior of Russia. Their hospitality is unbounded; they are, for the most part, humane to the serfs, are kind-hearted in the true sense of the word, and exceedingly amiable and polite to foreigners. There is very little ceremony, but much more heartiness in their welcome, and, rather than allow their guests to return home at night, they will put themselves to any inconvenience, and turn every apartment in the house into a sleeping-room, cause beds to be made up on sofas and chairs, and find accommodation for a couple of dozen acquaintances with as little care about the trouble it gives them as if it were merely a shake-down of straw in the stable: their principal concern is that everybody should be as comfortable as possible and *sans gêne* in their house; and what is more, the guests are welcome to stay as long as they please—one night or six.

The serfs are better off if the proprietor resides on the estate all the year: it is the land-stewards that make the most tyrannical and oppressive masters: being very often foreigners, generally Germans, they have no sympathy for the Russian race, and have besides two pockets to fill—their own and their employers'. They all seem to think that the poor peasants are fair game, and it is their object to squeeze as much out of them as possible. I have often accompanied my friends on visits to the country seats in the interior, and I speak from experience. In Novogorod, Jaroslaf, Kastroma, Vologda, Twer, Moscow, and other provinces, I have found many estimable people, ready to offer the same kindness and hospitality. Some of the proprietors undoubtedly abuse their power, are cruel to their people, vicious, intemperate, grasping, and hateful; of them I speak chiefly by report; they are not often met in really good society, and their company is generally avoided by families of respectability.

There is very little of *the country* to be seen on the post-roads, which generally run in a straight line through forests, plains, and morasses; and there being few elevations, there are no extensive views. Were there such, many beautiful spots might be discovered, widely separated from each other it is true, but consisting of woods and lakes, with hills to vary the scenery, verdant islands here and there in the broad sheets of water, reflected as in a mirror in the clear blue surface. The white house of the noble proprietor, half-buried amid the trees, and close by the church with gilded dome belonging to the estate, in which both lord and serf offer up their prayers every Sunday and saint's holiday. It is a different landscape in every respect from those in Old England, but it is beautiful nevertheless, and somehow becomes more firmly impressed on the memory than a more cultivated one, perhaps because there is more of nature in it.

It is dreary enough in the winter, when the ice has closed over the lake, and the trees have lost their foliage; when the snow lies three or four feet deep, like a white sheet over all, rendering it impossible to distinguish land from water, and silence and solitude hold their desolate reign. Plenty of wolves and bears then infest the woods near the house, and with stealthy step run across the frozen surface of the lake, while a few melancholy crows and sparrows hover in the vicinity of the village.

The wolves are sometimes rendered so bold by famine, that they will devour the dogs belonging to the villagers; and if an unlucky cow or horse be left out of the byre, its bones are the only relics remaining of it in the morning. One winter they even ate up a poor sentinel, whose post was near the palace at

Twer, and who had probably fallen asleep; but they seldom attack men except when driven to desperation.

A dreadful anecdote was told me of a peasant woman and her children, who were crossing the forest that stretched for many miles between her isba and the neighbouring village. They were in one of those small country sledges, in shape something like a boat, drawn by a single horse. Suddenly they heard a rustling sound among the trees; it was but faint at first, but it rapidly approached; the instinct of the affrighted steed told him that danger was near at hand, he rushed on with redoubled speed. Presently the short yelp of a wolf aroused the mother; she started up and gazed around; to her terror she beheld a mighty pack of wolves sweeping across the frozen snow, in full cry upon their traces. She seized the whip, and endeavoured by repeated blows to urge on the fear-stricken horse to even greater swiftness. The poor animal needed no incentive to hasten his steps, but his force was well-nigh spent; his convulsive gasping showed how painfully his utmost energies were exerted. "But courage! there is hope! the village is in sight! far off it is true, but we shall gain it yet!" So thought the unhappy mother as she cast a look of horror on the hungry savage beasts that were following in the rear, and saw that they were rapidly gaining upon her. Now they are near enough for her to see their open mouths and hanging tongues, their fiery eyes and bristling hair, as they rush on with unrelenting speed, turning neither to the right nor to the left, but steadily pursuing their horrible chace. At last they came near enough for their eager breathing to be heard, and the foremost was within a few yards of the sledge; the overspent horse flagged in his speed; all hope seemed lost, when the wretched woman, frantic with despair, caught up one of her three children and threw him into the midst of the pack, trusting by this means to gain a little time by which the others might be saved.

He was devoured in an instant; and the famished wolves, whose appetite it had only served to whet, again rushed after the retreating family. The second and the third infant were sacrificed in the same dreadful manner; but now the village was gained. A peasant came out of an isba, at the sight of whom the wolves fell back. The almost insensible woman threw herself out of the sledge, and, when she could find sufficient strength to speak, she related the fearful danger in which she had been, and the horrible means she had employed to escape from it.

"And did you *throw them all* to the wolves, even the little baby you held in your arms?" exclaimed the horror-stricken peasant.

"Yes, all!" was the reply.

The words had scarcely escaped from the white lips of the miserable mother, when the man laid her dead at his feet with a single blow of the axe with which he was cleaving wood when she arrived. He was arrested for the murder, and the case was decided by the Emperor, *who pardoned* him, wisely making allowance for his agitation and the sudden impulse with which horror and indignation at the unnatural act had inspired him.

When I was passing through a village in Olonetz, I remarked that the people were in great agitation. Upon asking the reason of it, the postmaster informed me that a child had been carried off by the wolves in the evening, and that the parents were half-distracted with grief at its loss.

Once I had a little adventure myself with one of these animals. It was in the autumn, and I very imprudently went to walk in a wood at a considerable distance from the house; presently I saw what I thought was a village dog, for there is much resemblance between the two. I wondered what it could do so far from a dwelling, and I noticed that whithersoever I went the creature followed, keeping a watchful eye on all my movements. I was engaged in picking hazel-nuts, and for a long time the idea of its being a wolf never entered my mind; but all at once the thought struck me: I however did not attempt to run away, as it would have been highly dangerous to have done so; but gradually backed out of the wood, keeping my face towards my companion. The animal advanced step by step as I retreated; fortunately I had not long to play the part, for I soon reached the open space; when I did so, and found I was no longer followed, I hastened home as quickly as possible. Search was instantly made by the villagers on the spot, and an enormous she-wolf and her cubs were found close by. She was apparently watching my steps, to see if I were going near her little ones; had I done so she would instantly have attacked me. My friends all congratulated me on my escape, and indeed I had reason to be thankful.

I do not know how true it may be, but wolf-hunters have often told me that the pack is almost always led by a female: that when a he-wolf is killed, the others will frequently stop and devour him; but if a she-wolf fall, they have never been known to do so, and at the cry of a she-wolf hundreds of animals will rush out of the forest to her assistance.

The *amusements* of the country ladies in the winter are very few—driving out in sledges, practising on the piano, and reading French novels, are the principal ones, now and then varied by a visit to a friend's house. They find *occupation* in their household affairs and in embroidery, chiefly in Berlin work.

The gentlemen who are fond of sport make up hunting parties, their game being bears and wolves: the former are hunted out by dogs and peasants and then shot, but there are several ways employed to destroy the latter. Sometimes a dozen sportsmen collect, and all go out in a large sledge capable of containing the whole party: they are well provided with powder and shot, a long rope, a bag of hay, a young pig, and plenty of refreshments to keep them in good humour. When they have reached a part of the country well known as being the resort of wolves they prepare for the sport: the man-servant who has charge of the pig gives its tail two or three pulls, which has the desired effect of causing as many loud squeaks; the bag of hay to which the rope is attached is then thrown out behind and trails after the sledge. A few more pulls at the tail and a few more squeaks as they go on cause the rushing sound of wolves to be heard at a distance, and very soon the pack is in sight, all eager to obtain the dainty bit of pork which the sounds warn them must be somewhere near at hand; their peculiar yelp brings others out of the forests, who all join in the pursuit. The repeated squeaks of the poor pig convince them that it is right ahead, and they fancy it must be in the bag of hay, consequently all their efforts are to reach it, whilst as fast as they advance within gun-shot they are picked off by the rifles of the hunters: the bodies are left on the snow, but the peasants are sent the next day to pick them up, as their skins are valuable to line cloaks with.

An old gentleman with whom some of my friends were acquainted was so fond of this sport that, even when years had rendered him too feeble to take his place with the others, he often accompanied them in his close carriage, and used to fire upon the wolves from the window. One day he shot an enormous one, that fell, as he thought, dead on the snow: it lay perfectly quiet and motionless; he saw that it was wounded, for its blood had already dyed the ground, and the old sportsman, delighted with his success, descended from his carriage, determined upon seizing his prey to show it as a trophy to his companions, who were now a considerable distance in advance. The cunning wolf let him come quite close without showing the slightest sign of life; he then suddenly sprang up, seized the old gentleman by the throat, and tore it so dreadfully before the coachman could interfere that he expired almost instantly. The animal had, it appears, only been slightly wounded, and was enabled to make good his escape into the forest.

The summer amusements are agreeable in the country, and are enjoyed with greater zest on account of the long dreary winter and the weariness induced by continually gazing on snowy plains during the previous six months. No sooner has the ice disappeared than summer commences ; the ground quickly becomes covered with verdure, the trees with foliage, and numberless lilies of the valley and buttercups (but no pink-edged daisies, alas !) are to be seen intermixed with what we call Canterbury-bells and various other wild flowers : even the dog-rose is often met with. There are no hawthorn-bushes, or May-hedges, or honeysuckles, or wild vines, blue-bells, cow-slips, or violets, such as we see in the shady lanes of merry England ; but the linden-flowers,* the white blossoms of the mountain-ash, the bright flowers of the flax-fields, the varied forest tints, from that of the sombre pine to the light birch, the beautiful sky, and the majestic eagle floating magnificently on the air, are sufficient to inspire us with admiration.

Immense quantities of strawberries and raspberries grow wild in Russia, also red and black currants are frequently met with in the woods. In the northern provinces there is a kind of yellow fruit, in shape like a mulberry, called maroshca, which makes an excellent preserve, and is also used medicinally as a remedy for the dropsy. Various wild berries, such as cranberries, bilberries, &c., abound in the forests, and numberless species of mushrooms ; of all these they make preserves and pickles, which they use in the long winter-season as a substitute for fresh vegetables. The peasant-women and children gather them in great quantities and carry them about for sale, by which means

* The Russians make a kind of tea out of these blossoms, which they take as a cure for a cold ; also of dried raspberries, which is used for the same purpose—a decoction of either producing a violent perspiration.

they obtain a little money for the winter. A party of these villagers, with their prettily-shaped baskets made of birch-bark in their hands, and wearing their national costume, make interesting groups of figures, befitting admirably their native landscape.

There is something quite classic in the Russian dress, and we frequently stood to admire the people at their employment. The straight, half-moon shaped head-dress of the girls is almost a copy of that on Diana's brow; the narrow band confining the hair of the men could find its counterpart on many antique heads; the closely-setting folds of the women's sarafane are very like those in Greek paintings and on Etruscan vases; the loose shirts tied round the waist worn by the men, their moustached and bearded faces, looked very like the figures on the friezes of the Athenian temples. Perhaps the reader may smile at the idea of comparing the half-civilized boors of Russia with the productions of the celebrated Phidias; but let him see those people in their native villages, not wrapped up in their sheepskin-coats, but in their summer attire, and he will alter his opinion; or let him witness a "chariot-race" between two peasants standing upright in their small country-carts and driving at the top of their horses' speed, holding the reins with outstretched arms, their heads uncovered, their fine figures clothed in the red or white shirt fluttering in the wind, and their faces, if not classically handsome, not devoid of manly beauty, and say then whether it does not recall to his mind the Greek chariot-races such as were depicted when Greece *was* Greece.

During the summer the inhabitants of a Russian château live almost entirely out of doors; they pass their time in sitting under the trees, reading or smoking (for many of the ladies smoke), embroidering, and chatting, or they stroll into the woods in parties to look for mushrooms, which form a favourite dish at their tables. Nothing indeed can be more pleasant than the life at a country-house; everything is easy and without restraint. There is not that splendour and opulence which we see in England; on the contrary, the rooms are but scantily furnished—only what is absolutely necessary for use is kept there, excepting when the family reside entirely on their estates, for the summer season lasts but two or three months in the year, so it would be scarcely worth while to go to the expense and trouble of keeping up an establishment there for the other ten. The peasants have their own recreations, and very often on Sunday afternoon they assemble before the proprietor's house, all dressed in their best, and dance and sing, not only for their own amusement, but because they think it agreeable to their master and mistress, who, with their family and guests, come out in the balcony to see them, and to scatter apples, sweetmeats, bonbons, and small coin among them, which they are quite as eager to scramble for as so many children.

Some of their dances are extremely pretty, and others are monotonous. I remember at one of the village fêtes a handsome young girl and a fine-looking man of about twenty-two stepped out from a group of their companions and performed a pas-de-deux, *the* national dance *par excellence.*

The girl had on the peculiar head-dress, her long hair hanging in a thick plait down the middle of her back; a crimson silk sarafane trimmed with gold lace and gilt buttons up the front; her white chemise gathered into a band round her shoulders and fastened before, the full sleeves tied up with sky-blue ribbon: gold-embroidered shoes from Tajock completed her costume. Her partner wore a crimson shirt confined with a narrow silver band round the waist (the peasants wear the shirt outside) over very full black velvet inexpressibles, the lower ends thrust into black leather boots. The dance was descriptive of courtship. At first the advances were treated with disdain; the suitor was not discouraged, he still hoped: he again made advances; *she* began to relent, then seemed pleased; he inspired her with love, but resolved to punish her former contempt with coldness. They at last become reconciled, and, after demonstrating their mutual happiness, the performance finished. Another dance, of which the villagers seemed very fond, was one in which a young man was enclosed in a circle of girls, who all joined hands and prevented him from breaking through the ring.

There is a game they very often used to play called garelki. They stand in a long double column, one pair behind the other, with a single one as leader. On the signal being given he runs forward as fast as he can ; the two next endeavour to catch him ; he or she that succeeds has him as partner, and the other takes his place, and so on in succession until the whole party are tired.

If this appear too Arcadian a picture, it is at least a true one ; but it must be remembered that these are the bright hours of their existence. God knows that they have many a stormy day, full of toil and trouble, suffering and slavery, to counterbalance the few pleasures they have in life, even though they should have the good fortune to be under a kind proprietor, and it is a real happiness to see them joyous and merry sometimes.

The serfs belonging to inhuman and cruel landowners, or ground down by the merciless grasping of a steward, must suffer incredible hardships—they are at the mercy of every one, and find none merciful. I have heard tales of their wrongs and dreadful evils in the provinces that it was impossible to listen to without indignation, and a hearty detestation of those by whom they were inflicted.

A few years ago, during our stay in the country, there was quite a famine in some of the provinces. Now, by the law, each proprietor must have granaries on his estates, and keep a certain quantity of corn in store, in order to be provided against such a misfortune. It was just at the time that England was buying up large provisions of grain for the Irish, and was consequently paying very high prices in foreign markets. The landowners in Russia, tempted by this, actually sent millions of tchetvas of corn out of the country, and left their own people in a state of absolute starvation : they emptied the granaries, and the unhappy serfs were reduced to dreadful extremities. It is true that the crown appoints officers to visit the estates and see that the granaries are filled ; but any one who has been in Russia, knows well how easy it is to bribe them, and induce them, for the sake of a few roubles, to shut their eyes to abuses and their ears to complaints. If the Emperor could have known it, the poor serfs would have found a protector, but how was he to be informed of it ? The officers sent affirmed that the granaries were full, and reported them as such to their superiors. Few of the slaves can ever escape to make their complaints in person, and, even if they should do so, the chances are that their owner has friends at court, who make out that the accusation is false, that the serfs are discontented, lazy, and disobedient, and deserving of punishment. I recollect seeing some slaves once in the country driven to their work by soldiers with bayonets fixed, and they had chains on their legs as if they were common convicts. We were told that they had gone to St. Petersburg to make some complaint ; that the Emperor had caused inquiries to be made, and, finding them to blame, had commanded that they should be sent back to the estate and made to work in the condition in which we saw them.

The upper class of the land-proprietors are often estimable people, but there are others unprincipled and immoral, intemperate and debased, unworthy of the position they hold, and of whom fearful and disgusting tales are told enough to make one shudder that they should possess any power over their fellow creatures. No wonder that the Russians look forward to a revolution, for, let the people be ever so patient, there is a measure of evil which cannot be borne forever.

Among the upper classes there are several whom I have heard lament the existence of slavery, and express their hope for the time when the name of serf would no longer be known in the land, but they seemed to regard it as a kind of necessary evil in the present condition of the nation. Necessary it can scarcely be. One would think that as, in the course of a few years under the enlightened government of England, the natives of New Zealand were turned into an almost civilized community, the same period of cultivation of the Russian mind would ensure amongst the people as rapid an advance in the march of intelligence and intellect.

CHAPTER XIII.

Government *employés*, their servility—Baseness, and its fruits—Duty of the senate—Dishonesty, bribery, and poverty—New way to pay old debts—Mistrust—Conduct of the ladies—Duties of those in office—The railway serfs—Police-masters in Russia—The military officers and the soldiers—The wretched fare of the army—Peculations of the colonel—Army regulation—A colonel in the Caucasus—Why *the people* are created.

THE most detestably mean class in Russia are certainly the government *employés*. There is no baseness too base, no dishonesty too dishonest, no cringing too low, no lie too barefaced, no time-serving too vile for them. "Do you see those men in their gold-laced coats, cocked-hats, swords, and ribbons ?" said a governor's lady to me one day ; "they are all coming to congratulate my husband. There is not one but would think it an honour to wipe the dust off his shoes." I fear, although severe, she spoke the truth, and knew well how to appreciate the character of her countrymen. There are, as far as we could learn, few exceptions to this servility, and unfortunately it seems to run through the whole of the different official ranks in Russia. It begins at the beginning : the ministers cringe to the Emperor, the heads of the departments to the ministers, the *employés* to their chiefs, and so on down to the very lowest writer or clerk receiving pay from the government ; and, what is worse, every one has his price according to his rank. When I was staying at the house of a provincial governor, the Emperor paid a visit to the place, and walked up and down in front of the station talking to his Excellency. His Majesty had no sooner left the town than the heads of the departments, the military officers, police, and *employés* rushed in full dress to the governor's to offer their congratulations on the occasion. If he had been promised the inheritance of the imperial crown itself, they could scarcely have magnified the honour more, or proffered a greater amount of flattery and adulation than they did on this event.

There were two of the *employés* in the province of which I speak who were exceptions to this: the governor respected them accordingly; they were almost daily at his house, and he esteemed them highly; they were the two principal adjutants, and were honourable men. Neither of these gentlemen came to congratulate the governor upon the occasion to which I have referred. One of them came in the evening, as usual, to take tea. He sat almost in silence, and seemed much out of spirits: at last he arose, and complaining of a headache, asked if we would like to take a walk round the garden. Madame declined, but I arose and accompanied him. As soon as we had reached the broad avenue, I said,—

"I fear it is more than a headache that you are suffering from; you have been annoyed by something."

"You are right, Madame," answered he; "I am vexed and ashamed when I think that I am obliged to be the witness of such degrading baseness in my own country-people as was shown to-day. What a dreadful thing it is that men should so lower themselves, and vilify the image in which they have been created!" He stopped suddenly, and he seemed overwhelmed with sorrow.

"They will behave more nobly," I said, "when more enlightened."

"Never, never!" he exclaimed, "until a dreadful revolution has swept over the land, and destroyed every vestige of the government now existing, and of the corruption throughout every rank."

"Hush! you must not talk so, Dmitri Ivanowitch; suppose any one should hear you."

"I am quite glad," he replied, "that I have had an opportunity of telling my feelings to some one: I know I am safe in speaking to an English person. You can sympathize in our cause of grief, as yours is a free nation."

Poor man! such noble sentiments were almost a misfortune to one condemned to serve in Russia.

"Without being base, it is impossible to get on," was the remark of another Russian to me one day.

The general rule certainly seems to be, that every encouragement shall be given to slavishness, and none to nobility of soul. "Do you know," said Dmitri Ivanowitch one day, "do you know why there are so many mean people? It is this: a young man, for example, enters the service with the determination to keep up a character for honour and integrity, and he does so for some time, and lives in poverty; in the mean while he sees those whose meanness he despises rise over his head in reward for their cringing; he gets no credit for being honourably poor; he wearies of the pursuit of honour, and so gradually becomes as debased as the others."

There is a senate of the empire; the senators assemble at the ministerial department in St. Petersburg. Their duties cannot be very fatiguing, as they consist in saying, "Sa Majesté a parfaitement raison" to everything that is proposed. One would be apt to think, also, that the law must be an easy study, as on the first page of the statute-book it is announced that everything is according to the will of the Emperor.

I am certain that the dishonourable actions to which many of these *employés* are addicted, and which I myself have witnessed, would scarcely be credited in England, where officers and gentlemen are synonymous terms. One day we saw an officer boldly pocket some money belonging to his neighbour, at cards. Another slipped some concert-tickets up his sleeve, that were the property of my friend. We both saw him do it, but neither of us could accuse him to his face. Many a time things were missing that could have been missing in no other way. One day a young officer called while the family were at dinner. The footman very carelessly had requested him to enter one of the drawing-rooms whilst he went and informed his master. He came back in a minute or two, and begged him to wait a little, but the officer politely said that he did not wish to derange the dinner-party, and, as he had to call elsewhere, he would shortly return. He then went away. No sooner had he done so than the servant discovered that his lady's watch had disappeared. The police were not informed of it, out of respect to his uncle, who was of rank.

Bribery is everywhere practised. There are some honourable men among the *employés*, undoubtedly, but they are generally so wretchedly poor, that really the temptation must be almost irresistible. Their pay from the government is so small that they can scarcely supply themselves with shoes and gloves out of it; so the money must be obtained somehow to enable them to make a genteel appearance. A few have, perhaps, private property, but the major part have only their appointment.

From all that is told concerning them, the Russo-Germans seem to be the most rapacious of any people in the country: they are the most cringing when in an inferior station, and the most tyrannical and merciless when in power.

"Immense numbers of our officers are Germans," said a nobleman to me. "They enter the service, and, as they have their fortune to make, they will submit to all sorts of insults, cringe and curry favour with their superiors, and do anything to get on. Now, *a Russian* will not do that; he will throw up his commission and leave the service upon a very slight provocation." My experience did not enable me to agree with him.

"Every man has his price," is said to have been one of Sir Robert Walpole's axioms; had he lived in Russia, he would have nearly hit the truth, and, he might have added, "every woman," too.

A lady in St. Petersburg, whose husband was indebted to the crown in the sum of about ten thousand silver rubles, and had not the means, or perhaps the will, to pay it, hit upon the following expedient :—It was the anniversary of the marriage of a personage of the most exalted rank, so she thought fit to address a letter of humble congratulations on the occasion. Humble enough! for it began thus :—"If a worm crawling upon the earth dare to offer," &c., &c., through a couple of pages, all in the same style. The letter deserved to be kept, were it only as a curiosity of literature, and to preserve it as an existing proof to what grovelling meanness a human being can descend. It was not in this light, however, that it was regarded by the personage to whom it was sent, or by those who had *the pleasure* of perusing it. The entire household was in an extasy of admiration for three whole days concerning Madame K—ska's beautiful address to the E——. The writer obtained what she so ardently desired; the debt was remitted. When I state that this was the person mentioned in a former chapter as having caused her poor servants' hair to be cut off, her character can be justly appreciated.

One day we went to pay a visit to an old lady. As all the drawing-rooms were thrown open for the reception of visitors, I committed no solecism of etiquette in rising to take a nearer view of some beautiful English engravings, of which I caught a glimpse in the next room. I was surprised and rather annoyed to find that I was followed, step by step, by the old lady herself, and that every movement of mine was closely watched by her. I was so vexed that I returned to my seat without having had the pleasure I expected. On going home, I mentioned the circumstance to my friend. "You must not be surprised at it, ma chère," answered she, "for really you do not know how many things are lost in such parties from the too great admiration of the visitors." At a ball, it is quite disgraceful to see the quantities of sweetmeats and fruit the ladies and gentlemen put into their pockets. The rush into the refreshment-room, when it is thrown open, is quite disgusting; it can be compared to nothing else than a swarm of locusts, and they leave the same desolation behind them. When the ladies go into the dressing-room, they will often actually take the packet of white gloves or hair-pins, which it is the custom to place on the toilette-table in case any of the visitors should require them. It would really be an insult to the lowest peasant in England to suspect him of such meanness as one meets with every day among the *employés* and *soi-disant* gentlemen and ladies in Russia. Dmitri Ivanowitch was perhaps right in saying that nothing but the hurricane of revolution could clear the social atmosphere of its corruption. Perhaps the figure of Justice on the *outside* of the ministerial department in St. Petersburg is an unintentional satire upon the state of affairs within.

Everybody seems to think that he is placed in an office for no other purpose than to fill his own pockets; and it is astonishing with what rapidity he manages to do so, especially if there be any public work on hand. We were staying in one of the provinces through which the railway from Moscow to St. Petersburg runs. While it was being constructed, the fortunes made by the engineers and *employés* were astonishing: from having nothing at all, they soon acquired estates, and became quite rich, and that at the expense of the crown and of the *miserable serfs* that laboured on the road. Once, when the trains began to run, we went to a picnic by one of them. When we stopped at the station, we found about four hundred of the workmen assembled. They eagerly asked if the governor were of the party. Being told that he was not, but that his lady was among us, they earnestly begged to see her. She very kindly came at their request. We then heard a sad story, showing the way in which these poor people were treated: they had not been paid any wages for six weeks; their rations were bad; and, more than that, a dreadful fever, something like the plague, had broken out among them, which had not been reported, and they said that their companions had perished by scores, and had been buried, like so many dogs, in the morasses along the line. The wretched looks and half-clad bodies of these ill-used men bore witness to their unhappy state, and showed too plainly how they had been wronged by the rapacity of the government *employés*.

The police-master and the officer of *gensdarmes*, with some of the chief engineers, were of the party. They pretended utter ignorance of the whole affair, and wished to make every one believe that they were quite shocked to hear of it; but undoubtedly they knew well whither the money had gone. They made so plausible a tale, and put so fair a face on the matter, telling the poor serfs that they would see it all righted, that one would have deemed them their guardian angels, instead of their robbers: not so thought the unhappy peasants, if one might judge by the look of despair and hopelessness that they cast on each other. They too well knew that vengeance would fall on them for daring to make the complaints we had heard, and that they had only rendered their condition infinitely more wretched than before.

At another time a large body of the serfs from the railway came to the governor's house, and made similar complaints; they waited and saw his excellency themselves, and he immediately caused their wages to be paid.

As for the police, they have been spoken of elsewhere, but I cannot avoid mentioning in what manner the chief master of the provincial police is regarded by the governor. He seems to be a kind of head lacquey, who is expected to run about as an errand-boy, and to perform all the dirty work of the government.

The police-master of a provincial capital in which we were residing was a colonel in the army, six feet high and stout in proportion ; yet, when he used to come to make the daily reports, he stood with the humility of a servant before his master, and bore all the insulting speeches and all the opprobrious names that the governor chose to bestow upon him, without showing the least indignation at them. He looked just like a great over-grown schoolboy being scolded by a little old pedagogue.

In regard to the military, if they are gentlemen by education *and fortune*, they behave as such ; but the major part, having nothing but their pay, resort to the same unjust means as the government officials, and the poor soldiers suffer dreadfully from the injustice of their superiors. I believe their lot is not quite so miserable in the capital as in the provinces, because by chance abuses *may come* to the Emperor's knowledge ; but it is a fact that sentinels on duty have frequently as we were passing begged in an under-tone a few copecks to buy themselves bread ; they saw perhaps, poor men ! that we were foreign ladies, and not likely to tell. One of them assured us (and from all that I know to be true there is no reason to think he spoke falsely) that he was really more than half-starved, and was so continually tormented by incessant craving, that it nearly drove him mad.

How many of the grand dinners given by the colonel are paid for by the hunger of the unhappy soldiers of his regiment, his conscience (if a Russian colonel have one) can best decide. Russians have often said in my hearing that they would prefer being colonels to having the rank of general, because the former have so many more advantages in a pecuniary view. It is true that there is an army regulation, that, when a general is sent down from St. Petersburg into the provinces (which takes place at certain intervals) to review the troops and to inspect military matters, he can call any man he pleases out of the ranks, and, taking him aside, ask him questions as to whether he has any cause for complaint regarding his rations, clothing, &c., against his colonel or commanding officer. It is supposed to be strictly confidential, and to be kept a great secret. The plan is certainly a good one, and was established for a humane purpose, to remove abuses as much as possible, and would doubtlessly act as a check if there were any trust to be reposed in the generals; but, from all that we have heard, *that man* must be a bold one who would dare to tell the truth: there would be too many opportunities to make him feel his commander's vengeance in case it should be believed. I have heard Russians relate the most dreadful tales of the way in which the poor soldiers in the Caucasus are treated. Some years since, the brother of a lady we knew in St. Petersburg (it was the same who suffered from the birch in Orloff's office) was under judgment for his conduct in the Caucasus; he had so starved his miserable regiment, and given such bad food for the men's use, that a pestilence broke out among them, and *ils se mouraient comme des mouches*, as it was said. It took half his fortune to bribe the authorities to hush the matter up. In fact, from all that is seen and heard in Russia, one would think that the lower classes are created expressly to become the prey of the upper, just as we see the smaller fish serve to support the larger, or to be regarded merely as a breed of sheep whose fleece the farmer takes whenever he pleases to do so.

CHAPTER XIV.

Description of churches—A devotee—Saints' portraits—The lower class of worshippers—Infant communion—Administering the sacrament—A funeral—Customs of oriental origin—Tartar burying-ground—A wake—Prayers for the dead—Horror of death—A baptism—Authenticity of Christ's portraits—A procession in Moscow—Miraculous portrait of the Virgin—Religious processions—Aquatic procession—Pilgrims—A pilgrimage—The miraculous image at Jaroslaf—Angelic artists—Monks and money—A holy tradition—Religious ceremonies—Confession in the Greek Church—Representation of Christ's interment—High mass in the Kazane church.

THE Russian churches are much decorated internally ; in some, indeed most of them, the walls are entirely covered with the pictures of saints, the Virgin and Child, and, the Protestant will be shocked to see, of the Creator also, who is generally represented under the figure of an aged man with long white hair and beard, having the triangle or symbol of the Godhead either in his hand or above his head. He is sometimes represented as sitting on the clouds, with his foot placed on the earth or globe ; indeed so depicted it appeared to be merely a copy of the heathen Jupiter or the northern Thor. Sometimes our Saviour and the Virgin Mary were painted one on either side. The circle of glory round the brows of the saints is ordinarily of silver gilt, but very often of pure gold, set with pearls and precious stones. Many of the dresses are of metal (either gold or silver gilt) and they so entirely cover the space that only the face and hands of the figures are visible out of the mass of rich settings of innumerable pearls, rubies, and diamonds. An anecdote was told us by the head of a judicial department, of a very devout lady, who was so exceedingly assiduous in repeating prayers, and in earnestly embracing the portrait of "Our Lady" in the Kazane church, that the priests began to suspect that so much unction was not purely spiritual ; they therefore set the police to watch, and "sure enough" they discovered that the devotee had actually succeeded in dislodging some of the valuable diamonds with her teeth : she was punished by being sent on a pilgrimage to Siberia. Many of the Saints' portraits are extremely ancient, and costly as regards the materials of which they are composed, but they are executed in the most barbarous taste, and possess no artistic excellence whatever. Some of them are so blackened by time, that at first sight the face and hands appear merely dark spaces left in the brilliant surface ; but the older and uglier these Virgins are, the more they are adored and the more miracles they are said to perform.

There is an immense deal of gilding about the churches, which, with rows of saints, all in their gold and silver dresses, lighted up by the innumerable little lamps suspended before them, the small tapers stuck in stands here and there, and candles of gigantic circumference in silver sconces, near the shrines and altars, makes a very glittering appearance, and harmonizes well with the splendid robes of the priests when they perform mass. More enlightened nations are apt to look with contempt on all these gewgaws, but undoubtedly they have their use in impressing a people so uncivilized and illiterate as are the lower classes in Russia, with respect for a religion which they are not yet in a condition to understand by precept alone. It is like teaching children to read by means of a pictured alphabet. Many and many a time have we seen deeply-felt devotion among the poorer portion of a Russian congregation ; certainly they *do* frequent their places of worship much more than their brethren in more polished countries, and believe what their pastors teach them. In the Greek Church, even the babies in arms communicate. I was present at a mass in which a child of about three months old took the sacrament. The reason given is, that they follow the command of Christ, that the children should be brought to him, from the text, "Suffer little children to come unto me, and forbid them not." The infant above-mentioned was that of a gipsy-woman, who, with a party of her tribe, had come to worship at the cathedral of Novogorod.

The manner of administering the sacrament in the Greek Church differs from that of ours. The priest holds the cup in his hand, and presents a portion of the wine in a spoon to the communicant, together with a small loaf, something in the shape of what we call a cottage-loaf, which is always made either by a nun or a priest's widow, but never by less sacred hands. A very small triangular piece is cut out of the loaf, which the communicant takes with the wine.

Everybody in Russia is expected to take the communion once a year at the least, and those in the government employ must produce a certificate from the clergyman to that effect.

We once went to witness the ceremony of electing the mayor of a town: it took place in the cathedral. The bishop, a venerable-looking old man, was standing in the front of the altar when we entered; on his right hand was the golden cross, borne by a priest, and the Bible placed on a stand. Each officer in succession first kissed the cross, then the book, and lastly the prelate's hand, as a token of his faithfulness to the chief of the commonalty. The address of the bishop and his benediction terminated the election.

There is a very curious painting on the walls of the cathedral in Archangel. It represents the parable of the mote and the beam; the former is depicted as a large branch of holly, stuck in a man's eye; the latter as an immense rafter traversing his neighbour's head. On the other side is a large view of the place of final punishment, in which hideous-looking devils, with bird's claws in lieu of hands and feet, are engaged in punishing the wicked.

A Russian funeral, if it be that of a rich person, is a very splendid sight. An old lady of rank, with whom I was acquainted, died suddenly. A description of her interment may serve to convey an idea of such in general.

No sooner had it been ascertained that life was extinct, than the body was carefully washed, and dressed in the handsomest gown she possessed when alive, together with all the remaining articles of toilet, even to the satin shoes and silk stockings, the beautiful laced cap trimmed with flowers, and the white kid gloves, just as if she were going to an evening party. Sometimes the face is painted, as it was not long ago in the case of a certain prince in St. Petersburg ; but in the instance of which I speak this was not done.

The body was then placed in the coffin, which is not like those used in England, but more resembles an ornamental box,* highly decorated with silver lace and large bullion tassels at each corner, and laid on the table in the great hall of reception. Priests came and sang mass incessantly night and day until the fourth morning, which is the time fixed by law for the interment.

During all this time the friends and acquaintances of the family came and stayed with them in succession night and day, so that they should not be left alone with the corpse for a single instant ; and even for a considerable time after the funeral, as they have a belief that the soul still haunts the abode for a stated period previous to taking its flight to the place of eternal rest. In all cases of domestic misfortune and trouble the Russians are unequalled in their display of kindness of heart and sympathy towards the sufferers, and unwearied in their endeavours to lighten the sorrows of their friends—a most estimable

* The coffin for an old person is generally covered with black and trimmed with silver, but for a young person it is pink or white, with a quantity of gold ornaments ; wreaths of flowers, according to the age of the dead, are laid on the top.

trait in the national character. It is at such times as these that their amiable qualities, their charity, and affectionate feelings ought to be witnessed: they serve to counterbalance the grave faults and errors of which they are guilty.

When the day of interment arrived, the cover of the coffin was placed on it, but was not fastened down—that is done at the very last moment; the coffin was then placed on an open hearse, a rich pall of cloth of gold was partly thrown over it, on which a silver cross was embroidered. But previously I should mention that a piece of paper was placed in the hand of the corpse, a kind of certificate from the priest, a passport to heaven. This may remind the reader of the Egyptian custom of judging the dead and the story of Charon.

When all was ready the procession set out; although it was midday, several men with lighted torches preceded it. They were dressed in long black cloaks, with very broad-brimmed hats, ornamented with streamers of white ribbon. Then followed the bishop, wearing his mitre, and carrying a golden cross, accompanied by several priests and deacons, habited in black velvet robes, trimmed with silver lace, bearing church banners and pictures of saints, followed by a number of choristers, chanting a part of the mass for the dead. After them came the hearse, drawn by four black horses, covered with cloth, escorted by more torch-bearers: immediately following were the nearest relatives; a long line of carriages belonging to friends and acquaintances closed the procession. After the interment was over, the priests and acquaintances returned to the house and partook of a magnificent repast, which it is the custom to provide on these occasions. I believe that it was on the fortieth day after the death that the nearest relatives went to the church, and made an offering of rice, bread, and salt, the reason of which they could not tell us, but said it was an ancient rite that ought to be attended to. Probably, like many of their customs, it is one derived from the

East. The ceremony of blessing the waters twice a year, which has been so often described, the reverence shown to doves and pigeons, although ascribed by the Russians to a Christian origin, must (if Asiatic travellers tell truly) have had a similar one.

The same may be said of their driving out to meet the summer, which seems to find its counterpart in China ; and the presentation of the egg at Easter might have been derived from the Hindoo religion, as we are told that the Brahmins affirm that the Creator was floating on the surface of the waters under the form of an egg. It is certain that some superstitions regarding this object must have a more ancient origin than the Christian era, so many traces of it having been found in Egyptian tombs ; nor can it have been since that time confined to the Christian Church alone ; for when we were at Twer a new road was being cut close to our house, and the men in digging came to a Tartar burying-ground ; hundreds of coffins were removed, and in many *eggs* were found ; some of them were brought to us. The bodies were all enclosed in strips of the birch-bark, but a few had the remains of the Tartar costume. In speaking on this subject I may mention that in one coffin a large bottle of some strong liquor was discovered, which the workmen had no sooner opened than they drank the whole of its contents, which they pronounced as some of the best they had ever tasted ! It had probably been some centuries under ground.

We were once at a grand festival given in honor of the memory of a rich proprietor on the anniversary of his death : it lasted three days, and was in fact a " wake," as the Irish call it. It differed in no way from an ordinary rejoicing, excepting that we went in the morning to church, in which all the peasants belonging to the estate were assembled. In the afternoon the villagers danced in front of the edifice, just as they would have done at a wedding, whilst the friends of the gentleman at whose house it was given dined together. There were all kinds of delicacies and every description of wine—champagne, œil de perdrix, burgundy, claret, &c.

A family with whom my friends were acquainted had the misfortune to lose their mother. The friends and relatives of the deceased as usual assembled to keep the survivors company, and the people below stairs actually played at cards whilst the clergy above were singing the mass over the corpse. The reason given us was "que c'était tellement ennuyant à s'asseoir et ne rien faire ;" but this was an exception to the general conduct on such occasions. The Russians believe in the efficacy of prayers for the dead, and for the good of souls in the intermediate state, but they do not seem to have any very definite ideas about purgatory. Indeed the Greek religion only teaches that there are two places : one for the good and the other for the bad. Yet they attend to the annual performance of a mass for those that are departed, and hold the communion of spirits in its literal sense. They endeavour by every means to render the prospect of death less terrible, yet perhaps there is not a nation upon the earth that contemplates it with so great horror and dread : like the ancient Romans, they cannot endure to hear it even named before them, and frequently, when death becomes accidentally the subject of conversation, they will beg that the subject may be dropped as being too disagreeable.

One morning the porter found a basket on the snow in front of the house in which we were residing, and brought it to the princess. To our astonishment on removing the numerous wrappings on the top, a little baby of not more than a few days old was exposed to our view. Madame, although she had six children of her own, immediately, with all the kindness of a Russian, declared that she would adopt it. "She would not," she said, on any account show such inhospitality to the little distressed stranger as to send it away ; it had been evidently destined by Heaven that it should be left at her gate, so that she might afford it the protection its own unfortunate mother was unable to give it." She therefore immediately sent to a priest, and requested him to christen the child, and she and the prince stood as sponsors. It is a curious thing that among the Russians the *father* and *mother* of an infant not only cannot stand as sponsors to it, but they are not allowed to *be present* at its baptism. The godfather and godmother, by answering for the child, become related to it, and to *each other;* and a lady and gentleman who have stood as sponsors to the same child are not allowed to marry each other. The form of christening differs materially from that of our Church. The priest takes the child, which is quite naked, and, holding it by the head, so that his thumb and finger stop the orifices of the ears, he dips it thrice into the water; he cuts off a small portion of the hair, which he twists up with a little wax from the tapers and throws into the font; then, anointing the baby's breast, hands, and feet with the holy oil, and making the sign of the cross with the same on the forehead, he concludes by a prayer and benediction.

In regard to the authenticity of the pictures of Christ, I have often asked my Russian friends how they could prove that the portrait before which they bowed really in any way resembled the Saviour or the Virgin. "In respect to that of Christ," was the reply, "we are convinced of its being like him, for when he had wiped the apostles' feet, to show a still greater humility, he immediately after removed the moisture from his own face with the same cloth, and his likeness became instantly miraculously reflected thereon. It is from this towel, which some say is still preserved, that all the portraits have been handed down to us."

"Well! but you have not accounted for that of the Virgin; we have no record of her wiping the feet of any one." "How you heretics talk!" exclaimed they; "why, have you never heard how many miraculous pictures of her have descended from heaven? they must needs be like her, for they were painted by the angels themselves who attend on her."

It appears that there are a great many of these portraits dispersed about Russia, for we saw several miracle-working ones in different parts of the country. In Moscow I frequently met a carriage and six, with postillions, coachman, and two footmen behind, all with uncovered heads, though it might have been in the depth of winter. It contained a portrait of the Virgin placed on the seat of honour, with two priests sitting facing it. All the people along the streets took off their hats and made the sign of the cross as it passed by, and seemed to regard it with as much respect as they would have done the Czar himself. During the time of the cholera I frequently used to see this carriage pass, and my Russian friends informed me that the presence of the image served to raise the spirits of the people, who believed that the dreadful scourge became lessened by it. I was even assured that, when taken, as it frequently was, into the chamber of the dying, their faith in it was so great that they had been often known to rally their failing energies and recover from a hopeless sickness, even after they had been entirely given over by the doctors that attended them. "But as it costs a great deal of money," continued my informant, "to cause a miraculous portrait to be brought to a house, of course only the rich can afford it."

In St. Petersburg there are very often processions of these pictures when the cholera is about, or any great event takes place; I saw them many times. The priests in their magnificent robes, bearing golden crosses and sacred banners, and several deacons carrying some miraculous portrait or other, go round the town accompanied by a band of choristers singing mass, and followed by immense crowds of the poorer classes, who considered themselves to be thereby performing an act of great devotion, every man having his head uncovered during the whole time. The picture is generally taken to some church, wherein mass is performed in its presence. When I was staying in Jaroslaf one spring, I had an opportunity of seeing the extent to which the superstition of the people and their reverence for these pictures prevailed.

As soon as the Volga was cleared of ice, hundreds of pilgrims and peasants from all parts of the country poured into the town, and they might have been seen in groups lying asleep on the bare ground, both men and women, there not being lodgings sufficient for their accommodation, but they probably preferred the open air, as they frequently sleep on the roadside on their marches. The custom of going on a pilgrimage is very general in Russia. We had a servant who went from St. Petersburg to Jerusalem and back again on foot. She went to the holy sepulchre to return thrnks for her son's recovery from sickness, and was absent a year. There is really something very affecting in such an act of gratitude and devotion.

The object of the pilgrimage to Jaroslaf was to assist in the procession of a wonderful miraculous picture of the Virgin, which was shortly expected to arrive from a monastery distant about eighty versts down the river.

The day at length came. Several barks with streamers flying and sacred banners displayed were seen from afar. On their nearer approach the sound of monkish hymns floating on the air caused a lively excitement among the people, who began crossing themselves with extreme assiduity. At last the Virgin disembarked: she was received by the governor with intense respect, who, together with the vice-governor, the maréchal de noblesse, the military, the police, and all the employés, were in their most magnificent uniforms. Those who had stars and crosses (which are about as plentiful in Russia as gingerbread-nuts at a fair, and as valuable) displayed them in their full splendour on this occasion in rows along their breast. The mayor and shopkeepers, and about twenty thousand of the lower classes in all their gala dresses, the pilgrims, and large numbers of children, accompanied the picture in the procession round the town, the governor walking next to it and the rest following according to their rank. It was then placed in the cathedral, where it was to remain for some weeks in order to receive the adoration (*and the money*) of the devout. Hearing so much about this wonderful portrait, I was induced to pay it a visit also. It was some time ere I could make my way into the cathedral, so great was the crowd, but at last my friend and I reached the altar on which it was placed. Certes, if the angels are no better artists they would assuredly starve on earth, for nobody, and certainly no *lady*, would wish her likeness taken in the same style. It could be compared to nothing but to a piece of a brown saddle, with some dark lines for the eyebrows, added to which the unfortunate Virgin had no nose—great age had deprived her of every trace of it. As usual in these old pictures nothing but the face and hands were visible : the crown and robes were sheets of gold set with precious stones. A priest was standing near singing mass, another by his side had a tray in his hands, a third had charge of a powder-puff and a bowl of flour. As soon as the worshipper had contributed to the tray, the priest with the puff powdered the Madonna's hand, and then the former was permitted to have the consolation of kissing it, which he did with many bows and crossings ; he then retired with the air of being highly edified with what he had done : hundreds of people in succession performed the same ceremony. The clergy must obtain immense sums of money by means of these miraculous portraits, for I am afraid to say how frequently, even during the short time we were in the cathedral, the tray was filled by the offerings and taken to a chest placed against the wall, and secured by three locks, into which its contents were emptied. To be sure, a great deal of the coin was in copper, but there was also a fair quantity of silver.

The history of this Madonna may serve to give an idea of the traditions taught not only to the common people but to those of education.

It was in the fourteenth century, they say, that a holy pilgrim, on his way to Jerusalem, rested a night on the banks of the Volga, and lo! whilst he slept a vision appeared unto him and told him that under a certain tree, on the opposite side of the river, he should find the portrait of the "Mother of God." In troubled agitation he awoke, for he knew that he had seen the blessed Virgin herself. On looking round him he perceived, to his unspeakable astonishment, that he had been conveyed in a miraculous manner across the rapid waters in the night, and that he was reposing under the very tree described in his dream. Near him was the heavenly portrait, mentioned by the spiritual visitant. He gazed on it in silent extasy, but on reflection he felt convinced that he ought to make known the event to the proper authorities: he therefore proceeded to a neighbouring monastery, and informed the venerable abbot and brothers of the facts. They immediately set out in grand procession to the spot, singing joyfully on the way, and there, as the pilgrim had said, was the miraculous portrait, now guarded by two bright angels, who instantly vanished. The abbot and the brotherhood interpreted the vision as the desire of Heaven that a church should be built on the spot, which was accordingly done, and the wonderful picture was reverently placed in it.

The service in the Russian Church is neither in Greek nor in the vulgar tongue, but in Sclavonic, which has about the same resemblance to Russ as old English has to the modern. Religious ceremonies are used on all the ordinary occasions of life; in removing from one house to another, when the priest comes and sprinkles the doorposts and the threshold, blesses the images, and says prayers; on the reopening of a school after the vacation; on the anniversary of alleged victories, when perhaps a dozen enemies have fallen and the rest run away; thanksgivings for having taken a flag from the Turks (which is then paraded round the town with a band of music playing); Te Deums for such triumphs as that of Odessa, when, indeed, they might have good reason to praise Heaven that their foes were *too merciful*, &c. &c.

Confession is one of the sacraments, but it is by no means of so particular a kind as among the Roman Catholics, but in a much more general sense, and is ordinarily made but once a year, during the first or last week in Lent. The six or eight days preceding the performance of this duty the penitents attend mass twice a day very strictly and fast conscientiously in order to prepare themselves for it. They assured me that it was not necessary to name any particular sin, but that, in acknowledging themselves guilty of having broken the commandments, they are exhorted by the confessor and advised to repent. The rite is generally performed at home, the priest attending for that purpose, and not in the church, but they go thither the next morning, or perhaps the same evening, to communicate: even the merest children are expected to confess, but it is not necessary that they should fast.

On Good Friday the ceremony of Christ's interment takes place: it is conducted in exactly the same manner as if it were a real funeral. I witnessed this ceremony at one of the cathedrals.

First came the priests and deacons bearing sacred banners, on which were depicted the lying in the sepulchre, the Resurrection, and various other incidents in the history of the Saviour; next two clergymen, who preceded the archbishop, a fine old man with a long silvery beard; four others followed him, who bore the coffin on their shoulders: the whole of the officiating clergy were dressed in black and silver. I followed the procession into the cathedral, and the service immediately commenced by the choristers chanting a psalm whilst the supposed body was being placed before the altar. On that being accomplished, the archbishop advanced and prostrated himself thrice on the pavement, each time being raised by the attendant priests, after which he kissed with great reverence the hands and feet of the image on the cover of the coffin, walked three times round the bier and bowed, signing himself with the cross at each corner; he then concluded the act of worship by prostrating himself as before. After the archbishop had retired, the different members of the clergy advanced two and two and performed the same devotions. The prelate then seated himself on a throne, a priest advanced and read a discourse to the people, which contained some excellent moral advice, and the service concluded with the usual benedictions.

The high mass in the Kazane church in St. Petersburg is well worthy of the stranger's attendance, especially when the metropolitan officiates. His venerable figure standing before the altar offering incense, the prostrations of the clergy, their splendid dresses, the beautiful voices of the two bands of choristers alternately making the responses whilst the high priest is in the seclusion of the Holy of Holies interceding with Heaven for the sins of the people, have an imposing and solemn effect. Although their creed may not be ours, still it is impossible to assist at such a service without being edified, or without feeling that it is the house of the great Father of all in which the prayers are being offered; but this feeling of reverence was greatly diminished by the scenes that were enacted on our leaving the church. The lower class, as usual, rushed forward to kiss the metropolitan's hand, when the police made a charge on them in a body, and there was such a scuffling and such a shower of blows given right and left as would have been a disgrace to a den of thieves.

At last, with great exertions, a space was cleared, and the prelate, surrounded by the officials, was hustled out more like a criminal than aught else, and safely lodged in the carriage. We then, amidst a crowd of whining beggars and mendicant nuns and monks, with difficulty made our way into the open air. It was really a pleasure to do so, for the smell of the incense, the smoke of so many lamps and candles, the bad odour that there always is in a Russian crowd (perhaps from the sheepskins), made the fresh breeze outside particularly agreeable.

CHAPTER XV.

The carnival—Amusements at the fair—Curious procession—Palm fair—Whitsuntide—The Resurrection on Easter-night—Easter-day—Easter privilege—Anecdote of the Emperor—Bell-ringing—Kindness of heart among the Russians—Household gods—Christmas—Midsummer-eve—Heathen custom—New-year's eve—A Russian election—Unfortunate orator—Russian maypole—Characteristic dance by a soldier, its beautiful execution—Military picnics—Disagreeable traits of character—Shopkeepers' balls—Splendid festivals—The Kremlin illuminated.

THE Carnival in Russia, although not so gay and animated as in Italy, has its pleasures nevertheless. There are continual parties, visits, and feasting, almost in as great a degree as during the Easter week. There is a grand fair held for the amusement of the people, in the great place opposite the Admiralty, in which whirligigs of all fashions, swings, ice-hills, and theatres *à la* Richardson, form the delight of their hearts. The Russians of the lower class are just like overgrown children : they are as much pleased with a ride on a wooden horse, or in one of the boats of a whirligig, in a swing, or down an ice-hill, as a party of school-children would be. In the grand theatre this last Carnival they have been intensely gratified with the "glorious battle of Sinope," fought over for their amusement about twelve times every day, in which not a single Russian got wounded, although the heads of the poor Turks were rolling by scores in all directions. It was, as they said, really a special Providence that nobody was hurt at all, and only shows *how just their cause is.* Of course the pleasant sight of the destruction of so many unbelieving dogs of Mahometans gave immense satisfaction to everybody, and tended much to their self-glorification, and the conviction of the Emperor's might, and so on.

CARNIVAL AT ST. PETERSBURG.

PAGE 198.

The "ice-hill" is an amusement peculiarly Russian. A framework, with steps up one side, is erected, and on the upper part is a small stage, covered with an ornamental roof supported by four pillars, and a rapidly inclined plane on the other side, which terminates in a long run, both of which are paved with blocks of ice, and rendered perfectly smooth by pouring water down, which quickly becomes frozen. The pastime consists in going up the steps and then sliding down the descent on small sledges. At the other end are a similar inclined plane and a similar flight of steps, which enable the slider to return to the first, and so on to and fro. The Russians are extremely fond of this amusement, and often have these ice-hills erected at some village at a little distance from the town, whither they repair in picnic-parties to enjoy the game for a few hours.

During the Carnival week, everybody feasts on blinnies, a kind of pancake, something like our crumpets, which are eaten with sour cream or melted butter. There are blinnies at lunch and blinnies at dinner, whilst the lower classes do nothing but regale on them all the day long.

"Well, Grushia," I once said to the servant, "and how many have you had to-day?"

"Thirty-four, Madame; but I am going to have some more."

The custom of going about masked from one friend's house to another's at the new year and in Carnival time is no longer *bon genre.* It was, some time since, very fashionable to go thus disguised, and dance a polka or quadrille in one place, and then proceed to another, and so on until they were weary of the amusement. I believe the various articles missing have contributed to render the custom obsolete.

During the week of the Carnival, there is the grand promenade round and round the place were the fair is held. Everybody that keeps a carriage or a sledge joins in the procession, which consists in a long line or single file of vehicles following each other at a foot's pace, marshalled by mounted *gensdarmes.* I could never, for the life of me, imagine what pleasure could be discovered in it, excepting that of staring at one's acquaintances and envying their new bonnets. But it pleases the Russians, *et cela suffit.*

I remember, when in Archangel, seeing a curious kind of procession at this festival. A large sledge, made to imitate a ship, having many stuffed animals on board, with skins and other objects, and accompanied by men in various disguises, was drawn round the town, in the same manner as our chimney-sweeps have their public show and Jack-in-the-green, raising contributions on the spectators, which they spend, *à la Russe,* at the whisky-shop. In no other part of the country did we ever see such; and I think somebody told us that it was not a national custom, but one introduced by settlers many years ago.

The day before Palm Sunday, another fair is held in the Nevsky Perspective, close to the Gostinoi Dwor—indeed, a part of it is under the piazza—where are to be seen immense quantities of toys, including little figures of John the Baptist lying asleep in a mossy cradle, with a cross by the side; the queerest-looking dolls that it is possible to imagine—some of them swathed up like mummies, and forming close imitations of Russian babies; for the nurses in the country confine the infant's arms down to its side, and wrap it up so that nothing but the face is visible, giving it the appearance of the papouse of the savages. Added to these are endless varieties of military toys for juvenile warriors, and palm-branches for the morrow's festival. These branches are variously ornamented, but the most common have the figure of a cherub with its wings spread, stuck on a small branch of artificial leaves, roses, and lilies, &c. Small boughs of the downy buds, which our boys call catkins, are also very generally used for this purpose. In the evening, the priest comes to bless the palm-branches, when he presents one to each of the family, which he or she is expected to carry to church on the next day, in commemoration of the entry of Christ into Jerusalem.

At Whitsuntide, the servants always place a large bough of the linden at the head of every bed, and also in the corner of the rooms, men carrying them about in carts to sell, in the same manner as they do the holly-branches at Christmas with us.

Easter is the greatest of the Russian Church festivals, and is a season of universal rejoicing, for the long fast of Lent is now over, or will be so when midnight strikes on Easter-eve. Everybody is dressed in his or her finest clothes: rich and poor, great and small, the Czar and the humblest serfs in his dominions, men, women, and children are all joyfully preparing to celebrate the Resurrection of the Lord. Service is performed at midnight in all the cathedrals. The sacred corpse that was supposed to have been buried on Good Friday will rise again at that hour, amid the songs of the choristers and the joyful thanksgiving of the people. At midnight the mass begins. The archbishop is in the Holy of Holies, praying for the pardon and absolution of the multitude that are waiting in silence in the body of the cathedral. Every one is standing, for there are no pews or seats in the Russian churches. The splendid silver doors are thrown open; the devotions of the archbishop are concluded. He appears standing on the highest step of the altar; he raises his hands towards heaven, and bestows his benediction on the people. Descending from the altar, he advances towards the bier, and, raising the cover of the coffin, he discovers that the body of Christ is no longer reposing therein; he announces it to the congregation, and then leaves the sacred edifice, at the head of the procession of the clergy. The people wait in silence, for he is gone to seek the body, which is no more "where it was laid." The sound of solemn voices is heard at intervals from without, whilst the procession makes the circuit of the cathedral three times in the search. Amid the breathless silence of the expectant multitude, the procession re-enters. The archbishop then, remounting the steps of the altar, and standing upon the highest, in front of the Holy of Holies, pronounces, in a voice whose tones reverberate to the remotest corner of the edifice, and thrill like an electric shock through the hearts of his congregation, the words "Christos vos chris" (Christ is risen). In an instant, the singers burst out into a joyful chorus; every one lights the taper in his hand; universal delight pervades the people, who turn and congratulate each other upon the happy event, and return thanksgivings to Heaven. The archbishop, bearing incense, followed by the priest, goes among the congregation, still proclaiming the welcome tidings; and, amid the cheerful voices of the choir, the fumes of incense, and the brilliancy of a thousand lights, moving with each inclination of the people, the gratitude of the Russians for their salvation ascends doubtlessly to the throne of the Creator, who, we are taught to believe, will not reject those that worship Him. The form of celebrating the resurrection of the Saviour is not according to our Protestant sentiments; but we must not condemn the Russians, who have been taught from their youth to reverence such ceremonies. The hour for a Sclavonic Luther is not yet come.

The service is concluded by reading a portion of the Scriptures in twelve different tongues; and then the benediction is given by the archbishop.

No organ or instrument of any kind is used in the Greek Church; the whole of the music is vocal; it is not joined in by the multitude, but is entirely performed by the clergy and the choristers. The celebration of the mass is really splendid: the innumerable lights, the magnificent robes of the clergy, the brilliant uniforms and costumes of the congregation, and the beauty of the psalms and choruses, make a *tout ensemble* that easily accounts for its taking so strong a hold on the minds of an illiterate and semi-barbarous people.

On returning from the church a magnificent supper is always laid out. Each family, like the Jews, holds a kind of Passover feast, at which twirock (a sort of white cheese), ham, hard eggs, and butter made in the form of a sheep with gilt horns, form necessary dishes. The ham, the Russians say, is a *sine quâ non* at Easter, because the eating of it is a proof that they are neither Jews* nor Mahometans; the butter represents the paschal lamb, and the eggs are in remembrance of the persecutions of the early Christians, who recognised each other by the presentation of one as a symbol of the Resurrection.

It is quite an amusement for the ladies and children to prepare these eggs, by staining them of different colours, by boiling them in pieces of silk several days previous to the festival. Very beautiful ones, made of china, sugar, chocolate, and various other materials, are sold at the shops, for Easter presents, and they frequently contain some valuable article of jewelry, such as a pair of diamond ear-rings, a broach, &c. &c.

If a Russian die during Easter, his soul is supposed to ascend immediately into heaven with Christ; and it is always rather a source of rejoicing than of sorrow when the decease of a friend takes place at this season, as a sojourn in the intermediate state is thereby avoided.

The lower class in Russia have a curious privilege during the whole of Easter week, that of becoming intoxicated with perfect impunity; it may therefore be easily imagined how many drunken men are to be seen at that season reeling about the streets.

On Easter-day everybody congratulates everybody: the

* The Russians have a strange idea that the Jews steal children to eat them, especially at the time of Pentecost, and no reasoning will persuade them of the absurdity and falsehood of this idea.

ministers and nobility go to pay their respects to the Imperial family, the *employés* to their chiefs, the servants to their masters, and acquaintances to each other.

We were told that His Majesty the Emperor kisses one man out of every regiment on this day.

One morning, as he was leaving the palace, he accosted, as is his custom, the first man he met, which happened to be a private soldier, with the usual phrase, "Christos vos chris." The latter turned instantly, and denied the fact, saying that Christ was not risen. "How!" exclaimed the Czar, in great astonishment; "who and what then are you?" "I am a Jew, your Majesty."

The manner of offering congratulations at Easter is to present an egg, saying, "Christos vos chris." The party accepting it answers, "Christ is risen indeed." Both then embrace, kiss each other thrice on the cheeks, bow, and retire.

The bells of the churches play a prominent part in all these grand festivals; and, as each place of worship prides itself on the size, number, and loudness of its peal, it may well be imagined what an awful din they make; added to which, the boys and men think it quite a treat to pull them, and are privileged to do so on every particular occasion, such as Easter, the Ascension, &c. In Moscow we were nearly stunned with the noise, for there are about three hundred and sixty churches, and some of their bells are enormous; so, when they were all ringing at once, the tintamarre was terrific.

On all these occasions of public rejoicing, the stranger may remark how kind and hospitable, how friendly and sociable, the Russian people are. Their hospitality is unbounded; from the highest to the lowest they will give what they can afford. They display their good will by making presents to those about them, to their relations and acquaintances, and their charity by freely giving alms to the poor. The clergy receive gifts from the members of their congregations: it is a period of pleasure and of profit to them; and they are frequently so extremely poor that it ought not to be grudged. They go about from house to house to sing hymns and consecrate anew the saints' pictures with which almost every room is furnished. From all the opportunities that I had of judging, I am convinced that there are many estimable and conscientious men among the superior grades of the Greek clergy, who religiously believe the creed they teach, and endeavour to set a good example to their flocks. In regard to the attachment of the people to their crosses and saints' pictures, although it may seem strange in a Protestant to say so, yet it appears to me a very natural feeling, and we ought not to be surprised at so great a reverence paid to objects which from their birth they have been taught to regard as holy. "I would not have a post removed which I had been accustomed to see," was the remark of a French philosopher: how much greater then must be the affection that these poor people have for these sacred things! besides which, they may feel that they have a friend always near at hand whom they can address in their grief and trouble, and who will not *betray them.*

I never saw a peasant carrying his picture of the Virgin and Child from one isba to another, holding it as carefully in his arms as if it were some treasure of incalculable price, without being reminded of the household gods of antiquity,—the Lares and Penates of nations that now exist no more. We have heard many turn these superstitions into ridicule, because to them a clearer faith has rendered such unnecessary; but let him that does so consult his own heart, and ask if he also have not some object that he regards with love and reverence, and prizes almost as highly as the Russian does his saint's picture.

In Russia, Christmas is not so great a feast as that of Easter, nor are there any national dishes set apart for that season, but the New-Year's Day is a very high festival. Similar congratulations between inferiors and superiors, friends and acquaintances, take place as at Easter, whilst hospitality, generosity, and charity are shown in an equal degree. On Midsummer Eve a custom still exists in Russia among the lower classes that could only be derived from a very remote antiquity, and is perhaps a remnant of the worship of Baal. A party of peasant-women and girls assemble in some retired, unfrequented spot, and light a large fire, over which they leap in succession. If by chance any one of the other sex should be found near the place, or should have seen them in the act of performing the heathenish rite, it is at the imminent hazard of his life, for the women would not scruple to sacrifice him for his temerity: I was assured that such instances had often been known. Numberless charms and acts of sorcery are supposed to succeed on this eve, among which may be mentioned the sitting alone for about an hour before midnight with the eyes fixed on a looking-glass, in order to see the reflection of the future husband's face thereon when the clock strikes.

On New-Year's Eve the Russians "try their luck" in a great many ways. They pour melted wax or lead into water, and exercise their imaginations regarding the varied forms that it assumes: they fill two bowls with water, one of which is for the men and the other for the women, and stick slips of paper round them, on each of which is a name, either male or female as the case may be: a wax taper is then set afloat on the surface, and those whose names have the good fortune to be burned will be married ere the next year. The ladies send out their servants and the gentlemen their valets to watch at midnight for the passers by; the first one that is perceived is asked his or her name, which, of course, will be that of the future spouse, &c. &c.

Numerous superstitions of this kind are practised, and too often believed in, by the upper as well as the lower classes.

Among the festivals ought to be mentioned the elections,

which, even in despotic Russia as well as in Britain, are attended with speeches, votes, and opposition.

I was present once at one of these public ceremonies : it was the election of the Maréchal de Noblesse, a kind of officer chosen in each province from among the landed proprietors. His duties are various, but the most important one is his guardianship of orphans whose fathers have died intestate : he is a kind of provincial lord-chancellor, and, next to the governor, is the most important personage in the county.

The election is perfectly free, and supposed to be entirely unbiassed by the government authorities : even the governor himself is not allowed to be present or to have the least voice in the matter.

The ceremony takes place once in three years, and is looked forward to with as much interest and anxiety as the choice of a member of parliament could be with us, and perhaps even more so, for it is the only opportunity the people here have of making a *free election* of anything.

On the morning of the election the carriages of the pamestchicks or landowners rolled into the town from all parts of the province. Innumerable gentlemen descended therefrom and entered the assembly-rooms, in which the extraordinary event was to take place, with all the *manière affairée*, the bustle, the importance, the seriousness, and the chattering of the members of a " Constitution République " or a Congress. Two or three were gravely consulting upon somebody's pretensions to the honour ; two or three in another place were laughing him and his pretensions to scorn. The noise was so great that I could only catch a word or two here and there, which, rising above the din, reached the ladies up in the gallery. " We won't have him, he's a rogue "—" A most amiable man "—" Don't let S——ff speak "—" Hold your tongue, S——ff is the man "—" Hush ! N—toff is going to make a speech "—" Speak more loudly, we can't hear"—"What does he say?" and so on.

Amid all this noise and confusion, a gentlman placed his chair on a table and mounted thereon, intent on addressing, not *the people*, for there were none, but the *free and independent* electors. Scarcely a word of what he said reached us; whether he proposed himself or anybody else it was impossible to make out, but apparently, his speech did not meet with general approbation. He however became more and more excited, made frantic gestures with his arms, tossing them above his head as if he were mad. His speech was suddenly cut short by his rapid disappearance from the table, chair and all; whether intentionally or accidentally there was no evidence to show, but he got up again as well as he could, and, amid shouts of laughter from the audience, he was glad to hide his diminished head among the crowd. The next speaker was a little, round, bald-headed old gentleman, who made a long and energetic discourse upon the moral excellences of one of the candidates. The audience listened to it with attention, so probably there was truth in it. The third was an orator who, by all appearance, was "unaccustomed to public speaking," &c. &c., for he quickly got into a labyrinth, and did not know for the life of him how to get out of it: he soon descended amid intense and general disapprobation. Several others "trespassed upon the time and attention of the assembled electors," and put their patience to a sore trial, some with greater and others with very indifferent success, after which the meeting was adjourned until the following morning. The second and third days offered but a repetition of the scenes of the first: at last the election was referred to the ballot, and the candidate who had the majority of votes was declared duly elected.

The whole affair terminated in a grand dinner and ball, whereat the opposition and the maréchal side seemed equally to enjoy themselves. The next day the landowners and their carriages left the town: they had all had their say, they had strutted in "brief authority," and were now going home to bury themselves in their woods and forests for the next three years, until another such opportunity of exercising the freedom of election should occur.

Among other ancient customs of Oriental origin is a species of maypole dancing, but it has little or no resemblance to what was once the delight of the merry lads and lasses of Old England. The peasant-women and girls fix upon a small fir-tree or bush; they then attach streamers to it of as many gay colors as they can obtain; the ends are held in their hands, and they continue to walk round and round the maypole, singing a monotonous chant one after the other until they are tired.

The different provinces in Russia have dances peculiar to each as well as different costumes. I remember at a picnic we were all greatly delighted with the picturesque dances of some soldiers from Malo Russia. One dance in particular, executed by a private soldier to the singing of his comrades, was descriptive of the love and occupation of a peasant-girl. It began by a song, during the performance of which the supposed maiden was seated on the ground, imitating the making of thread so well that we could almost fancy we saw it between her fingers, and the distaff in her hand. Presently she pretends to be listening to the chorus, the subject of which is her absent lover. Her fingers move faster and faster as she becoms agitated. At last she throws away the distaff in despair and weeps bitterly. The chorus goes on to describe the warlike exploits of the loved one, the thoughts of her and his far-off village that occupy his mind. Hope begins to spring up; joy reanimates her features; the spinning is resumed; she makes responses to the singers, who tell her that a horseman is in sight, that he comes nearer; they perceive he is the absent warrior. She can no longer contain her emotions ; she springs up, dances a beautiful descriptive pas-seul, and then rushes among the chorus as if for the purpose of welcoming the supposed lover to her cottage.

It is perfectly impossible to convey an idea of the charming manner in which the story was told by the very expressive and graceful movements of the dancer, or the wild and beautiful air to which the whole was executed.

In speaking of this picnic I may mention, just to show how everything in Russia is *à la militaire,* and how the love of the wild life of their nomadic ancestors is not yet banished from the hearts of their descendants, the way in which these amusements were conducted, at least all that I witnessed.

On some place being fixed upon, little tents of boughs were erected, and a number of watch-fires lighted, round which the company were seated in groups : there were always a military band and a great number of soldiers hired to sing the national airs, to dance, and to amuse the guests. They stood in parties at a distance, one composed of the musicians, and the others of the dancers and singers. As soon as one party had finished their performance another commenced, and so on during the whole time. Whilst we were at supper the band marched round the wood and played the soldiers' war-song, and the others stood as sentinels and videttes. It was really a great treat for foreigners to go out to one of these military picnics, and they seemed never to lose their novelty. One of the principal amusements at them was firing pistols at a mark, and, from the display of skill on these occasions, I should say that the Russian ladies are much cleverer at it than the gentlemen. There were generally several officers of rank present, yet the ladies hit the target certainly four times as frequently as *they* did. Parties of the peasantry always formed the spectators of these scenes, and they came in for the remains of the good things that happened to be left. On the national festivals, such as the coronation-day, the Emperor's birthday, &c., as well as at Easter and the new year, the governor of a province holds a levée, as the representative of his majesty, and receives the congratulations of the military and government *employés*. It is at such times the Russian character shows to disadvantage : respect sinks into slavishness, politeness into fawning, civility into adulation, and the conversation throughout is a mass of hypocrisy and deceit. Heaven only knows how many centuries it will take to teach the Russians to speak the truth. The wives and grown-up daughters of the *employés* congratulate the governor's lady just as the husbands do his excellency, when it is customary to invite them to a ball and supper in the evening. The government allows three hundred silver roubles per month to pay for their entertainment. The same ceremony takes place on the anniversary of the governor's birthday as on that of the Czar.

Balls in Russia are much the same as in other civilized countries, but it is a disagreeable fact that it is absolutely necessary to burn scent in the rooms. "I will really speak to the policemaster's daughters," said the lady of a governor after one of these general balls ; "and I will advise them to put on *clean linen*, otherwise I will not invite them to the ball !" There is also another disagreeable custom, that of leaving the lady in the middle of a room after the dance is over, instead of escorting her to a seat.

I went several times to balls given by merchants, generally on the occasion of a daughter's marriage ; they were all in the same style. It seemed to me that the grand object in view with the shopkeepers' wives and daughters was not to dance, but to show off their finery. They sat in a straight line all round the room, dressed in a most splendid manner, with magnificent diamonds, rubies, and pearls, their hands folded over each other, loaded with valuable rings ; just as if they were so many portraits or waxen figures, placed there for exhibition. They scarcely moved, excepting when they partook of some refreshment handed round. A very few of the younger portion danced, but the sole amusement of the remainder seemed to consist in criticising and admiring the costume and jewelry of each other. A room was always on these occasions set aside for the governor's family. As soon as we entered, the host and hostess stepped forward, and respectfully indicated with many bows and inclinations the apartment prepared for our reception ; it was sure to contain several tables completely loaded with refreshments of all kinds, immense cakes, trays of fruit, preserves, bonbons, &c., twenty times as much as it was possible to require. Nothing would ever induce the host and hostess to sit down ; they came in occasionally to entreat us to do honor to the feast and to show their hospitable wishes for our sakes ; they appeared never so pleased as when they saw us eating ; indeed they seemed to expect us never to leave off for a single instant from the time of our entrance to that of our departure.

The most splendid fêtes at which I was present during my stay in Russia were two given by the Emperor : the first was on the occasion of the Archduchess Olga's marriage, and the second on the twenty-fifth anniversary of his own accession. The former took place at Peterhoff, the marine palace, not many versts distant from Cronstandt. The banqueting, illuminations, and rejoicings lasted three whole days, and cost, as the Russians said, "des millions de roubles." The bride was one blaze of diamonds, but she looked anything but happy. All the riches and magnificence of the court and nobility were displayed on the occasion : the variety of national costumes, Georgian, Circassian, and others ; the glitter of the innumerable military uniforms, belonging to every regiment and race in the Czar's dominions ; the foreign ministers and visitors—all formed a *coup-d'œil* of extreme splendour : not the least conspicuous among the throng were the negroes belonging to the court in their rich and picturesque oriental costume.

The court-ladies wear an uniform taken from the national dress; the *married ladies* of honour wear a train of green velvet embroidered with gold over a white robe, and the *maids* of honour a train of crimson velvet; the headdress is in the shape of a crescent, similar to that of the peasants, only much enriched with diamonds and other precious stones; on the shoulder is a bow of blue ribbon, in which are the Empress's initials in brilliants. A long blonde veil is thrown over the head and descends in folds behind. Notwithstanding the richness of the costume, there is a stiffness about it, and there are not many faces to which it is becoming, as it can be so only to classic features. There were very few handsome or pretty women in the whole assembly; indeed, generally speaking, beauty is rare among the Russians. It is very uncommon in every rank, yet, perhaps, no people value exterior appearance so much as they do, or are so vain of their persons. One proof of the latter failing may be seen at every step, for there is not a single shop in St. Petersburg in which a looking-glass is not placed for the benefit of the customers. Mirrors hold the same position in Russia as clocks do in England; with us time is valuable, with them appearance.

Every night during the festival the gardens of the palace were illuminated; Russians said that there were ten millions of lamps. Perhaps there were two or three millions at the most; but they always multiply every number, like the Orientals, who slay tens of thousands, when probably a few hundreds only are meant. Twenty thousand soldiers were engaged in relighting the wicks as they became extinguished by the wind. Walls of light were on each side of the walks and avenues, pyramids and obelisks from fifty to seventy feet in height, resplendent stars seemingly suspended in mid air were everywhere to be seen, but the most beautiful sight of all were the fountains. The palace is built on an elevation, and the water falls in artificial cascades from this height, forming a pretty stream. Below, in the hollows of the overhanging rocks, rows of lamps were placed, over which the fluid rushed from the cascade like a shower of diamonds, whilst the flashing lights beneath had an indescribably brilliant effect ; the fine bronze figures untarnished glittered like statues of gold in the rays of thousands of beaming stars ; the long avenues of splendid pines that border each side of the artificial stream below were also illuminated ; and the view was terminated by an enormous sun, sixty feet in diameter, that appeared to be hovering over the sea in the distance, invisibly suspended in the air. There were not many coloured lamps, and those were placed among the flowers in the gardens, which had an extremely pleasing effect. The others did not resemble those used in England, but were merely little earthenware saucers, filled with grease, and furnished with a wick ; these were placed on a frame-work of wood, painted black, and made into various designs. Soldiers stood at intervals on it, or were mounted on ladders behind, in readiness to relight the lamps that might accidentally become extinguished. One little fact connected with this magnificent festival deserves to be recorded, if it be only to show that enthusiastic cheers and delighted shouts can be made to order, and according to the regulations of the police, by which everything in fact is conducted in Russia. A general assured us that there was a number of men stationed among the crowd whose duty it was to shout in extasy whenever the signal was given them on the appearance of any person of rank on the balcony whose position demanded notice. This was the key-note for as many as liked to join in the chorus, otherwise they did not dare to make any exclamations of pleasure or satisfaction. Disapprobation was of course entirely out of the question, as the least sign of it would subject the delinquent to disagreeable con-

AN IMPIRIAL BALL.

PAGE 214

sequences. There were also a great many spies doing duty among the crowd, who were placed there in order to hear what might be said of the whole affair.

The second festival, that on the anniversary of the Emperor's coronation, took place in Moscow. A description of it would be merely a repetition of what has just been stated. There was one sight, however, that could be seen nowhere else but in that city, and that was the Kremlin illuminated. Its numerous churches and towers decorated with what appeared from below to be a vast number of brilliant little stars,—the gilded crosses glittering in the dark azure sky,—the high and massive walls covered with one immense design resembling embroidery in light, —the Alexander gardens below, illuminated with thousands of lamps,—the showy costumes of the Circassian guards,—the gay dresses of the people,—the bright uniforms of the military, as they passed in crowds to and fro,—formed altogether a splendid sight, well worth the trouble of a journey from St. Petersburg to Moscow to behold. The illumination was at the expense of the city merchants and shopkeepers, who subscribed an enormous sum for the purpose. Magnificent though it was, yet for the large sum subscribed it ought to have been more so; but as it was necessarily under the direction of the police authorities, they doubtless took a good percentage for their trouble.

Illuminations in St. Petersburg are paid for by a kind of tax which the police demand of each house; and as the Russians illuminate for everything, they must form a good source of profit to these "honourable men." Not a single baby belonging in the fiftieth degree to the imperial family can either be born or christened without a round of five hundred cannon and an illumination; not a score of Turks can be killed, or half a dozen guns taken, without a similar demonstration of public rejoicing. The latter may be a "make-believe," very convenient in the time of defeats and retreats to blind the nation's eyes to the truth, especially as no authentic accounts are ever published for the people. The manner of illuminating in Russia is different from ours. Little grease-pots are placed at intervals along the kerbstone of the pavement, at about the same distance apart as are our lamp-posts in London. The effect is not at all imposing; besides which, they are at the mercy of the wind and rain, which generally cause an ugly hiatus here and there.

Whilst speaking of illuminations I must not omit to mention one that we saw in Archangel; it was certainly not to be compared to the two already described, but it had a very beautiful effect from the lamps being placed in holes made in the snow. The weather was very cold, and the damp had frozen in crystals on the trees, so that it looked like a scene in northern fairy-land, or as if some silver grotto of the gnomes had been suddenly thrown up on the surface of the earth.

The night on which the news reached St. Petersburg that the Russian army had crossed the Danube, there was a great illumination by order of the authorities. The weather was fearful; the high wind and beating storm soon effaced all traces of the lights, and the streets shortly became as dark and as desolate as before—an evil augury of the misfortunes so soon to follow.

CHAPTER XVI.

Travelling in Russia—Monotony of scene—Want of animation—Style of dwellings of the nobles, the gentry, and the peasantry—Poor gentry—Pride and poverty—Peasants' isbas, the furniture they contain—Vermin—The breaking up of the ice—The Dwina—Distressing occurrences—The peasant and his dog—The aged peasant—The commandant's gold cup—Native barks: the peasants on board of them—Neva boats—Concerts al fresco—numerous imperial palaces.

I HAVE given no account of our various journeys in Russia, as it would be merely a repetition of the same terms, in which forest, sand, and morass would figure as the leading objects, and would indeed be only wearisome to the reader. Not but that there are some pretty places here and there, but they are very wide apart, and the trouble of wading through two or three hundred versts of monotonous travels over the unchanging post-roads would be but ill repaid by being told that on such a spot stands such a town or such a village, the name of which is never heard beyond the frontiers of the province in which it is situated, and which possesses no interest whatever for any one but the traveller himself, who in journeying through the country is apt to hail the sight of an inhabited place with much the same feeling as he who in making a voyage across the ocean welcomes the appearance of a strange ship in the offing: so inconceivably wearying is the constant view of the endless tracts of forest-land and waste. Descriptions of provincial towns would be almost as tiresome as those of pine-woods and marshes; the same style of houses, the same kind of churches with green roofs and gilt domes; the streets badly paved, or rather unpaved; the same unvarying background of firs and sky—in fact "*sameness all.*"

Besides all these objections to a detailed account, so many descriptions have already been published, that the road from St. Petersburg to Moscow must be almost as well known as that from London to York. Nothing perhaps is more striking to a foreigner travelling through Russia than the utter want of animation in the people; there are no merry laughs ringing joyously on the ear from some light-hearted maiden; no lively bustle at the post-stations when the diligence stops to change horses, such as was seen on similar occasions when stage-coaches ran on the level roads of England, when the arrival of the London mail caused quite an excitement in the village. The sound of songs may be everywhere heard, it is true; but they can scarcely be called joyful ones—they are almost always sad and mournful, being in the minor key; their melancholy cadences, as a French writer remarks, "might be said each to contain a tear." The peasants' downcast looks and inexpressive faces—their cowed manner, as if they were shrinking from an uplifted lash—the want of intelligence which the absence of civilization causes in their countenance, give them an almost brutish appearance, and cause a painful sensation in the stranger's heart. Even the cattle seem to want that air of life which makes our fields and meadows so gay; there are no snowy flocks and frisking lambs, no shepherd's dog with joyous bark, no robin on the flowery thorn: it is, as my friend remarked, not the "repose of the living," but the "slumber of the dead," that reigns over the land of Muscovy.

A nobleman's mansion contains as much beautiful furniture, as many articles of taste and luxury, as we could see anywhere else; the apartments are, generally speaking, much larger and loftier than with us; the whole of them are thrown open for the reception of guests and for the free circulation of the air; and a long suite of rooms thus disclosed has a very pretty perspective effect. The floors are not covered with carpets, but are composed of parquet, or inlaid oak ; very often each room has a floor of a different design ; the doors are shaded by rich portières, matching the window-curtains of each room ; splendid chandeliers are everywhere suspended from above ; many of the ceilings are richly painted in fresco, and a great deal of gilding adds to the effect ; the chairs and sofas are covered with velvet or flowered silk of the most beautiful and delicate colours ; marble statues and elegant vases are placed here and there, with objects of virtù, &c. The lady of the house has a boudoir which is often a complete gem ; the splendid furniture, covered with light blue or rose-coloured satin or brocade ; the inlaid floor partly covered with a Persian carpet ; the tables in marqueterie, enamel, and ormolu, on which elegant trifles of the most exquisite taste are placed ; fine and valuable pictures decorate the walls, which are probably covered with flowered silk or satin, instead of paper. The gentleman's cabinet is but plainly furnished in comparison. I do not know where I read, some time since, 'A Description of the STIES of the Russian Nobility.' It was certainly with indignation that I did so : whoever wrote the description could never have seen or entered the house of a nobleman either in St. Petersburg or Moscow ; nor is it fair or just to speak so of a people, merely because our nation is at war with them ; the truth ought not to be affected by any sentiment of hostility we might feel to the government. The above description may serve to give a slight idea of what *really* exists. The less wealthy of the nobility take a suite of apartments (flats as they are called in Scotland) in some large hotel, built on the plan of those in France. Some of the extremely poor gentry do, it is true, live in a very comfortless state, of which an anecdote has already been given in these pages ; their pride of birth preventing them from gaining a livelihood by following any profession, for fear of losing caste ; and their natural indolence making them prefer a life of poverty, and almost of want, to the doing anything to increase, by their own labour, the slender means furnished by the serfs of some insignificant estate, who generally are doubly miserable from the pressing indigence of their owners. To these people and their dwellings the names of *sties* and their usual occupants may be justly applied, for they live in dirt and discomfort, in the midst of filth and vermin that could only find their equal in an Irish lodging-house ; they sleep on the sofa, which is so dirty that the silk with which it is covered is almost invisible ; their clothing is so abominably unclean, that it is quite offensive ; and they live "littéralement de pommes de terre," as we were often assured. Yet when these people go out their filthy under-clothing is hidden by a showy silk gown and cloak *à la mode.* They pay visits in their own carriages, which are wormeaten and worn, with four horses half-starved—a coachman, footman, and postilion in miserably soiled and tarnished liveries; they look down with contempt upon respectable merchants and shop-keepers, and, to use a vulgar expression, they turn up their nose at the industrious, "parce que leur naissance est noble." I shall never forget the disdain with which one of these second-rate people mentioned one day at dinner that an English merchant in St. Petersburg had made her daughter an offer ; "but how was it possible?" she said, "un homme qui n'est pas noble!"

The sleeping apartments in the houses of very rich people are elegantly arranged and separate from the drawing-rooms ; but in many they form a part of the suite of salons. They are divided by an ornamental screen from the other part of the room, so that a stranger may frequently have been in them without having had the least idea that they were the sleeping-rooms. Each room is heated by a kind of oven, which, when the wood is burned to ashes, is shut down so as to confine all the warm air and prevent it from escaping, and thus an equal temperature is ensured. If this stove happen to be closed too soon, the vapour diffused through the apartment is extremely injurious, being the fumes of charcoal, which find no egress from the double windows, and produce a terrible headache, and a sensation as if water were running over the brain: it is soon cured by being a short time in the open air.

The isbas, or cottages, are constructed by the peasants themselves; the exterior is formed of balks, cut of precisely the same length and thickness, laid horizontally one above the other, the ends of which cross each other at each corner of the building; the interstics are filled with moss and tow; the roof is somewhat like that of a Swiss châlet (indeed, in general appearance, an isbas resembles one); the eaves are decorated with wood-work *à jour;* pretty balconies are very often to be seen, and windows, round which the same ornament is carried; these are the cottages of the wealthier peasants, but the poorest isbas are destitute of any of these gay docorations, and sometimes even of windows, and consist of merely a small balk cottage, with a plain roof. The furniture inside is in almost every case the same: a wooden settee, a deal table, and a chair or two, a samovar or tea-urn, a few earthenware pipkins and basins, some bowls of birch-wood and spoons to match them, and a picture of the Virgin or of some saint, which is always suspended in the corner; and, if the peasants be rich enough, a lamp filled with oil is burning before it. The bedroom in a cottage is the one in which the inmates live and cook; the bed for the family is the flat top of the stove, where they enjoy their sleep and fairy dreams in company with the cockroaches, tarracans, and brown beetles, in a heat that seems sufficient to bake them, and in an air foul and close enough to stifle any one but a Russian. We were once travelling near Velsk, and stopped for a short time at one of the cross-road stations; it was in the middle of the night when we arrived. On going into the room, we looked around, and, at the first sight, we all thought that the walls were papered, a small tallow candle alone serving to make darkness visible; but on approaching nearer, to our horror and dismay, they were completely covered with insects that must not be named to ears polite; myriads swarmed even upon the ceiling. We rushed breathlessly down the stairs, and, when we had reached the asylum of our carriage, we trembled lest we should unwittingly have transported a colony on our dresses.

In the summer-time, the peasants sleep on the bare ground, and generally in the open air. When the weather is not wet, they throw themselves down anywhere, in their ordinary dress and sheepskin, and usually turn their faces to the earth.

When the foundation of one of their isbas becomes decayed, they raise the whole of the upper part by means of beams inserted between the balks, and reconstruct the lower part, which operation renders the cottage almost as good as it was before.

To a stranger, one of the most interesting sights is the breaking up of the ice on the large rivers. As spring advances, everybody is anxiously expecting the day when it will take place. Groups of people may be seen standing along the quays or banks, with their eyes all fixed on the same object, giving their opinion from past experience, drawing inferences from the black and watery appearance of the ice, and gravely debating upon the probability of its disappearing "either to-day or to-morrow." Gentlemen bet wagers on it, ladies chatter about it, peasants quarrel over it; every person is interested concerning it, and, when it is first seen to move, pleasure is expressed on every face.

The breaking up of the ice of the Neva is by no means so magnificent a spectacle as that of the Volga or the Northern Dwina, although the whole of the frozen masses from the lake of Ladoga descend by its stream.

How delighted I was when, for the first time, I saw the breaking up of the ice in the Dwina! Sometimes the immense blocks seemed to assume the shape of a lion, a dog, a swan, and every kind of figure, beautiful or grotesque, according to the fancy of the spectator. The rushing and crashing of the enormous masses in their onward journey to the ocean; the force with which they became heaped one on another, as if they were really endowed with life, and were struggling to obtain the foremost place in the watery race; the deep blue sunny sky that had succeeded the cloudy canopy of the dreary winter months; the flocks of wild swans; the solitary sea-mew, skimming with snowy pinions the liberated waves—formed a scene altogether strange and beautiful. Sometimes some huge bark would float by, like a wreck vainly struggling with its fate amid the sea of ice, and carried along with irresistible force; sometimes an uprooted pine or sombre fir might be seen dashing against everything in its way.

Many fatal accidents occur at these times. I remember a sad day we once passed at Jaroslaf when the Volga was breaking up. The ice is a long time floating past, from the immense length of the river and the numerous tributaries that empty themselves into it. We used, when the weather was fine, to go in a party to the shore to enjoy the sight. It was on one of these occasions that we perceived a bark rapidly descending the stream. On its nearer approach it was discovered that there were several people on board. It came so close to the shore that the men could hail it. To our horror they informed us that they had been seven days on board, and that they had eaten up all their provisions "three days ago." They begged and prayed that some help might be given them, for they had not a single piece of bread or any other article of food remaining. Loaves were instantly brought, and every exertion was made to throw them on the deck. Some men even drove at full speed along the banks, so as to precede the vessel, and have the better chance of succeeding; but, alas! all was in vain. Every attempt failed; and the bark, with the ill-fated peasants, was carried away by the rapid current far out of sight.

"And what will become of these poor men?" I asked of one of our party.

"The probability is, that they will be driven with the ice down into the Caspian Sea, unless, as sometimes happens, a stoppage may occur by the masses being jammed together in some narrow part; they will then be saved; but, if not, nothing but starvation is before them."

Can any one imagine a death more dreadful than to be dying of want while passing through so many inhabited places, within a stone's throw of them, seeing crowds of people on the shores, all anxious to afford aid, yet unable to do so?

Apparently the waters were unusually high that year, for several isbas also floated by that had been swept away by the flood, indicating that one or more villages had been overflowed. At Twer the flood was so great that the governor's family all went in boats, with hundreds of loaves in each, down the centre of the streets, and the servants were employed to throw them into the windows of the poor people's houses, lest they should be starved. In Petersburg there are stones inserted here and there with the date 1824 inscribed on them, to commemorate the dreadful inundation of that year. During it thousands of people perished, whole villages were washed away, the coffins of the dead were seen floating down the streets, and the names of those enclosed therein were read on the plates as they passed by. Each spring the capital is in a similar danger. One other like misfortune would be almost the ruin of it. A lady told me that she was residing on the quay at the time, and mentioned a curious circumstance. The countless rats infesting the banks suddenly made their appearance by thousands, and sat on the window-sills, or any place where they could be in safety, until the waters had subsided: they then as suddenly disappeared, and were seen no more.

It seemed that we were destined to witness misfortunes on the day above alluded to on the shores of the Volga, for we were just on the point of returning home when another bark hove in sight. We waited, out of curiosity, to see it pass by. Only one man was on board: he and a dog were standing together on the deck. At last, perceiving how near they were to the shore, he resolved to make a desperate attempt to reach it. He seized a pole, and, calling to his companion, leaped upon a large sheet of ice that was floating past. The people on shore, admiring his courage and agility, cheered him to the utmost, and, with shouts and acclamations, stood ready to welcome him to land. The poor dog, having less boldness than his master, or warned by instinct of the imminent danger, remained for a few seconds upon the fast receding bark, whining with grief and dismay, and then made up his mind to run the same risk. He soon stood by the side of the man, whose steps he followed as he leaped from one sheet of ice to another by the aid of the pole. All eyes were eagerly watching their movements. They really seemed to have a chance of success. Another and another leap, and they were now within twenty yards of the shore. "Courage!" shouted the multitude; "there is but one leap more, and the danger is over." The man looked at the crowd of eager faces, all anxious to extend a helping hand, when he was seen to hesitate, and he trembled violently. Was it possible that at the last effort his heart failed him? The dog had already leaped the watery space, and had reached the shore in safety, on which he stood barking encouragement to his master. "Courage!" again shouted the people; "Courage!" The piece of ice on which the man was standing was floating on: there was but one chance, and that was going from him. He summoned all his energies A cry of despair was heard, answered by one of horror from the spectators, as the body of the unhappy peasant was swept rapidly past us down the river, impelled onwards by the crashing massses under which he had disappeared. Poor fellow ! the ice that had been strong enough to bear the weight of his light-footed companion, gave way with his, and the fate he so earnestly sought to avert overtook him at last.

A friend of ours related to us that some years before, being at Peterhoff when the Neva was breaking up, she was at the window one day, when she thought she perceived an object at an immense distance off on the ice. By means of a telescope she was enabled to see a poor old peasant on his knees, his white hair streaming in the wind, his hands raised in imploring despair towards heaven, apparently praying for that aid that none, alas ! could render him. His horse and telega were standing by, soon destined to become the prey of the rushing waters that surrounded them. He was swept gradually from her sight, but, as long as it were possible to discern him, he still remained on his knees, in the same attitude of devotion.

In St. Petersburg, as soon as the ice has disappeared, the commandant of the fortress crosses the river to the winter palace on the opposite side. Several boats, with flags flying and bands playing, form a kind of aquatic procession. The custom was, that, on the commandant's presentation of a gold cup on this occasion to the Emperor, his Majesty should return it filled with ducats ; "but," said General P——, "his Majesty, perceiving that by some unaccountable means the cup became larger every year, was under the necessity of limiting the number of ducats to a fixed sum, since which time no change has been observed in the size of the cup." It is not until this ceremony has taken place that any boats are permitted to cross the Neva, as the rapid descent of the ice may cause fatal accidents.

Immense numbers of native barks come down from the

interior as soon as the river is clear. They are large, unwieldy, flat-bottomed boats, constructed in a very primitive fashion, with an enormous barbarous-looking helm, at which a long-bearded peasant, in loose shirt and trowsers, is generally standing. Several others propel the vessel with long poles, which must be very fatiguing, as they are obliged to walk to and fro incessantly. A gallery is often erected outside, on the upper part of the large corn-barks, with a long wooden seat, on which the men can sit when the vessel is at anchor. When a couple of these boats run foul of each other, the people on board run hither and thither, shouting and bawling with all their might, making clumsy attempts to get free, and perform a frantic pantomime, as if the accident had driven them completely mad. At last, *slavo Bogen!* they part company with their bulky friend, and are in no more danger from his awkward embraces, so all goes on as before, until a similar event again occurs, when they become animated by another *accès*.

These poor men have perhaps come a thousand versts or more from their native villages, pursuing patiently their toilsome and weary journey, pushing themselves onwards with those long thin poles, walking three times the length of the whole distance in going to and fro as we see them now, to bring the produce of their proprietors' estates—corn, flax, linseed, deals, and hides. Their cargoes are destined mostly for the English market, and will be taken in this manner down to Cronstadt,* where they will be transferred to British vessels. Theirs must be a dreary life, one would think ; yet on the banks of the Volga I have often passed an agreeable hour in listening to their wild songs,

* Cronstadt, the celebrated port of St. Petersburg, although strongly fortified, which of course is to protect the capital, is in itself a wretched town ; most of the houses are of wood, the streets unpaved, and containing scarcely a single handsome building. There was much talk of immense batteries and mines under the water ; but people who had resided there for years assured me that it was not possible that it could be true.

as the sounds were borne to the shore from the strange-looking barks, during the calm evenings of a Russian summer.

The little ferry-boats that ply on the Neva are slight, dangerous-looking things, with a very elevated stern, painted with all sorts of colours, and in every device that may suggest itself to the owner's fancy: sometimes there is a fine landscape at the back of the seat, sometimes extraordinary tulips and marvellous roses, most unhappy-looking fish, or a melancholy lady and gentleman staring at each other. The boatmen are like the peasants, with long beards and loose shirts, and generally civil and obliging; indeed, it must be allowed that the lower class of the Russians are remarkably so, not only to their superiors, but to each other. The most unpolished boor in the country will always take off his hat when he meets a companion or acquaintance, and that with quite as much respect as to a person above him in rank.

A little pleasure-trip in these small boats to some of the numerous islands in the vicinity of St. Petersburg is extremely agreeable on a summer's evening. These islands are formed by different branches of the Neva and by canals, which serve to drain the marshy ground of which they are composed. Although everything about them is purely artificial, Nature having done little enough to embellish them, yet the effect produced is very delightful. Pretty little country houses, or fancy isbas, built of wood and fantastically decorated, show themselves here and there among the foliage of a forest of trees and shrubs; a Chinese temple or Turkish kiosk placed on some little promontory arrests our attention; a Greek statue or Corinthian column ornamenting some sequestered spot, and half buried in the creeping plants that twine around it. The whole scenery is entirely flat, there are no hills or even elevations, and its chief charm consists in the bright-green verdure with which the islands are covered, the clear blue streams everywhere meeting the eye, and the glorious sky of a northern summer. Bands of musicians play in various spots on certain days : they are mostly Germans. These al fresco concerts are excellent, the pieces (generally selections from operas) are admirably performed, and crowds of ladies in beautiful dresses, and gentlemen in country costumes, repair in the evening to attend them. Now and then there is a benefit-night, otherwise the amusement is entirely gratuitous. As the entertainment takes place in the open air, even the humblest classes can enjoy it, and numerous groups of the people may be seen standing at a respectful distance among the trees, for they are very fond of music. No disturbances ever take place in Russia, even when a crowd is assembled ; but then, as Count Custine said, when the remark was exultingly made to him by a Russian nobleman on some public occasion, " Mon cher, c'est très bien, mais je ne vois pas de peuple !"

Yalagen is among the islands, and is a very favourite place of resort : the grounds belonging to the palace are beautiful and the flower-garden charming.

Pavlofski is another place whither many go to reside during the summer: there is a palace there also, and a Vauxhall, whereat concerts and balls are given. Tzarskoselo is a large estate belonging to the crown, the grounds of which are laid out in the English style : of course there is a palace there also. At Gatchen there is another ; indeed there seems no end to imperial residences. Go where you will, there is a country house belonging either to the Emperor, the Empress, some grand-duchess or other, nephew or grandchild of Nicholas the Czar. They almost seem to have descended in some hailstorm, they lie so thickly on the ground. The expense* of

* The expenses of the Russian Court, we were informed, amount to about forty millions of silver rubles per annum, or rather more than six million three hundred and thirty-three thousand pounds sterling.—*From a Russian authority.*

supporting them must be almost equal to that incurred by the "million of men," the mighty boast of the Russian nation, which is not yet enlightened enough to perceive who pays for them all.

CHAPTER XVII.

Education—The highest studies—Russian history—Infallibility of the Czar—Moral excellence—Devotedness of a young lady—Profiting by instruction—Noble culprits—Education of the serfs—The University—The students' costume—Naval school—School for the deaf and dumb—Academy of Fine Arts—Driouts—Education of boys—Studies—Ladies' institutes—Plan of education—Uniforms—Private education—Remarks on education in Russia.

Education in Russia, unless strictly private and superintended by tutors and governesses at home, is entirely under the surveillance and control of the government, in which undoubtedly there is great policy. "Train up a child in the way he should go, and when he is old he will not depart from it." This is a truth from too high an authority to be called in question, and it is on this principle that the government acts, justly judging that what is instilled into the mind of youth is the most difficult to efface, and possesses an influence in after years that can never be entirely shaken off, although it may become weakened. Even ordinary schools are visited by inspectors appointed by the authorities, who examine the pupils, the branches of instruction studied by them, the books used, &c. By this means, they possess immense power over the rising generation, as of course only such an amount of knowledge as the government approves of is allowed to be taught—history, in which the names of the Czars and the dates alone can be regarded as true, the remainder being merely an historical romance written for the glorification of Russia and all that apertains to it or to the imperial family, in which every prince that ever reigned in Muscovy, excepting the false Dmitri,* is recorded as having been possessed of all the virtues under heaven, while not the slightest notice is taken of their violent exit from the world; geography and statistics, which magnify every object within the frontiers of the empire, giving the most fabulous account of all the possessions and might, the resources and riches of the Czar, and diminishing those of every other country; and so on of every other study that can be turned to advantage by the government.

Religion is also taught by priests at all public establishments, and it must be confessed that one of the chief uses to which it is put is to inculcate the most slavish reverence for the Emperor, who, according to them, is infallible in all spiritual and temporal matters, and as holy as the Pope is in the eyes of the fanatical Roman Catholics.

Submission and obedience, or rather slavishness and servility, are qualities infinitely more valued by the authorities than any other virtue. On making inquiries of students concerning rewards, &c., we were always answered, "O, good conduct (*i. e.* submission) is the first consideration, much greater than the progress we make in our studies."

All St. Petersburg was in extasy some months ago at an anecdote that ran the round of the court, and was cited everywhere as the very climax of moral perfection. It was this: A young lady in one of the first Institutes of that city, whose brother had been slain at Kalafat by the Turks, received one morning the news of his death. On this being communicated to her, she smiled and said that she was "rejoiced to hear it, as he had died for the Emperor." A sentiment so elevated and noble

* This unfortunate prince, although thus named, might have been the true heir: there are many more circumstances to prove that he was so than that he was not; his extreme resemblance to his father, his public recognition by his mother, and the cross that had been placed round his neck at his baptism, &c. But it was too much against the interest of his successors for them to acknowledge his rights; his name is still yearly anathematized in the Russian churches, to keep up the belief in his imposture.

was of course repeated to imperial ears, and the pseudo-Spartan damsel was handsomely rewarded by a splendid dowry, and the assurance that her future fortune should be cared for. "Pour encourager les autres," as Voltaire said on another occasion. When such encouragements are given to youth of both sexes, and what we should consider as a vice is held up as the highest point of excellence, and inculcated from the earliest age, when the heart can be moulded to any form, it would be worse than useless to expect a just sense of moral independence, nobility of soul, or true sentiments on liberty, from men and women so educated. To do the Russians justice, they have "minded what their teachers said," and have perfected themselves in the lesson, for, notwithstanding many good natural qualities which they undeniably possess, I think it would be impossible to find in any country so much baseness, deceit, and hypocrisy as are to be met with every day in Russia, and especially in the capital.

One of the greatest punishments to the nobility is the being banished from St. Petersburg and from the light of the Emperor's countenance. I remember a few years ago, when four ladies of rank, one of whom was, they say, a Countess O——f, thought proper to go to a masquerade and afterwards to a restaurant, where they all became "tellement ivres" that they were taken home by the police, on droshskies. Two of them were exiled to their estates for five years, and it was remarked, *par les mauvaises langues*, that his Majesty had shown his usual discrimination, for the two who were endowed with pretty faces were allowed to remain in the capital (where, I believe, they are still an *ornament* to his court), and the others were sent away.

The government, in its excessive care regarding instruction, has established colleges and schools for every branch and for every rank in society excepting *the serfs*, who, poor people! know very little more than the cattle they drive, or beyond their own name and that of their village. It is not an exaggeration to say that they do not know their grandfathers, for among the serfs there are no surnames; like a dog, they only bear one name while alive, and leave none behind them when they are dead. Nine out of every ten cannot tell you how old they are, so it may readily be imagined what the extent of their knowledge is. In speaking of this wronged and "evil entreated" class, I may mention, as *à propos* to the subject of education, that I once went to a school which M. S——, a gentleman of the province of Twer, boasted he had established on his estate. He was possessed of nearly four thousand souls (*i. e.* men), so, of course, I expected to see a noisy crowd of merry boys all busily engaged in learning their A B C. I was shown into a small room in which were six or eight young lads standing with a dull and heavy look over some dirty books, the contents of which I had the curiosity to examine. The first one I took up was a Latin catalogue of the names of plants, with the pronunciation in Russian letters and the translation on the opposite page. No wonder, poor boy! he looked dull and heavy, to be obliged to con over those long botanical names in a language of which he knew nothing, and to repeat them like a parrot to the master, without feeling the least interest or meaning in the study. I expressed my surprise at his having to learn out of such a book, when I was informed that the lad was destined to be a *gardener on the estate!* and every one of those eight unhappy youths was only being taught to serve his owner's interest. One was to be a steward, another a village apothecary for the serfs, and so on, just as if they were so many machines of flesh and blood which might be put to any use that their master pleased. This circumstance accounted sufficiently for the absence of the others, for, as they were destined to be merely field-labourers, it was not thought worth while to teach *them* any more than the horses and oxen on the estate!

The University at St. Petersburg is a long white-faced building on the quay of Vassali Ostroff. The students are taught as much as it is thought proper for them to know, and their studies are conducted under the watchful eye of the authorities; from all I could find out, astronomy seems to be the only science that is permitted to be thoroughly investigated by Russian subjects;* for the revolutions of the stars have not much to do with those of monarchies, nor the precession of the equinox with the advance of civilization.

Some years ago I was told an anecdote, which I was assured was a true one, and my informant affirmed that he knew the parties well. I will relate it here, as it may serve to show how matters are conducted in the Russian *alma mater*. I premise that the students do not reside under the roof of the university, but have to find lodgings elsewhere, and that many of them are extremely poor. Among the latter class was a young man of more than ordinary talents, who by great perseverance and industrious application had twice merited the prize; but there were two obstacles to his receiving it; the first was his poverty, which forbade him to offer any of those golden bribes which cause the superiors to discover wisdom in a fool and talent in an idiot; the second was the dislike one of the professors bore to him and his jealousy of his talents.

The young student having been twice cheated of his just reward, was yet determined upon making a third effort to obtain it. His finances were become so reduced, that it was only by great privations and excessive economy that he could manage to exist, and pay for the humble lodging he occupied; indeed it was almost beyond his means to remain long enough to pass his examination. He was sure of the prize if it depended only on

* A learned Russian traveller assured me that even the account he gave of his journeys in the north of Asia was not allowed to be published; only those parts wherein the desolation of the land were not exposed were permitted to be printed.

the knowledge required to obtain it; and it may readily be imagined with what anxiety he awaited the day which was to decide his fate. I should remark that more than the actual honor was involved; his daily bread, his very rescue from utter starvation, depended upon his passing the ordeal with credit; as so doing would entitle him to some post under government, which would furnish him with at least the means of subsistence. The time at last arrived; the examination was passed, and nothing remained but the receiving of the reward which he had so justly earned. All the professors, excepting the one before mentioned, had testified their approbation; *his* voice alone was necessary to complete the votes that would decide the affair. All eyes were turned on him, when suddenly he arose and announced his intention of retaining his "suffrage," making some remarks concerning the conduct (*i. e.* submission) of the student as the excuse for his hateful injustice. The unfortunate young man, before whose eyes starvation and want presented themselves in grim and terrrible reality, who had been buoyed up to the very last moment with the certainty of reward, now saw all his hopes scattered to the winds, his prospects for the future dashed to the earth, his plan for his own support and that of his mother (for he was a widow's son) crumbled into dust. Indignation at the injustice, grief at his loss, anger, rage and despair, seized upon his heart, and, urged by an irresistible impulse, he rushed forward and struck the villain whose envy and hatred had caused him so great a misfortune. He was immediately arrested, brought to trial, and condemned by the Emperor himself to receive a thousand lashes of the knout.

This instrument, which happily is unknown out of the Muscovite empire, inflicts so dreadful a chastisement, that a single blow, when struck on particular parts of the back or side, is sufficient to deprive a human being of life; and I have often been assured that, if the criminal be rich enough, he pays the wretch destined to be be his executioner* to put him as speedily as possible out of his pain, by striking him in a vital part. When the day arrived on which the unhappy young man was to suffer for his imprudence, the whole of the students and professors were ordered to be assembled to witness his punishment, the horrible details of which can scarcely be conceived ; at every blow of the barbarous knout a long line of flesh flew off, until the bones were quite bare and the heart was exposed to view. Of course long ere this the unfortunate victim had ceased to breathe, but the sentence was a thousand lashes, and, whether he was alive or dead, the number must be given. Several of the horror-stricken students, the spectators of this disgraceful sight, were lying insensible on the ground, having fainted with dismay ; and my informant shuddered as he mentioned that a piece of flesh fell on his own sleeve as the knout was uplifted. The Almighty will be the judge between this wronged man and his assassins ; but what real civilization can exist in a land where such savage acts are done ? Scenes such as this are sufficient to show from their cruelty the barbarous state of the nation at large, and would do more to retard its enlightenment than a whole university of professors could contribute to its advancement.

Whilst speaking of this horrible punishment I may mention another execution which took place in St. Petersburg, although it has has nothing to do either with the university or education. A certain *gentleman* (?), who was rich in "blood and ore," employed his faculties in the invention of what may be designated a truly "infernal machine" for the castigation of his slaves : it was constructed in such a manner that, when the unfortunate delinquent was placed in it, so that he could not move, a piece of mechanism, ingeniously contrived, was put in

* The executioner (it is said) is always made intoxicated before inflicting the punishment of the knout.

motion, and inflicted severe blows on his back. The slaves, at last driven to desperation at being made the victims for his amusement, one day placed *him* in the machine, and let him feel by experience the pain he had so often out of mere wanton cruelty caused them to endure. How he escaped from their hands I never heard; but he did find means to do so, and immediately lodged complaints against them; they were cited, and condemned to be knouted. An eye-witness of their punishment assured me that the same fearful details took place as those mentioned in the preceding example; but he also added that carriages filled with ladies (to their shame and disgrace) were drawn up in a line, and their occupants were the spectators of this diabolical execution. Well might our friend have pronounced that "c'était le siècle de Louis Quinze," for does not this remind us of the crowd of ladies of *his* court who were witnesses to the awful punishment of his would-be assassin, and of the *amiable* countess who so *feelingly and gracefully* gave a description of the horrid scene at an evening party on the same day on which they had seen it?

But enough of these horrors; let us return to the subject from which their recital has formed a long digression. The University men eschew the long black gown and square-topped cap of Oxford and Cambridge, and have a uniform assigned them in which a cocked hat and sword figure as the most remarkable features. As regards the hat, there is nothing against that, as we may suppose a cocked one answers the purpose of covering the head as well as any other; but the utility of the sword is incomprehensible. A great number of the students are Germans, or rather Russo-Germans, and some of them are excellent musicians; they give a concert about once a fortnight during the winter season, for the benefit of their poorer brethren. These concerts are well worth attending, not only for the pleasure of contributing to a laudable purpose, but also from the excellent manner in which the music is performed.

There is a naval school at the Admiralty, in which maritime affairs are taught by theory, and fresh-water sailors manufactured.

"Have you ever been to sea?" I asked of a young officer of three-and-twenty.

"Oh, yes!" was the reply, "certainly; I have been to Helsingfors!"

There is a corps forestier, an establishment in which the mode of cultivating land, planting trees, &c., is taught. The gardens belonging to this corps are about four miles from St. Petersburg, and are very interesting; they contain a great variety of shrubs and flowers, to which much attention is paid. The grounds are laid out in the English style.

Not far from this college, on the Viborg road, is one for the deaf and dumb. I frequently saw the boys out at play in the garden attached to the establishment. The utter silence reigning among so many unfortunate youths had a mournful and oppressive effect, but they seemed happy and even merry. I had no opportunity of learning anything touching the mode of instruction pursued, or to what occupation the young men were destined upon quitting; perhaps the government finds them *useful*.

In St. Petersburg there is an academy for actors and actresses, near the Alexander Theatre; they are educated at the expense of the crown, and for the first fifteen years after completing their training, they are obliged to give up the greater part of their salaries to the government; this arrangement cannot be very gratifying to the artistes one would think, for those fifteen years must be the very best in their lives, supposing that they commence their histrionic career at the age of eighteen. After the expiration of the above term they are free to retain for themselves all they earn by their engagements.

A large square building in Vassili Ostrof is the Academy of the Fine Arts, where the productions of modern painters are exhibited every year for a certain length of time. Great encouragement is given by the government to the students, and he who gains the first prize is sent at the expense of the crown to travel in various countries for the space of two years, so that he may have the advantage of seeing the works of men of genius, and of profiting by them.

As the Russian government is a military one, there are of course innumerable establishments for the education of officers: there are the Gymnasiums, the Corps des Pages, and fifty others, in which warlike studies are pursued. "Notre Empereur aime à jouer aux soldats," said a Russian; "ce n'est pas sûr qu'il FAIT des soldats."

There are commercial schools for the bourgeoisie, and priouts, or establishments on the Bell and Lancaster system, for poor children, such as those of petty shopkeepers, domestic servants, and such like. Immense numbers of the scholars in all the colleges and different establishments are maintained at the expense of the crown; others are paid for by their parents.

The boys are always under the embarrassing restraints of a strict surveillance; even young men of seventeen and eighteen cannot go home or return from school unless they are attended by a relation or a servant. This plan, although it may be thought proper for young ladies, seems excessively ridiculous for young men; and of course, as a natural consequence of such a measure, as soon as they become their own masters they do not know how to govern themselves; and this is doubtless the cause of a vast deal of evil in Russia.

The study of the greatest importance in the Russian code of instruction is that of modern languages,—French, German, and English. The classic tongues are but little studied. Very few gentlemen know Latin, and still fewer have any acquaintance with Greek. Although it is agreeable to be able to converse in all these different languages, yet upon the whole it must be a defect in the plan of education to learn so many at once; for the time thus taken up in acquiring so many words and grammatical rules would be better employed in obtaining useful and solid information in one's own, and that is what the Russians are extremely deficient in. A great many really know nothing beyond the frontiers of their own country. The appearance of knowledge given by the facility of chattering fluently in so many languages is a kind of imposition unless accompanied by the acquirement of the wisdom contained in each.

The establishments set apart for young ladies are under the surveillance of the authorities in an equal degree as those of the other sex. The principal colleges, or institutes as they are called, are—the Catherine, in which none but girls of noble birth are admitted; the Smolnoy, which is divided into two parts, one of which is for noble children and the other for the bourgeoisie; the Patriotic, for ladies of inferior rank; the Elizabeth, for the daughters of merchants, employés, &c.; the Foundling, for orphans and others; and the different Priouts, similar to those for the education of boys.

The branches of study are various. As usual, languages take the first rank, followed by geography, religion, ancient and modern history *(à la Russe)*, physics, &c. &c.; for each of these there is a professor appointed by the crown. Music, drawing, dancing, and singing form the accomplishments, to which much time is devoted.

In the Catherine Institute there are nearly four hundred young ladies of rank, and it is an excellent establishment, admirably conducted, under the direction of a lady of high rank who is responsible to the Empress; she is assisted by three ladies who have the title of inspectresses, and surveillantes, and called dames de classe. The directress is always designated Mamma by the pupils, which has a pleasing social sound. The ladies who conduct the establishment are obliged to wear an uniform, which consists of a dark blue dress and lace cap: the pupils, who are divided into two great classes, have also their uniform ; the high class wear a puce-coloured stuff frock, the lower a dark green; but they all have white aprons, sleeves, and tippets, similar to those of our national schools.

The young ladies enter for six years, three of which are passed in the lower class, and the remainder of the term in the upper. During the whole of this period they are not allowed to be absent on any pretence whatever ; they never go out for a walk, and only twice a year for a drive, and they live quite as retired from the exterior world as if they were buried in a convent. In the establishment there is a church, an hospital, and a splendid ball-room, and attached to it are a priest, a comptroller of the household, an architect and carpenters, a band of musicians, a guard of soldiers, and an immense number of servants, who have been educated for the purpose. The greatest order and regularity prevail; but the influence of a military government is felt even in a school for young ladies, which gives a kind of mannerism to those brought up under this system, as every action has its drilling before going on parade. One day when I was there I noticed an unusual shouting in the ball-room; one of the inspectresses was continually entering and quitting it; each time she did so I remarked the same simultaneous cheers as before. Curiosity led me to inquire what it meant. "Oh!" I was answered, "it is only the young ladies practising the salutation to the superior when she arrives, for she is to come the day after to-morrow from the country, and they are therefore rehearsing 'We hope you are well, Mamma,' so that they may all say it together."

Notwithstanding the brilliant education that the young ladies receive by the aid of so many first-rate professors, and the care and trouble taken in their surveillance, it is still a question whether it is wise to have so many young people together; at least, it does not agree with the ideas usually entertained in England. There is another great defect in this plan; the pupils have so very little leisure that they can take neither exercise nor recreation; the only unoccupied time they have is one hour after dinner, which they spend in walking up and down the immense corridors which run the whole length of the building. The even tenor of their existence is varied by balls among themselves on the anniversary of an imperial birthday, that of the coronation, the saint's day of the Institute, &c. On these occasions the invitations are restricted to female relatives of the young ladies. They have also a long recess during the summer; but they often used to tell me in confidence "that they would rather the masters came, for it made a little variety." A sortie or breaking up takes place once in three years, when the whole of the upper class leave the school, and then the lower take their place and become the first. A public examination takes place on these occasions, at which most of the imperial family are present; prizes are awarded, the highest of which is le chiffre or the Empress's initials in diamonds, and the others consist in gold and silver medals. The young lady who gains the first prize becomes immortalized by having her name inscribed in golden letters on an oval board, painted dark blue, which is suspended in the ball-room, which the others have the pleasure of reading every day, and which serves to incite them to obtain a like distinction. She is also honoured by a kiss from the Empress. At the sortie the friends and relations attend, when some excellent performances on the piano, beautiful singing by the pupils, and the examination of their drawings and embroidery, form a part of this interesting ceremony.

In addition to the studies and accomplishments before mentioned, there is a week, at certain intervals, in which the young ladies are taught to embroider, and attend in the kitchen to learn the culinary art. I have taken the Catherine Institute as an example, as it is the first in the empire, but the others are conducted nearly on the same plan. The Smolnoy Institute contains a greater number of pupils, because several classes of society are received: there are eight hundred in the two divisions. In the Patriotic, there are three hundred and fifty; in the Elizabeth, three hundred; in the Foundling, six hundred. There are similar establishments in Moscow.

Everything is found for the use of the pupils by the crown: their dresses, linen, shoes, and even their pocket-handkerchiefs. The surveillantes, or dames de classe, are "de service" every alternate day, the other is entirely at their disposal.

Private education, that is, education conducted under the parent's roof, is, in almost every instance, directed by foreigners —French, English, or Germans. If the family be rich, generally an individual of each nation is resident in the house, by which means the practice of speaking the three languages is ensured. It is very rare that a Russian is engaged either as tutor or as governess. The Russians are extremely kind to those who undertake the education of their children. Certainly, in respect, consideration, and *manière d'être* towards them, they set an excellent example which might, with advantage, be followed elsewhere; for they judge truly when they say "that, if they be wanting in these points themselves towards those intrusted with the care of their children, they could not expect those children to profit from their instruction, or respect them as they ought to do." In speaking of education in general, I should say that in Russia there is a great deal too much restraint and watching, leaving the young person no time for reflection, by which the mind may be strengthened, and by this means so much distrust is displayed in the conduct of a youth of either sex, that, as a natural consequence, lying, deceit, and cunning are produced, for no human being likes to know that his every action is the subject of an established espionage, and he will inevitably resort to meanness to avoid detection. Too much attention also is paid to exterior and showy accomplishments, such as dancing, music, &c.; if they make a good figure in these, *peu importe le reste.* In Russia there are few, it must be confessed, whom we should call well-informed people, among either the ladies or gentlemen.

The whole system of education in Russia seems to have been, indeed, expressly devised for stifling all feelings of independence in the heart of youth, so that they may submit without a struggle to the despotic government under which they had the misfortune to be born. Their minds are formed to one pattern, just as their persons are by the military drill; their energies are made to contribute in every way towards the aggrandizement of the Czar's power, and to render more solid the chains of their country. "We can have no *great men,*" said a Russian, "because they are all absorbed in the name of the Emperor:" meaning that *individual* glory could not exist. The Mussulman teaches his child, "There is but one God, and Mahomet is his prophet." The Russian as piously inculcates the precept that "Nicholas is his general." "God and the Czar know it," is often the reply of a Muscovite when he can give no direct answer to a question. A gentleman was one evening giving us an account of the Emperor's journey to Moscow, and of the manner in which he had been received on the route. "I assure you," continued he, "it was gratifying in the extreme; for *the peasants knelt* as he passed, just as if 'c'était le bon Dieu lui-même.'" Whatever pleasure *he* might have felt on the occasion, I could not help regarding with astonishment and intense disgust a person who could thus exultingly speak of the moral degradation of his countrymen.

CHAPTER XVIII

Moscow—Poushkin's verses—The Moscowites—Dislike of foreigners—Antipathy to the St. Petersburg people—Ancient devotees—Places of amusement—General remarks—The Kremlin—The churches—General view of the city—Napoleon—The miraculous image—Ivan and his recompence for genius—The Gostinoi Dwor—The shopkeepers' brides—A wedding coach—The Tartar—The Persian—The Metropolitan of Moscow—The Jews—The shopkeepers—Smoking—The Tiramà, or ancient palace—The new palace—The Treasury—The diadems—The Tartars of the present day—The church of Warsaw—The last fight for freedom—Various curiosities—Spoils of the *grande armée*—The officer's widow—French refugees: their gratitude—The model of the Kremlin.

Although this is no book of travels, but merely a sketch of the Russians and Russian life, yet, as I have frequently spoken of Moscow, perhaps a description of it may be acceptable. This beautiful city strikes the stranger with admiration, as much from its fine situation as from the semi-Asiatic barbarism of it splendour. Poushkin, the national poet, speaks of its gardens and its palaces, it crosses and its cupolas, that "form a crescent," and appeals to the hearts of his countrymen in some beautiful stanzas that find their echo in every Russian breast, for there is no place in the empire for which they have so great an affection. "Mother" Moscow is the endearing epithet they bestow on their ancient capital; and they would rather see St. Petersburg buried in the morasses on which it is built than that any evil should befal Moscow. Patriotism in every people is to be admired; and certainly the love the Russians bear to their country, although mixed up with much fanaticism, is worthy of our respect. Moscow has all the prestige of a holy city, and is still regarded by the *nation* as the capital. The Moscowites themselves look down on the inhabitants of St. Petersburg as a kind of *parvenus* and mushrooms—people of no caste, and a race of mixed blood, descended from foreigner and adventurers—whilst they hold themselves up as the true sons of Old Russia, and are in every respect much more truly Russian than the St. Petersburg people. The feeling against foreigners, although their society is much courted by the upper classes, is, as a national sentiment, very strong. Were a revolution to break out, I have heard it said a thousand times, they would be the first to fall victims to the people's rage, for they are looked on as heretics, and subverters of the manners and customs of their forefathers, to which they cling as tenaciously as any oriental nation. If the lower class were to rise, as some fear they will do, a Russian massacre of St. Bartholomew would inevitably ensue. The English *were* the most liked and respected by them before the late events; they are now the most intensely hated of any.

The general rule appears to be, that what is liked in St. Petersburg should be hated in Moscow, and *vice versâ;* if, therefore, an actress or singer *fait fureur* in the western city, she is immediately hissed in the eastern. If people be in an extasy of delight at some grand discovery, such as table-moving, which has occupied the *powerful* intellect of the inhabitants of St. Petersburg for the last year and a half, it is, of course, but coldly received in Moscow; and so on. In religion the Moscowites are in everything the most orthodox "Greek." It seems an established rule that old ladies superannuated from society should go to reside in Moscow, in order to spend their last years among the ancient churches, bigoted priests, monks, and nuns, with which the city is perfectly crowded. When the world has lost its charms for them (or, rather, they have lost their charms for the world), they retire thither, and assiduously fast, pray, and *pay,* in the hopes of more surely paving the road to heaven, and removing the brambles of youthful sins and follies out of their path. The time that was formerly spent by them at balls, the opera, and card-tables, they now devote to nightly vigils in the churches, attending mass, and in visits to the convents and their musty inmates. The money which they used to throw away in gambling and extravagance, they now employ in making rich gifts to religious houses, in purchasing dresses for the priests, and in giving presents to pilgrims; so that, as may be supposed, the prospect of living merrily in Moscow is rather clouded; but fortunately there are people neither so old nor so bigoted but that they have amusements of their own. There are an opera, a French theatre, assembly-rooms, which are very splendid, and every social entertainment the same as in St. Petersburg; but the truth must be told, they are all in very second-rate style. The streets in Moscow are irregular, narrow, and badly paved, but there is an Asiatic look about them and the inhabitants that pleases from its novelty. Some of the houses are magnificent in appearance, and the elevated situation of many of them adds greatly to their effect: they lie scattered here and there among gardens, which serve greatly to embellish the general aspect of the city. The views presented by almost every opening are really beautiful, and possess so great a variety that they never cease to delight the eye. The churches are extremely curious; many of them are very ancient, and, were it not for the gilt crosses on the top, they might be mistaken for oriental mosques. Some of them have the most strange galleries on the exterior, the most extraordinary embellishments of paint and colours, twisted towers, and wonderful roofs, that can be imagined. But let us take a walk into the Kremlin, and have a general view of the whole city. We are now passing down the Kousmitski Most, or Smiths' Bridge, which is the principal street, the Pall-Mall of the Moscowites; there are some good shops, nearly all French or Italian, yet everything bears the stamp of a *second* capital. The faces we meet are quite in a different style from those we saw in St. Petersburg: some of them are extremely pretty, and others very much the contrary. I believe it was in Moscow that I saw the most frightful countenance I ever beheld. There are not many pedestrians: the Moscow people are too Asiatic to be fond of exercise. The carriages that pass contain numerous portly old ladies and gentlemen, some of them with very Tartar-like faces, and looking solemn and grave. A few minutes' walk, and we are at the far-famed Kremlin itself. Its massive walls, and curious towers tapering to the sky, with small loopholes and windows, the terrace of earth on which it is built, may all recall to our mind the time when it formed the stronghold of Muscovy, when men fought with bows and arrows, and the besiegers were repulsed from lofty battlements. The general appearance almost reminds us of the pictures of the old palaces of Hindûstan, so perfectly oriental does it seem. What a number of churches crowded together! What a variety of domes, cupolas, and crosses, all glittering in the sun! That long, narrow garden, which forms a walk under the walls, was formerly the moat which rendered the Kremlin a more secure abode for the Czar, for here is still the ancient palace of the Muscovite monarchs. That huge white building yonder, audaciously lifting its staring front over the walls, is the new imperial residence, which joins on to the old one. It certainly spoils the picturesque *ensemble* of the Kremlin, and looks infinitely more like a range of barracks than aught else. Crossing the sloping way over the Alexander Gardens, we perceive that the wall encloses within its precincts not only innumerable churches and convents, but an arsenal and casernes, before which are displayed, in a very prominent manner, several handsome guns, a part of the spoils of the *grande armée*, as they say. As we proceed we see a variety of curious old churches, each more quaint and interesting than the last; and now we have a good view of Ivan Veliki (or the Cathedral of John the Great), the pride of the Moscowites, in front of which is the celebrated great bell of which everybody has heard or read. Several monks sweep past us in their long black gowns, and innumerable military men saunter about, making a fitting group in the foreground. If we stand and look over this wall on the side of the walk, we shall have a view that is worth coming a thousand versts to see. Below us lies the city; what a gay-looking place! The gilt domes and golden crosses, the star-bespangled cupolas, the belfries with their lofty spires, the palace-like buildings, the gardens, the gaily-painted roofs, the very irregularity of the streets, lend an additional beauty; the hills on which the city is built, rising from the Moskwa's banks, succeed each other until lost in the distance. The only object wanting to render the panorama perfect is water. What a pity that the river is so narrow and scanty! The view of Moscow, for an inland town, if it only had the broad Volga running through it instead of this poor shallow stream, which scarcely serves to float the river-boats, would be unequalled, excepting perhaps by the city of Mexico, which filled Cortez and his iron warriors with so much delight. That enormous square building with a church in the centre, that we see yonder to the left, is the Foundling Hospital: it contains some thousands of inmates; the children are brought up to serve the crown, or as servants and needlewomen, according to their sex. The present state of affairs in Russia renders such establishments necessary, in order to prevent the crime of infanticide, which would otherwise be a common one. Far away to the right are the Sparrow Hills, a very pretty place of resort for picnic parties, &c.

It was near the spot on which we now are that Napoleon the Great is said to have stood and gazed on the flames of the burning city beneath him, in whose red glare of fiery light he read, as Belshazzar did of old upon the wall, that his empire had passed away. Why did not Nicholas learn of a mightier man than himself how dangerous it is to invade the hearths and altars of another race, when ambition and not justice prompts the deed?

We could remain here for hours and yet never be tired of gazing on this beautiful tableau; but there are many other objects to see, and so we will continue our promenade.

In crossing the space within the Kremlin we pass more churches and more barracks until we reach the Holy Gate: the picture of the Virgin and Child is above it—of course it is a miraculous one. One of the greatest miracles it ever performed was the remaining where it is when the French invaded the city; for that gay and frolicsome people tried, so the Russians say, with all their force to remove it, but in vain; so, *sous entendu*, it could be nothing but a supernatural power that kept it fixed where we now see it. We heretics may imagine, from its shabby appearance, that they let it stay because it really was not worth their while to take it away. The Russians regard it with extreme reverence, and the sentinel placed near has strict orders to let no one pass through the gateway unless he uncover his head. We ladies are exempted from this penalty, and having unceremoniously walked through the arch we reach the large space in front of the Gorod or Gostinoi Dwor. That strangely-built church to the right, painted of all sorts of colours and twisted into all sorts of contortions, is one that was erected at the command of Vassili the Blessed, or, as some say, Ivan the Terrible, the Muscovite Caligula,* who was so enchanted with it when it was finished that he ordered the architect's eyes to be *pulled out*, lest he should ever construct another similar in beauty. What a pleasing encouragement to genius!

That heavy statue in front of the Gostinoi Dwor was, they say, cast to commemorate the defeat of the Poles when Poland

* It is almost a compliment to Ivan IV. so to call him.

was more powerful than Russia. That ponderous arm appears disproportioned to the figure. The Gorod is much larger than the Gostinoi Dwor in St. Petersburg, but it is neither so clean nor kept in so good order: I think the shopmen are still more tiresome with their "What do you wish?" Some of the shops contain things of great value, although not displayed to view. That decent-looking woman is inspecting real cashmere shawls. "How much is this one?" she asks.

"Seven hundred silver roubles" (110*l.*); and he adds, "not a copeck less."

That young girl standing near her is her daughter; she is going to be married, and one of these expensive shawls must always form an item in the dowry of a shopkeeper's bride. Generally, the most extravagant furs, brocades, jewels, and satins are to be seen worn by the women of this class: they frequently have no bonnet, and wear merely a silk handkerchief tied tightly round the head and fastened in the front with a diamond brooch. That splendid carriage with six horses, three postilions, coachman, and two footmen behind, all richly bedizened with gold lace, and having cocked hats trimmed with white ostrich-feathers, is one sent to fetch another bride of the merchant class: she is probably the destined wife of one of the shopkeepers in this Gostinoi Dwor. I remember once seeing the dowry of one of these people; it was being carried by on the heads of about sixty men one after another. Such quantities of fine things, enough to raise the envy of all the damsels in the city. Certainly there was nothing hidden under a bushel, for every article was frankly displayed to the greatest advantage in midday and in the public streets. Formerly it was the custom to marry the daughters at twelve and thirteen: there are many now alive who were married at that youthful age, but an ukase has since been published forbidding any girl to be espoused before she has attained her seventeenth year. That man with a covered dish is selling hot blinnies (pancakes); he seems to find numerous customers. The one next to him is a Tartar; his shaven head is covered by a light-coloured felt hat, and he wears a long blue caftan, which is their usual costume: he is vending Kazane soap, made of eggs, and very much prized by the ladies. Like all Mahometans he abominates pork. We used to see the village children, as one was passing, hold the two corners of their apron in their fingers, imitating the shape of pigs' ears, which invariably filled them with unutterable disgust, and which they always showed by spitting several times over the shoulder. The man opposite, standing in front of an eastern-looking shop, is a Persian: notice his high black sheepskin cap of a conical shape, such as those seen on the Nimroud sculptures, and his long open sleeves tied in a knot behind his back: he is speaking to a countryman of his in a language that seems to equal the Italian for its softness. His Asiatic countenance and elegant appearance form a marked contrast to the group of peasants near him, who are standing admiring the shoes and boots of coloured leather embroidered with gold and silver, for which the town of Torjock is celebrated.

Yonder goes the metropolitan of Moscow in his coach and six, exactly similar to the one we saw in St. Petersburg. They say that he would not be long primate here if his Majesty had the power to remove him, for even *his* authority finds a check in the reverence and respect with which his Eminence is regarded by the Russian people. He is the author of several theological works, and bears besides so exemplary a character for piety and good works, that it is no wonder they look upon him as a saint: indeed there are many so designated in the Greek kalendar who have not merited the title half so well.

Many of those whom we meet have the unmistakeable traits of the Hebrew countenance, yet there are no Jews allowed to reside either in Moscow or St. Petersburg unless they produce the certificate of their baptism. Can it be that the temptation of gain has caused them to *call* themselves Christians and to forswear the creed of their fathers?

The people of Moscow seem even greater lovers of tea than those of St. Petersburg, for almost every shopman is comforted by a glass of it, which is constantly standing on the counter beside him. On the other side you may remark a small frame with strong wires stretched across it, on which wooden or ivory beads are threaded, by means of which he makes his calculations very rapidly, the Russian money being in decimals. It is most probably an invention introduced by the Chinese, as Mr. Davis speaks of an instrument exactly similar in common use in the Celestial Empire, and very likely the merchants from that country, at the grêat fair of Nishmi Novogorod, might have first taught the Muscovites its utility. It is true that with this instrument they can instantly calculate any sum of whatever amount, but it must be a bad practice after all to do so, as without its aid they can do nothing in arithmetic, and appear quite at a loss in counting the most trifling sums.

That gentleman opposite is making a bargain with our friend the Persian; he wishes to buy some narghilés. See what a number of pipes he has brought out, of all fashions and prices; some of them are beautifully ornamented: he finds a ready sale for them, the Russians being as much addicted to smoking as any Oriental nation, but it is strictly forbidden to do so in the streets; any person seen so occupied would be taken to the police-station. There is a story they used to tell in St. Petersburg; I do not know whether it be a true one, as so many anecdotes are invented about the Emperor. One morning he was walking down the Perspective, and a French gentleman, who was on a visit to the capital, was sauntering along with a cigar, the tip of which was as red as a ruby, and pretty wreaths of smoke were gaily ascending in the frosty air. The Emperor looked at him, and he in return looked at the Emperor. He then, with all the grace for which the *grande nation* is celebrated, accosted him in elegant French, and turned to enter into a little chat. His Majesty took it all in good part, and they continued their walk until they came near the palace ; but on the way he mentioned to the stranger that the strictest orders were given concerning smoking, and asked if he had heard of them. The Frenchman replied that he believed somebody had told him something about it, but he was going to leave Russia in a day or so, and he would not care if he met Nicholas himself. Just at that moment the guard turned out and saluted his Majesty. "Ah !" said the Frenchman, "who are you, mon cher ?" "I *am* Nicholas himself," answered the Emperor. The gallant Français immediately put his cigar in his pocket.

The Kremlin we have just visited contains, among other interesting buildings, the Tiramà and the Treasury. The first mentioned is the ancient palace of the Czars. Among other apartments shown are those formerly occupied as a kind of harem. The Russian women in former times were kept as secluded from the world as are the ladies in eastern countries : they were veiled and jealously guarded, and were not allowed to quit the palace nor even to go to church : the place on which they were accustomed to stand to hear the mass sung in the adjoining cathedral was pointed out to us. The rooms in the Tiramà are small, with vaulted ceilings, the whole of which, as well as the walls, are completely covered with arabesque paintings exceedingly rich and curious : they were executed by Byzantine artists : the doors are *à jour* and similarly decorated.

The chair, table, and Bible of the Czar Alexis, father of Peter the Great, are carefully preserved in one of the apartments : the book was securely locked, so we could not see in what language it was written, probably in Sclavonic. The window still exists out of which the so-called false Dmitri leaped when the insurgents had effected an entrance into the palace to assassinate him. The story of this unfortunate prince still remains an enigma in history: certainly it was greatly to the advantage of Shuisky, his immediate successor, and of those that followed him, to endeavour to prove that he was an impostor. Outside of the palace is the terrace on which the Czars appeared after their accession to the throne, to show themselves to the people in all the pomp and circumstance of imperial power.

The church adjoining the Tiramà is curious and very ancient; there are a great many paintings and ornaments in the old Byzantine style.

Connected with this antique palace is the new one built by the present Emperor: it is certainly magnificent in the interior, from the immensity and splendour of the suite of state apartments, each of which is designated after one of the orders of knighthood. I do not know which is the most imposing of these grand halls; each one is perfect in itself and of its kind, but the largest is that of St. George.* The walls are completely covered with gilt arabesque carving, relieved at intervals by the insignia of the order; enormous chandeliers depend from the ceiling, and the floors are of inlaid oak. Even in the daytime the effect of so much gilding was dazzling, and when the lamps are lighted it must be almost overpowering. So much glitter and overcharged ornament do not accord with our English taste, accustomed as we are to Gothic architecture and buildings of simple grandeur; but the Russians are extremely fond of show and barbaric splendour, so that perhaps they look with equal *dégoût* on our public edifices.

The treasury contains a great variety of interesting objects. In the jewel-room, placed on pedestals, are sixteen crowns, among which is the imperial diadem of Russia, the crown of

* St. George with the dragon is the insignia of the Russian order, as well as of the garter in England.

unhappy Poland, and those of Siberia and Astrachan. Both of the latter are extremely curious, and resemble a highly ornamented skull-cap of gold, trimmed round with black fur. Whilst gazing on these, it is impossible to avoid reflecting upon the vicissitudes of nations. I remember when we were staying near the Volga, in the summer-time, we frequently took a walk along the upper bank, whence we could look down on the river and watch the numerous barks heavily laden with corn and other raw produce, being tugged up the stream by gangs of Tartars; they were harnessed together like so many cattle, sometimes as many as forty in a company, with a headman or driver. Now and then they were allowed an hour or so for rest, and, just like so many beasts of burthen, they threw themselves, leashed together as they were, upon the bare ground, and were soon asleep. When the leader thought that they had reposed long enough, he went about from one to another, kicking them up with as little ceremony as if they were dogs. Having received a sufficient number of these gentle admonitions, the men arose, and immediately re-commenced their toilsome journey, singing with sharp piercing voices the barbarous songs they had learned far away amid the plains of Tartary, and with which they awoke the echoes in a land where their forefathers once caused their scarcely less savage war-cry to resound. The very cities through which they were wearily marching bore the monuments of their ancestors' triumphs, and many a high wall of earth or solid tower pointed out the spot over which they reigned in other times as the conquerors of the land. In gazing on these Tartar slaves, whose faces had no more expression than that of a brute, one could scarcely believe that these were the descendants of a race at whose name not only all Asia but the whole of eastern Europe trembled, who founded empires and dynasties, who overran kingdoms and carried monarchs away captive, and who have left the traces of their conquests from the Yellow Sea to the

Neva. Among other objects to be seen at the Treasury are the throne of Poland, her sceptre, and, alas for her! the keys of Warsaw. How sad must be the feelings of a Polish heart at the sight of the spoils of his miserable country! When I was at Warsaw I saw the church at which the unhappy people made their *last* stand against the overwhelming armies of Russia. When every other part of the city had fallen into the hands of the enemy, the Poles shut themselves up in the church that is to the right as you enter from the St. Petersburg road, determined in their despair at least to sell their lives as dearly as possible, and to perish rather than to become the degraded slaves of the hated Muscovites. They fought until, faint and weary, they could defend the place no longer; they were forced to give way, and the Russians entered. Heaps of the dying and the dead, weeping women who were on their knees praying for the aid of Heaven, infants wildly clasped in the arms of their frantic mothers, wretched girls shrieking with terror or vainly begging for mercy, wounded children and bleeding patriots were presented to the sight of the savage soldiers in their *career of glory!* The victors did not remain long in the church, and when they quitted it there was not a man, woman, or child left alive within its walls—"thus was *Warsaw* lost and won!" The lady who was with me spoke in guarded whispers as she recounted the sorrows of her country, and looked round several times in fear lest she should be heard by some passer by, so dangerous is it to speak the truth under Russian rule.

Perhaps the time will come when the blackened walls of this doubly sacred edifice will be replaced by a glorious monument which shall proudly meet the gaze of the Muscovite traveller in future years, when Poland shall be again a country, and the Poles a people; for surely so much patriot blood has not fallen like rain upon the soil, though now trodden down by the iron heel of oppression, without bringing forth a rich harvest of noble hearts who will sweep the name of Russian from their land, and restore that land again to its place among the nations. It is to be hoped that the days of adversity have not been entirely lost, nor the lesson taught by it unheeded; perhaps the chastisement has been dealt them by the hand of Heaven, that the evils may be swept away, and that they may rise once more a wiser nation and a better people. How many scores of sad and mournful tales have been told me by my Polish friends, showing the miserable state of their country! The brother of one of them, who was in the revolution of 1830, was obliged to take refuge, with another patriot, in the wild forests of the west of Poland: they remained there during several days, subsisting on berries and crude fruits; at last the latter was determined to make an effort to leave the country, but previous to so doing he wished to obtain an interview with the young lady to whom he was going to be married, as he could not think of quitting the country without informing her of his fate, lest she should imagine that he had been slain. He accordingly found means to let her know that he would meet her on the next night at a peasant's cottage, and when the hour came he set out for the purpose. My friend's brother accompanied him as far as he dared, but he had scarcely left the forest, and was not out of sight, before some soldiers suddenly appeared who had been sent to scour the country in search of them: they seized him immediately, and shot him dead before the eyes of his companion, who hastened to quit the spot. How he crossed the frontier I was not told, but he did find an opportunity to do so, for my friend informed me that he was then in the service of France. The last time that news was heard of him he was with the army in Algiers, and perhaps ere this he has taken part in those grand struggles now going on between the soldiers of freedom and the slaves of despotism, in which he will have a noble opportunity for avenging the death of his brother patriot.

The Treasury contains many other remarkable curiosities besides those I have mentioned—the coronation robes of Peter the Great, Alexander, and the present Czar, together with the canopy borne at the ceremony ; a curious chair richly set with turquoises and precious stones ; an ivory throne, &c. In glass cases were a number of bâtons, crosses, stars of knighthood, and insignia ; a quantity of plate was also displayed on shelves round the room of a very ancient appearance—forks that must have been made about the time when they were first invented, the prongs of which were three inches long, so that they looked much more like warlike instruments than any destined for the festive board. Another apartment was appropriated to curiosities in armour and weapons. Some wax figures upon pedestals were dressed in the ancient national costume, which did not much differ from the modern, and also in that of Muscovite warriors ; their shirt of mail and the formidable axe might recall the armed figure of some Norman knight. This warlike instrument, which the soldiers formerly *threw* in battle with so unerring an aim that they rarely missed cleaving the enemy's skull, resembles in every respect the axe of the modern Russian peasants. There is something very Saxon about the features and figures of these effigies, so that one might almost imagine that the supposition of some historians is a true one, that the original race of Sclavons was nearly related to the one from which we are descended, but the admixture of the Tartars has changed the Russian face. I do not know how true all these suppositions of the learned may be, but the Highland Scotch whom I met in Russia have often assured me that Russ resembles Erse so much that they found it extremely easy to learn ; according to them the numerals are almost the same. As I do not know the Celtic language, I could only judge by the sound, and certainly, when ten were counted, I had no difficulty to understand the words.

In a room further on we were shown a collection of muskets, pistols, &c. &c., which we were told had been taken from the French : they had most likely been collected after the terrible retreat from Moscow in 1812. I was acquainted with a lady whose first husband was an officer in the *grande armée ;* her history would furnish ample incidents to make an attractive romance. She was only sixteen when she crossed the Borodino sitting on a telega, with a baby a few weeks old on her lap, and was present in that battle, or rather she was left in her husband's tent : she never saw him more ; and in the evening, when she was anxiously expecting his return, she was terrified by the appearance of several Cossacks, who with their drawn swords rushed into the tent : they were on the point of seizing her and her infant, when she pulled out a pistol which she always had by her loaded, and, boldly taking aim, she vowed that she would fire at the first who dared to touch her : the savage soldiers did not, of course, understand what she said, as she spoke only in French, but they easily guessed her intention, and drew back. Just at that moment M. K., a Russian officer of rank, happened to pass near the spot, and, hearing a female voice, entered the tent. Struck with the lady's youth and beautiful countenance, as well as with her courage, he ordered the Cossacks out of the place, which command they reluctantly obeyed, and then, as he spoke her language, requested an explanation. She informed him who she was, that her husband was a French officer, and begged M. K.'s protection. A soldier belonging to the army of Napoleon entered whilst she was speaking, and informed her that her husband was killed, and that he himself saw him fall. Her situation was now really desperate, for she was alone in an enemy's country, ignorant of their language, with an infant in arms, and destitute of means. M. K., sincerely pitying her misfortunes, offered her the shelter of his mother's roof until she could be forwarded to Paris. She accepted gratefully his kindness ; he procured a country cart with a sufficient escort, and she was enabled to reach Madame K.'s estate in safety. When the campaign was over, the gallant Russian returned home, made an offer of his hand to the young French widow, and they were married. He died of the cholera in 1832, and she again became a widow. I am still in correspondence with her daughters, and therefore am well acquainted with the family.

Another old lady with whom we were intimate often gave us the most fearful accounts of the scenes she had witnessed during "la retraite," and of the dreadful sufferings of the unhappy French soldiers. She told us, among other anecdotes, that she herself had sheltered some officers and men who came to her once in the depth of the night to beg her aid. They had been flying before the Russians for several days, and had at last reached her estate. It was awfully cold, and the poor foreigners were nearly starved; so her womanly compassion, surmounting her antipathy to the enemies of her country, prompted her to afford them assistance. She did so at the imminent hazard of her own life, for the people were so exasperated against the invaders, and so infuriated against those who offered the least protection to them, that they would infallibly have sacrificed her as a traitor. The utmost caution was therefore necessary : she bade the unfortunate Frenchmen to go away for the present as quietly as they could, lest any of the household should hear them, and directed them to a wood not far from the mansion, where they would find a hut filled with hay, promising them that she herself would come to relieve their necessities. They did as she requested, and she instantly slipped on her fur cloak and hood, and, filling a basket with all the cooked provisions and wine she could find without the aid of her servants, she fearlessly left the house and hastened alone on her mission of charity, although the neighbourhood was much infested with wolves rendered ravenous by the excessive inclemency of the weather. The gratitude of the poor refugees may well be imagined, and every night, let the weather be what it would, she repeated her kind visit for a long time, until by heavy bribes she found the means to get them across the frontiers, and they returned in safety to their beautiful France. It was not until some years after that she heard what had become of them, when one day she received a splendid piece of plate illustrative of the Retreat, on which was an inscription expressive of the most grateful remembrance of her benevolence, and accompanied with many prayers for her happiness and prosperity.

By the side of the spoils of the *grande armée* were some richly ornamented saddles set with turquoises, pearls, and diamonds, with frontlets and bridles to match, mostly of Persian manufacture.

In the lower story of the building is shown the model of the Kremlin* as Catherine II. wished it to be re-constructed ; but although the long line of Greek columns would have had a fine effect, it would neither have been so picturesque nor so truly national as the present structure.

* Kremlin is a Tartar word ; it means a fortress.

CHAPTER XIX.

English people in Russia—Sudden change of sentiment—Intolerant feelings of the Russians towards them—Opinions of the people—Ideas of the Russians on the English ministry—Their hope of aid from the Americans—The lower classes—Losses of the Russians—Disagreeable remarks—Their manner of speaking of the French—Political ideas—The Americans in St. Petersburg—Invented news—Odd ideas of a war-ship—The English in fault—Mr. Pim's designs—Russian disgust at the new warlike inventions—Dread of the British—The serfs—The troops in the capital—Vanity of the Russians—Their disappointment about Turkey—False ideas—Evil effects of the conscription and slavery—The recruits—Deserters—Dissatisfaction—The Czar's ambition—Aspect of St. Petersburg—Wretched recruits—Embarrassments of the Russians—A bivouac—The dying officer—March of the army—The future of Russia—A review—Anecdote of the Emperor.

The English in Russia have always been much more respected than liked; and latterly they have become most intensely hated, from the political position in which Great Britain stands towards that country. Among us, if a Russian were in company, it is not probable that he would find any difference in the manner in which he was received because the two governments are at war; but the Russians are really not enlightened enough to separate the individual from the nation, and think it a proof of patriotism to show their resentment to any son or daughter of England whom they may chance to meet. As soon as the Declaration of War was known, there was a marked and very disagreeable change in the manners of even my oldest and most attached friends: it seemed that those few words were sufficient to sever the bonds of amity, and to place a barrier of ice between those who had previously been on the closest terms of intimacy; indeed, I verily believe that they would just as readily have touched a toad as have shaken hands with an English person. This intolerant feeling of course found vent in words, as well as in silent indications; and at last it reached so great a height, that it became almost impossible for any one to remain in the country who was obliged to come into daily contact with them. No opprobrious term was too coarse for us: "those dogs," "those swine, the English," were expressions so general, that we were not surprised to hear them even from the lips of ladies of rank and education. Added to this was the impossibility of making any reply, unless in the most guarded terms; for the immense number of spies, and their excessive pleasure at catching a stray word or so, would have subjected either a lady or a gentleman to the most disagreeable visits of an emissary of the secret police, and a summons to Count Orloff's office. Indeed, I was told of two Englishmen who were requested to present themselves at that place, for speaking disrespectfully of the Russian journals in a coffee-house, and expressing some well-founded doubts of the veracity of their contents. I was informed that they received a severe reprimand, and were *ordered to believe* all that was written under the government sanction—a thing extremely difficult to do, seeing the extraordinary falsehoods inserted in the papers, and the wonderful triumphs of Russian valour recounted; but, to be sure, the word *victory* is as easily written as the word *defeat;* and it certainly sounds much more agreeably to the ear. Although we English did not believe the accounts published, yet it was extremely annoying to hear the exulting remarks of the Russians on the supposed advantages obtained by their armies. The majority of the people professed to believe the accounts given, and very likely they really did so, as only a select few are acquainted with anything like the truth. I was told that even the Emperor himself is not always informed of the extent of his losses, because so few have the courage to tell him of them. A friend of mine accidentally heard two military generals* talking of the great reverses the Russian arms had experienced ; they were speaking in an under tone, but she distinctly heard the words—

"It is very strange that three generals should have fallen, and so few soldiers slain !"

"How !" exclaimed the other, "few ? why, we have lost altogether forty thousand men !"

This was before the fatal siege of Silistria, or just at its commencement : so the thousands that have perished altogether by the sword and pestilence must have amounted to a fearful number. Even while I was at St. Petersburg, it was affirmed that the Russians had lost, since their entry into the principalities, at the lowest estimate, seventy thousand men !"

The absurd fasehoods daily published for the amusement of the Russians, and the abuse of our nation, we can well afford to laugh at in England ; but it is widely different to one standing alone in a foreign land, and among the enemies of one's country. None but those who have been placed in such a position can have any idea of the grief and heartburning causes, nor how very difficult it is to remain silent on hearing such expressions as, "There will be plenty of English blood shed this year, thank God !" "We must have some new hospitals built for the wounded when the British fleet is destroyed !" "Count Besborodku has made a present of cannon to the Emperor, to shoot those swine when they approach us !" "There won't be many of the British that will ever return home again !" "The first victory we gain over those dogs of islanders," &c., &c. Amid all their resentment and hatred towards the English, it was strange to remark how tenderly the French were treated, as if they were a people too insignificant and helpless to merit any other sentiment but that of the most profound pity and compas-

* In Russia, civilians as well as military men have the title of general ; it is, therefore, usual to distinguish them by the designation of military or civil, as the case may be.

sion, the victims of English policy, and as if they were merely a cat's paw to serve the turn of our government. The Russians expressed the greatest contempt for them in the light of antagonists: "We have beaten them before, and we will beat them again," was a phrase a thousand times repeated, for they vauntingly boast of having defeated *la grande armée* in 1812, and of having hunted the French out of their country as if they were sheep; but all Europe knows what truth there is in Russian history.

The Russians expressed great friendship for Lord Aberdeen, and intense hatred of Lord Palmerston, whom they blamed as the prime mover of public affairs, and as the author indirectly of all their misfortunes. I may mention, *en passant*, that the names of Napier and Palmerston inspired the lower classes with so great a terror, that the women used to frighten the children by saying that the English admiral was coming! And among the common men, after exhausting all the opprobrious terms they could think of (and the Russian language is singularly rich in that respect), one would turn to the other and say, "You are an English dog!" Then followed a few more civilities, which they would finish by calling each other "Palmerston," without having the remotest idea of what the word meant; but as the very climax of hatred and revenge, they would bawl out "Napier!" as if he were fifty times worse than Satan himself.

There was an English lady of influence in St. Petersburg, of whose great wit and penetration the Russians stood in the most profound dread and awe. I shall never forget the unbounded rage with which they related an anecdote of her, which showed how deeply they felt the cut they had received, and how true they knew her words were. Soon after the *Battle* (?) of Sinope, one of the Russian nobles was so obliging as to call on her, expressly to hear what she would have to say concerning that *glorious* feat of valour or cowardice, and in the course of conversation remarked that it must be very disagreeable to her to reside on the quay.

"Why so, your Excellence?"

"Because," replied he, "it must be so annoying to you to hear the cannon fired in honor of our victories!"

"Oh! dear, no!" was the reply; "not in the least; it happens *so very seldom.*"

The Russian, finding he was no match for the English lady, remained silent, and was soon glad to beat a retreat to hide his discomfiture.

In revenge we were told that "she would not be invited to their balls," as if to be excluded from their dull feasts of frivolity were a severe punishment and an irremediable misfortune. It was really ridiculous to see what puny efforts the Russians made to show their anger at the English: they would pass you in the street, and not bow, although they had previously been well acquainted with you. It may be judged to what an excess they carried their resentment, when I mention that even children behaved in the same manner. I was well acquainted with a lady who resided at one of the Institutes in St. Petersburg, and I was in the habit of frequently calling to see her; before the Declaration I was always met with smiles, and, according to the established custom, the young persons used to bow as they passed us; but as soon as they knew that the war had commenced, we heard them continually make the remark one to the other, "Ne la saluez pas ma chère, c'est une Anglaise!"

All the shop windows in St. Petersburg were filled with plates inscribed "The Glorious Battle of Sinope," as the Russians are pleased to call that fearful act of cowardice. On my arrival in London I found the very same representations, or facsimiles of them, displayed, with the far truer designation of "Horrible Massacre!"

Among the upper ranks, the most ridiculous ideas concerning

the war were prevalent; they were kept so entirely in the dark by all the government accounts, and by the absurd severity of the officials at the Censor's office, who carefully erase every article that has any reference to political affairs or to Muscovite losses, that it is no wonder that their conjectures were sometimes laughable, and if related in England, appear incredible. The Emperor in their eyes was a martyr, and the English his persecutors; they blamed them as the most cunning of people, nor could they conceal their spite and vexation at having been outwitted by our government. They were convinced that the union with France could not possibly last, and that the Americans would come to their rescue; that English money was the chief instigator in the whole affair; and that it was mainly the curry-favouring spirit of our people, who hastened to congratulate Louis Napoleon on his being elected Emperor, that had prevented a friendship between Russia and *la grande nation.* "Ah, quel malheur!" exclaimed one of the Czar's aides-de-camp, "that our Emperor did not call him 'mon frère;' how different it would have all been!" To hear them talk, one would imagine that all the evils existing in the world are to be ascribed to British influence, which at least proves how very powerful they must deem it. It was usual to hear them affirm that the revolution in China was all our doing, and that we were trying to raise Poland against Russia; that the Indian empire was in imminent danger from their army in Asia, which they declared had been sent against Hindûstan; that we were on the point of learning a great deal from their teaching in military matters, meaning by that, that our soldiers never had so powerful an enemy to contend with as the Russians. "Deceitful England" was to receive condign punishment. "If," said an old general, "Napoleon the Great called England 'Perfide Albion,' our Emperor should name her 'Fausse Angleterre;'" a sentiment that met with universal approbation. The Greeks, according to them, were a nation of saints and martyrs, who were worthy of the utmost admiration, and the French were to be despised and pitied for being so led astray ; yet, notwithstanding their pretended disdain of the latter people for their inferiority to themselves in every respect, they still had a dash of hope that they would ultimately be induced to change sides and serve the turn of Russia.

It was extraordinary how the Russians clung to the idea that they had secured the aid of America* to save them from their embarrassments. They spoke of the help they were to receive with as much assurance as if a treaty had already been signed on the subject, and they appeared to regard the President of the United States with as much respect as a sailor does his sheet anchor in a storm. To do the Americans justice, they took all the advances in perfect good faith, and rather encouraged the hope : they were courted in all companies, feasted, petted, and, as they say, "made much of," and seemed rather pleased than otherwise. It is odd that the citizens of a republican nation like that of the States should have so great a reverence for titles, orders, stars, and the like trumpery, for surely, if a person *be* a gentleman in the proper sense of the word, it is not necessary that he be ticketed as such like a prize-ox at a cattle-show ; and in Russia, above every other country, a glittering star, or a cross suspended by a scarlet ribbon round the neck, would be a most fallacious criterion that the wearer merited so high an appellation. Indeed it often happens that the subjects of the Czar, the breast of whose coat is like a cushion, on which all the family jewels are pinned, have the vilest souls and the blackest hearts, together with the most empty heads, in his dominions. I do not know if a foreigner would not really form a more correct estimate of their character if he judged of their baseness by the num-

*Yet they always spoke of the United States as a half-savage country, and of the Americans as half civilized.

ber of orders they display. The Americans in St. Petersburg did not seem to think so, for, the very morning I left it, one of the attachés of their embassy showed my friends, with the greatest exultation, the Easter eggs with which the Princess so-and-so, and the Countess such-an-one, and several officials of high rank about the court had presented him: he also exhibited the portraits of the whole of the Imperial family, which he intended to hang up, he said, "as household treasures, when he returned to New York," whither he was going "right away," as he assured us.

The Russians, upon the strength of their hopes, were always threatening us with the American fleet in the Baltic, which would place the Allied fleets between two enemies. Is the old adage about extremes meeting really so near the truth? Whether there were any substantial foundations to all these castles in the air, we had no means of knowing. The French have a proverb, "Il n'y a pas de fumée sans feu."

Almost every morning we were hearing news of the discomfiture of the Allies, the destruction of at least a part of the fleet, and so on. One day I went to call on a lady, and an elderly gentleman there present informed her, as a piece of pleasing intelligence, that *four more* of the ships in the Baltic had been sunk. As this was about the tenth time that reliable information had been received of a similar event, upon a fair calculation there were already forty of them put *hors de combat.* In speaking of Sir Charles Napier one evening, I was informed, "He is the most savage monster breathing; he never shows mercy to any one, because he really does not know what the word means; and as the parliament has ordered him to spare nothing that is Russian, God knows who would live to speak of the scenes we shall witness when he comes to St. Petersburg."

Notwithstanding the terror which was universal, they still affected to laugh at the idea of a naval invasion. "Look at Odessa; what did the fleet do except making themselves ridiculous, and what is that place compared to Cronstadt and our other forts?"

We were much amused once by the account an old gentleman gave a whole company concerning the manœuvres of the Allied fleets near Denmark. According to him, the splendid "men" of war now floating on the Russian seas were constructed somewhat in the fashion of hens and chickens; for he gravely told us that the hulls were made to open, and a whole progeny of little gun-boats made their sudden appearance, which, after having fired off the cannon and done all the mischief they could, ran back like lightning to the shelter of their great parent's wing, the hull of which opened and closed by means of machinery, and were thus enabled to place all the young fry in safety!

Instead of the Russians being the aggressors and the cause of the war, the English were always accused of it, and, according to the people in St. Petersburg, our Queen would have declared war long before she did so had our government been sure of the co-operation of the French. "Vous prenez la France par la manche, because if you do not guide her she may turn against you." At another time we were told that the chief object for which the English made war was that of obtaining possession of the gold-mines in Siberia. In England people would scarcely credit that anything so absurd could be believed even in Russia, yet it undoubtedly was so. I remember when Mr. Pim, the naval lieutenant, came to St. Petersburg, proposing to cross overland to the north of Siberia in search of Sir John Franklin, all the Russians were convinced that he was sent merely as a spy to look out for the gold mines,* whilst some went so far as to

* A Russo-French gentleman, who is the possessor of large property in these mines, assured us that the idea that the Emperor derives much from them is entirely false; that the expense of working them is enormous, and the time that they can be excavated in each year is very short; added to which is the charge of transport; and, above all, the

say that his designs were to corrupt the nomads of Asia, only they forgot to add what we intended to do with them when we had them.

We heard a Russian gentleman remark that, in fighting with the Anglo-French powers, they should at the least have the advantage of doing so with people more enlightened than themselves, and, gain or lose, they should still profit, for, even if they were beaten, they should acquire greater civilization; and he adduced Prussia in illustration of the proposition, "for she would never be the nation she is were it not for her wars with France."

Intense indignation was also expressed on account of the new warlike inventions. "Look at those long-range guns and asphyxiant balls; it is a perfect disgrace to any people to invent such, and it is cowardice and baseness to make use of them." The knowledge of the superiority of English mechanism and wonderful machinery, of which even the lower classes in St. Petersburg have some idea, seemed more than anything else to inspire them with terror, and by them nothing was considered impossible for the English to perform. I heard a common man say one day to another, with a grave shake of his head, "The English, ah! there is no getting on against them!" and such seemed to be the universal impression. I was informed that many of the lower classes in the capital had the idea that, if the English conquered them, they should be no longer slaves, and not have a poll-tax to pay. If this be true, and I was assured it was so, who can calculate what the consequences of such a belief spread among the populace might be, or how

necessity of their productions passing through the hands of the *employés*, who, according to Russian custom, rub off a great deal in the process. "It is true," said he, "that sometimes large amounts are forwarded to the capital, which make a figure in print, but they omit to say what expenses were incurred in obtaining them. You may be sure that very little in the way of profit reaches the Imperial Treasury, but private speculators make them pay better because they themselves superintend them."

soon the hollow fabric of the Russian government would fall into ruins? If this conviction once enter into the national mind, the nobility may soon find that they have a greater enemy in their oppressed peasantry than in a foreign army. They have a thousand years of wrongs and slavery to avenge, and, like the heaving of ground in an earthquake, they will shake and topple down the mighty strongholds and towers of those who vainly hope to tread them under their feet for ever. It was the opinion of many when I left St. Petersburg that the eighty thousand soldiers (as the Russians said) bivouacked in the strees and billeted on the houses, were a great deal more for the purpose of ensuring peace within the barriers of the town than for that of repelling a foreign invader *au dehors*.*

Everything that could be done by the government for raising the anger and fanaticism of the people against the English was resorted to, and it was nothing uncommon to hear many of the lower classes declare that they would cut the throats of all the heretics within reach, as soon as they heard the sound of the cannon at Cronstadt, as the sacrifice of a certain number of them was necessary in order to ensure the victory on their side. A pleasant prospect for our poor countrymen left in the capital! But it is not astonishing, taught as they are that we are heretics, that all their fanatical feelings are raised and all their barbarian antipathy set in antagonism to us and the French.

The upper classes were equally enraged against us, and even in society they sometimes could not restrain the expression of their anger and spite within the bounds of politeness or propriety. One day I called on a lady of rank, and I had scarcely entered the room ere she began to attack me in a rather violent manner concerning the present war. It was in vain that I

* In order to ensure the fidelity of the Finnish people, the Emperor took a journey to Finland. and, after having exerted all his talents *pour faire l'aimable*, he promised them fifty years of immunity from taxation, &c.

assured her that I knew nothing at all about it, and that it was the affair of our government. "Ah!" said she, "you pretend to be very cool and unconcerned now, but you will tell another tale when you see the Russian flag flying over the Tower of London!"

Before the war began, the Russians were always boasting of their navy and the excellence of their seamen. "Our sailors," said the senator L—ski, one day, "are, you must allow, quite equal to those of England—le mâtelot Russe ne cédera jamais à qui que ce soit." Since the declaration of war, they have wisely been silent. It is strange, however, that a people possessing nautical qualities in so admirable a degree should be glad to run behind stone walls and keep there whilst the enemy's ships are sailing merrily over their seas. "What inconceivable insolence," said a court-lady once, as she was reading the gazette, "what inconceivable insolence of those English to call their squadrons by the names of the 'Baltic fleet,' the 'Black-Sea fleet!' the seas are our Emperor's and not theirs." I had a great mind to ask her why they did not assert it in a stronger manner than by words only; but I reflected that I was in an enemy's land, and the vision of Count Orloff's office and the birch had a great deal to do with my prudence.

The boastings of the Russians are intolerable. To hear them talk, you would think that, like the Khan of Tartary, their Czar bids all the kings and potentates of the earth to eat their dinner; and I do believe, if St. Petersburg were demolished by the Allies, and Moscow in ruins, they would still declare that they were invincible. If their Emperor is not exactly the brother of the sun and moon, he is Heaven's first lieutenant at the very least. Perhaps this fanfaronnade is a remnant of their Asiatic habits, which may possibly shortly be cured by European remedies.

How much soever the Czar might have sought to disguise his intentions concerning Turkey and Constantinople, his nobles did not attempt to do so, and that even two years ago, long ere this war was certain.

"Quant à Constantinople, nous l'aurons ; soyez tranquille," said a nobleman one evening.

"But perhaps it would be advisable to ask the permission of France and England," I remarked.

"It is not necessary," replied he ; "what could your fleets or the French with their armies do against our brave troops ?"

"We shall see that, perhaps, some time or other."

"We shall, but Turkey is ours !"

This is a phrase I have heard them repeat scores of times, even before the English dreamt of a war, with as much confidence as if the double eagle were already stretching his black wings over Stamboul and the Bosphorus, and the Czar were issuing imperial ukases from the Sublime Porte itself.

When the Anglo-French fleets entered the Black Sea, and a few troops were forwarded to Constantinople, nothing could then exceed their rage and indignation. "There is no such country as Turkey now," said they, "and no longer a Sultan, for henceforward the game will be played by France and England." The Russians would not believe that England seriously intended to declare war against them. "It is not possible," said they ; "she will never do it ; how could she ever exist without Russia and Russian commerce ?" This was the illusion they had ; in fact, they really seemed to imagine that all our national prosperity depended upon the flax, hemp, tallow, and corn of their steppes and fields ; but when the news came at last, with a copy of the Queen's declaration, there was a complete panic. I was informed by my acquaintance that the merchants on 'Change looked perfectly aghast and were silent with terror, for they and the nobles equally felt how serious the effects would be to them, and, with the continual draining of the young men from the estates, and the money from their pockets, ruin and distress stared them in the face. No one can have any idea of the effect on the population these continual conscriptions produce, unless he has seen it. When we were leaving the country, we passed through nearly twelve hundred versts of Russian and Polish land : excepting recruits, we scarcely saw a young man in any of the villages. There were only very old peasants with the women and children ; even young lads were drawn away, and the chaussées or post-roads were all being mended by women and girls. What desolation will reign in these districts ere the war is over it is impossible to imagine. But the loss of life is not the only evil that attends the wretched system of a military despotism ; the dreadful effect it has on the morals of the people will be felt generation after generation. These young men, totally ignorant and illiterate, are drawn away from their homes and families in all probability for ever ; they have no means of communicating with their relations or wives, as they do not know how to read or write, and the loosening of all social ties, the forgetfulness of duty and affection, causing them to feel that none sympathize with them or even know that they are still in being, produce a fearful amount of vice and crime that will be an inheritance for many a year to come. I remember hearing a Russian noble say that "true communism is only to be found in Russia." From that assertion, it may be imagined what the state of morality must be in the villages. The condition of slavery must also contribute to this evil state of things ; for the domestic servants, who are often separated from their parents when very young, perhaps apprenticed or taken to some place hundreds of versts distant from their native village, entirely forget each other, and for years, consequently, never hear or know anything concerning their relations. Most of the men-servants are married, and many of them have their wives in the country, whom perhaps they do not see even once a year. When the young men are taken for soldiers, their relations do not even expect to see them again. One morning a poor woman came to me crying most bitterly, and saying that her two nephews had just been forced from her house to go into the army. I tried to console her, saying that they would return when the war was over, but this only made her more distressed. "No, no," exclaimed she, in the deepest sorrow, "they will never come back any more ; the Russians are beaten in every place." Until lately, the lower classes were always convinced that the Emperor's troops were invincible, but it seems, by what she said, that even *they* have got to know something of the truth. A foreigner in St. Petersburg informed me that he had "gone to see the recruits that morning, but there did not seem to be much patriotism among them : there was nothing but sobs and tears to be seen, among those who were pronounced fit for service, whilst the rejected ones were frantic with delight, and bowed and crossed themselves with the greatest gratitude." The most distressing scenes may be seen in the streets among the bands of recruits—they, their mothers and sisters, or wives, all weeping together as they walk along ; for the women, with innate tenderness, accompany them for many miles out of the town, unwilling, until the very last moment, to bid the objects of their affection adieu for ever, whilst the latter, in entering the Russian army, like the condemned in Dante's "Inferno," leave all hope behind.

Before the war began it was the universal custom among the landowners to send all the worthless characters into the army, and, as men of *any* size are eligible to serve therein, it was a convenient manner of getting rid of those that were idle or disobedient. I have often been present when a lady or gentleman, in writing to the steward, would say, "Since you can do nothing with Vassili, Ivan, or Gregory, you can hand them over to the recruiting officers at the next conscription."

"Do you know," said one of these proprietors, "if you say to one of our serfs, 'I will send you for a soldier,' he will tremble at the words, and not forget them either for two years at the least." By this we may form some idea of the light in which the honourable profession of arms is regarded by them, and of the treatment they expect when they are forced to embrace it.

Desertions are, of course, extremely frequent, and since the commencement of the war they are fifty times multiplied, if one may judge from the numerous groups of miserable wretches, heavily chained, met with almost hourly in the streets of St. Petersburg. I am sure it was enough to make cne's heart ache with sorrow and indignation to look on their grief-stricken faces and thin figures, which seemed as if they had been wandering with the wolves in the wilderness to escape from the cruelty of their fellow-men. Once or twice I met a group even more horrible than these. Several soldiers with fixed bayonets were walking on each side of a droshsky, on which was seated one of their comrades holding in his arms what was certainly the *corpse* of some unhappy deserter who had just received the punishment for his fault, his head shaking listlessly from side to side, and his arms hanging straight and rigid, the livid shadow of death on his sharp and painful features, showing that the heavy lash had at last released him from his misery. In looking round on the broad streets of the capital, and seeing, in contrast with so much suffering and misfortune, the gaudy carriages of the nobles and their gaily-dressed occupants, who seemed so wholly busied in the pursuit of pleasure that they could not spare a single moment to reflect on the unhappiness of their fellow-creatures, I was often tempted to ask myself whether, if entreaty were made, as in times of old, "to spare the city for ten's sake," the domes and towers of St. Petersburg would still stand to cast their shadow on the earth.

The numerous conscriptions levied since the Russians entered the Principalities have taken away not only the worthless slaves but the very flower of the estates, and great was the dissatisfaction even openly expressed by the proprietors: "Notre Empereur se trouvera en face de son peuple," said one of them; from which an inference may be drawn. On all sides universal disapprobation was heard; but they were careful not to lay the blame on the Czar, so their anger was vented on the English and Lord Palmerston, whom they still persisted in saying was the prime mover of all, and on whom, of course, their own government was glad to throw the odium. It was not known, nor would it be believed when affirmed, that the Allied Powers had caused the rights of the Christians to be recognised in Turkey; and even when the "Confidential Correspondence" was published, they actually, with the Emperor's letter before them, declared that the whole was a forgery and a tissue of falsehoods.* In conseqence all their hatred, anger, and fanaticism were roused against the English as abettors of infidels and downright liars; their monarch was a martyr, and the English his persecutors. At last, when they could no longer shut their eyes entirely to the truth, the upper classes said that they supposed the Emperor wished to acquire the surname of Great, and that he was willing to become the admiration of future ages and be spoken of by posterity. If the latter reason be a true one, there is every probability that his expectations will be realized, only in a manner rather contrary to what he desired. Perhaps the illusion concerning the wonderful power of Russia will be further dispelled when they have been enlightened by a few flashes of the cannon of the Allies, and have been made to feel that of France and

* So little do the Russians know of the true state of affairs, that, since writing the above, I have received two letters from Russia, in the first of which my friend begs me to "excuse the faults, for she is so much interrupted by the cannonading in honour of their *great victories* over the Turks." In the second it is stated that "thirteen thousand English have been slain near Anapa!" which, according to the writer, took place about a month before the army left Varna; and I was further told that "the manner in which we treat the prisoners of war, in giving them neither food nor money, is disgraceful to a Christian country." To one of these epistles is a postscript, giving me to understand that the British fleet were too frightened to remain before Cronstadt, &c.

England, for as yet scarcely any of them are acquainted with the resources of the two countries, thanks to their education and the government books of instruction. They are truly like people walking in darkness, and are now moved liked chessmen anywhere that the player pleases.

One morning I went to call on a lady, and as usual the parties present were railing at the English. At last I asked my friend why they did not say something about the French as well. Her answer was naïve enough: "Oh, we don't mind them; but I believe they talk about the English so much because they fear them the most. Our people you know," she continued, "are accustomed to think of the former as a nation they have vanquished, but they were not prepared to see your countrymen in the light of enemies, the two countries have been so many centuries friends." Certainly the communication with England has existed from time immemorial; even in the remotest ages commerce was carried on between the two countries, although it was only *established* in the reign of Ivan IV.; and it may be remembered by the reader of Russian history that the daughter of Harold the Unfortunate married a Russian prince.* I remember a gentleman near Orenburg informing me that, in digging among the ruins of an ancient Tartar city near his residence, fragments of English pottery were frequently turned up, yet the very name of the town had disappeared and was forgotten. An English gentleman in Moscow once showed me a gold coin, half the size of a fourpenny-piece, of Ethelred, or Ethelbert, I am not sure which, that had been dug up or found near the lake of Ladoga, and, as he supposed, had been dropped there by some British merchant on his way to the fair of Nisny Novogorod, which has been annually held at that place for centuries beyond record, and was in former ages the grand emporium of Europe and Asia, whither merchants of both continents repaired to

* Vladimir, Prince of Novogorod.—*Nestor.*

exchange the manufactures and produce of each. It is still held in the month of July, and lasts six weeks, and is also still resorted to by dealers from most of the nations of Europe to purchase cashmere shawls, &c. I was once very near the place during the time of the fair, but, as it is not considered "comme il faut" for a lady to be seen there, I did not visit it. It is the grand market for tea, which is brought thither by the Chinese to exchange for Russian money. Formerly the Russians gave their own manufactures of cloth instead of paying in coin for the chests of tea, but I was assured that their speculations on that head had been entirely ruined by themselves; "for," said my informant, "with true Muscovite dishonesty they, finding that the Chinese did not unroll the bundles of cloth, hit upon the ingenious plan of making the first few arsheens of good quality, and the remainder of the veriest rubbish: the unsuspecting Celestials took them as usual, without much examination, at the word of the western merchants, and carried them back to China, the Russian cheats meanwhile laughing in their sleeve to think how they had taken them in. But they were severely punished the next year, and have been ever since, for the Chinese tea-dealers were not to be duped a second time; they attended the fair with their well-packed chests, but obstinately refused to receive anything but silver money in payment; so the Russians, who had prepared a vast quantity of cloth, were obliged to carry it all back again; and as the people cannot do without tea, they were forced to purchase it for ready cash, and bear the loss as they best could." Any one that knows the Russian character and their want of foresight will have no difficulty in recognising this anecdote as a true trait of the national mind.

In London we may walk through every street, and, from any indication we see of the fact, we should never guess that the nation was at war with anybody. It was far different in St. Petersburg when I left it; there not only every street but every house gave some intimation of the struggle in which they are engaged: trade was almost at a stand-still; scarcely any of the shops had customers in them; everybody seemed to be economizing their money lest poverty should come.

Long lines of cannon and ammunition-waggons were drawn up here and there, outworks were being thrown up, parks of artillery were being dragged through the streets continually, regiments marching in and marching out, whilst whole armies were being sent to the Baltic provinces, which I was informed were to be occupied by four hundred thousand troops, but, as the authority was a Russian one, there is no reason to believe it. Every morning, look out of the window at what hour I would, hundreds, nay thousands, of raw recruits, torn from their villages perhaps a thousand versts off, were tramping wearily along, with all their worldly riches in bundles at their back, with dresses wet and muddy, and faces stricken with grief, as they marched in the direction of the palace in order to receive the Emperor's approval. I know not what the feelings in that man's breast can be as he deliberately scans the downcast countenances of so many miserable wretches, and then sends them down to the seat of war, really and truly for nothing else than to become food for cannon, and the prey of vultures and jackals. Does he ever reflect that for each life he thus sacrifices for his ambition he will be called to account and stand arraigned as a murderer before the judgment-seat of God, who has committed them into his hands that he may be the protector and not the slayer of his people?

Reviews were held almost daily: Cossacks, Circassians, guards, and the line, all had their turn and their destination assigned them. I was told that the Czar, in reviewing a number of troops previous to their being forwarded on their march to the south, was struck with the sad and dejected air of the poor men, and even the officers. "Hold your heads up," he angrily exclaimed ; "why do you look so miserable? there is nothing to cause you to be so!" Perhaps the soldiers saw more plainly than he the evils that threatened them. From all that I could learn, the government was at its wit's end to know what to do with the forces: they were marched hither and thither, to and fro, according as some fresh intelligence arrived, bringing news of intended attacks just in the opposite points to those reported before, and by this means wearing out the men's strength and spirits, until they would be too happy to surrender as prisoners to whoever would have the charity to take them. The daily expense of supporting all these myriads amounts, as a Russian informed me, to about a million of silver roubles, or rather more than a hundred and fifty-eight thousand pounds. To the English, who pay their troops more liberally, and feed them with better rations than the detestable black bread and salt with which the Russian warriors are furnished, this may seem a small sum for so vast a number as they boast of possessing, but perhaps, with the national failing concerning numbers, they might have put in a stray figure or so to look well on paper.

In speaking of the Anglo-French invasion, the Russians declared that, if the enemy took Cronstadt, they would themselves burn St. Petersburg, as they did Moscow in 1812. Indeed it looked somewhat as if they had the idea in view, for all the great families were sending their jewels, plate, and valuables into the interior, whilst many of them went to their estates with the intention of remaining there a whole year. I was informed that the treasures from the palace were also taken away, and, among other articles worthy of removal, the state prisoners from the fortress, who were transported to some unknown place at a distance. There was also a grave discussion as to the propriety of forming another capital near the ancient city of Novogorod, which in former times, under Rurick, in the ninth century, was the metropolis of his dominions. If they do so they will incur the danger of falling into the *status quo ante* Peter's reign, for, if cut off from easy communication with Europe, civilization, which is still but an exotic in the country, and has not yet taken a firm root in its soil, will die away, and barbarism, which is the normal state of Russia, will assert its supremacy. In short, the Russians are in that agreeable position that any prospect would be preferable to that which they have before them.

Perhaps the sentiments of a gentleman in St. Petersburg, concerning the present state of affairs, may be interesting: he is of Polish descent, a man of talent and education, and one of the best authors in the country. A great many visitors were assembled, and during their stay my friend assented to everything that was proposed; but when they had all departed, he frankly told me that he was convinced the Russians had no chance, and that he was sure they would be dreadfully beaten. On my asking him what he really thought of the whole affair, he replied, "In a few words I will tell you. This Emperor Nicholas seems to me to have been placed by Heaven on the throne in order to punish the wickedness of his people: how otherwise could he have been tempted thus to risk his country, crown, life, and all, upon a single turn of a card? vous verrez qu'il sera flambé. No one has ever yet stood against Lord Palmerston, and neither will he. Look at Louis Philippe; who caused him to repent of kicking against the pricks? And that Queen of Spain—you will see how long she will rule. Lord Palmerston is one of the greatest statesmen the English have ever had, and you may be sure he would not be so much hated in Russia were he not feared, and with good reason too."

I remarked that it was a pity the Emperor did not withdraw ere it was too late.

"He would be glad to do so," was the reply, "but he dares

not; he has raised a legion of demons that he cannot lay. What would the proprietors say? What would the ruined merchants say? and what would become of him if he were thus publicly to acknowledge that he is in the wrong? No; now that he has advanced so far, he is obliged to continue, and leave the bill he has drawn to be dishonoured by those that come after him." He also expressed the conviction that the allies could take St. Petersburg if it suited them to do so. "But in regard to that," he said, "they would do well to destroy what the efforts of barbarians have erected. This city," continued he, "is but a false imitation of a civilized capital. What barbarism has planned and fostered, let civilization demolish: we shall then perhaps see the nation reduced to a savage state, and so much the better, as they will have to learn by experience, instead of having the outward appearance of a civilized people thrust upon them by a despot's sword. Peter the Great made an enormous mistake that it will take centuries to correct."

On my expressing regret that so many fine buildings should be destroyed, "It seems so at the first sight," replied my friend, "but it ought to be done for more than one reason, for the sake of the human race thousands of years to come, who would bless the hands that had dealt chastisement to a tyrant, and had shown an example that would be felt to the end of time." He finished by presenting me with a copy of the imperial proclamation concerning the miraculous preservation of Odessa, which he laughingly bade me keep as a precious document, one of the most wonderful productions of the age, and a most astonishing proof of the extent it was possible to lie in the face of Heaven. I believe that, although I had been acquainted with the family seven or eight years, my friend would not have dared to speak so freely, had he not been aware that the next day I was to leave Russia probably for ever.

Whether my friend's ideas be just or not, I cannot tell ; but how can we expect that a blessing will be on a city, every stone of whose foundations was laid at the cost of a human life ?* The Russians themselves have ever had a foreboding that St. Petersburg will not long exist, and that evil will befal it. Perhaps they feel that the myriads whose clay has long ere this mingled with the morasses into which they were thrown, still cry for vengeance unto Heaven, and that they will be heard at last.

When I was on the road to Warsaw, I saw the large army that Russia was sending through Poland to the south and the Principalities ; as nearly as I could calculate there were about sixty thousand men, chiefly infantry of the line, in three divisions, perhaps at the distance of fifty versts apart. It was not without a feeling of sincere compassion that I gazed on the poor people's faces, and thought how few, how very few, of all those would ever return again. One division of many thousands was bivouacked on the plains *à la belle étoile ;* most of them were fast asleep on the bare ground, their arms piled up near them, with sentinels guarding different points ; videttes were stationed at a distance, looking in their dark coats like bronze statues, with the twilight sky in the background. Here and there were watch-fires, with a few soldiers sitting around ; scores of ammunition-waggons and gun-carriages were at a little distance further on, with men standing under arms, and the horses grazing on the scanty grass of the fields close by. I came up with the second division early on the next morning ; the soldiers were all marching merrily along to the voices of those in the van

* Peter the Great caused immense levies to be made throughout his dominions to furnish men sufficient to construct his capital ; crowds of Cossacks were also brought from the Ukraine after Mazeppa's defeat, who, together with the prisoners of war taken from Sweden, were all employed in the work of excavation ; and in laying the foundations hundreds of thousands, it is said, perished from fatigue, pestilence, and ill-treatment. One hundred thousand died from famine alone.

of each regiment, who were singing the war-song of the Russian army ; and they really seemed, in the excitement of the moment, to have forgotten the scanty rations and infamous treatment they receive, and for which they are compensated by the munificent pay of *nine shillings per annum!* I remarked that the officers were dressed precisely the same as the privates ; a small piece of twisted gold lace, from the neck to the shoulder, was the only distinguishing mark by which they were known. The reason of their being so attired was because so many had been shot by the enemy, who, it was affirmed, took aim at their more showy uniforms ; but from all that I was told, the rifles of the Turks are not the only ones of which they stand in fear, nor are the Turks their only enemies ; their oppression has caused them to find both among their own ranks.

At one of the stations an officer belonging to this division got into the mail-coach ; he was evidently in a deep decline, and was so extremely ill that he could scarcely stand : it was truly sad to hear him talk. He informed me that he had received orders to join his regiment, living or dead, and that he was obliged to obey, although he feared it would only be to leave his corpse on the route, as he could be of very little service to his country in the state in which he was. It was plain enough that he would never again be able to bear arms in the field ; but he was going to the war nevertheless, although he must have perished not many days after I saw him. His brother officers appeared very kind to him, and rode several miles by the side of the diligence, cheering him with their conversation, and endeavouring to instil some hope into his heart, but in vain ; he smiled faintly, and shook his head with mournful significance, for he felt that his march in life was over, and that ambition and a soldier's name had found an early grave. But he seemed resigned to his fate ; and when we stopped at the wretched village in which his company was to rest for the night, I doubt whether he ever quitted it again, and most likely rose no more from the miserable bed in the peasant's isba to which he was supported. We were all very grieved to see him, yet perhaps some of his gay companions have ere this met a worse fate still; for they may now lie with thousands of their poor fellow-soldiers in their dismal graves amid the pestilent marshes of the Danube, or in the ghastly trench that forms the grave of thousands on the heights of Alma—a horrible sacrifice made to the hateful ambition of their imperial master. The third division was crossing the Vistula in flat boats and rafts at the time we were doing so; indeed many of the men and horses were on the same raft with us: their cannon and ammunition-waggons were drawn up in a long line on the opposite bank. I asked some of them whither they were going, but I met with the usual answer of the Russian boor—"Ya nisnaiu" (I don't know); on listening, however, to the conversation of a group of officers who stood near me, I concluded that a part were to remain in Poland, and the remainder to proceed further south.

There must have been immense numbers of soldiers wounded in the affairs of Oltenitza and Kalafat; for, go into whatever house you would at St. Petersburg, the ladies and children were all occupied in preparing lint, by unravelling linen rags, for the use of the army; and all the ladies in the Institutes were so engaged by order of the Crown: the enormous quantities they made, and the repeated demands for more, proved how many poor men had been sufferers for the Emperor's sake.

The check that the Russian arms are receiving at our hands, we may be well assured they will neither forgive nor forget; and even centuries to come, they will, if they have the power, take their revenge for it: it is their national character, and they will never rest until their thirst for vengeance is slaked, if it be possible. How fairly soever they may speak—how plausibly soever they may act—they will ever be on the watch, like a cat for its prey, for the slightest weakness, or the least slip, that could give them the most trifling advantage, or tend to the attainment of their object. Remember the taking of Moscow by the Poles, and see for how many centuries they were lying in wait for Warsaw, and how patiently generation after generation they set traps and pitfalls to catch the Polish people tripping, although their enemies were at that time one of the most civilized and powerful states of Europe, whilst they themselves were scarcely recognised as a nation, and were almost unknown to the west. Like drops of water undermining a bank, they venture little by little, and work in silence until their object is gained—then woe and desolation to those that fall! But now that "vaulting ambition has o'erleap'd itself," let us hope that the children's children of England and France may bid defiance for ever to their schemes of vengeance!

One of the most splendid sights in the world is perhaps the *grande révue*, in St. Petersburg, of the troops, previous to their proceeding to the summer encampment; it lasts nearly a whole day, and takes place on the *Champ de Mars*, a large space in front of the summer gardens. We went several times to see it; on the last occasion there were eighty thousand men assembled—a hundred thousand, a gentlemen who was with us affirmed, which he pronounced "effrayant pour le monde entier." There is usually a great crowd to witness the spectacle, but we were so fortunate as to have seats secured for us at a friend's house, whence we could have a good view of the whole field. On reaching the *Champ de Mars* my first feeling was one of disappointment, for I could scarcely believe that so great a multitude of men and horses would have occupied comparatively so small a space. The square is not more than one-third of a mile in length, yet there seemed ample room left for performing their military evolutions. The men were all standing under arms, awaiting the arrival of his Imperial Majesty and staff—they and the horses immovable

CHARGE OF TEN THOUSAND CAVALRY.

PAGE 290.

as statues of bronze; the solid squadrons of Cossacks, like a dark cloud, were drawn up at the further end of the field; their long spears held quite upright had the effect of an endless line of palisades, so even and motionless did they appear. The Czar was expected every minute, so we anxiously kept our gaze fixed in the direction of the palace; at length he arrived: tremendous indeed was the effect of the salutation which he received from the multitude of warriors. He, followed by his glittering staff, passed close to the spot where we were seated, mounted on a black war-horse, his noble figure dressed in the full uniform of the guards, his brow surmounted by the magnificent helmet with a golden eagle, whose widely-spread wings form the crest; he looked like another Atilla reviewing the descendants of the Huns. It was with a feeling almost of sorrow that I gazed on that brilliant group as they swept proudly along the serried lines of the living mass, and thought that, long ere another century had fled, not one of all that mighty multitude would exist to speak of that splendid sight, and that the magnificent pageant of that day was doomed, like thousands of others that had passed before, to fade away like a shadow, and be remembered no more.

It was only when the masses began to move that I could form any idea of the myriads assembled; then indeed the sight was magnificent. As to the military evolutions, of course I could not attempt a description of them, but the beautiful costumes of the various nations, the handsome uniforms, the glittering casques and flashing swords, the wild strains of the martial bands, formed a scene that could perhaps be only equalled by the *Champ de Mars* in Paris on a similar occasion. Now would come sweeping past a regiment of Circassians, like a band of warriors from some gay tournament, heroes of song and romance awakened from their sleep of ages into a new and stirring life; presently a squadron of the guards, their eagle-crested helmets flashing in the sun ; then would rush by the sombre cloud of Cossacks, their lances couched as if to attack the ranks of an enemy, their rough-looking horses galloping at the top of their speed ; then again regiments of infantry, until there seemed no end of the long line, their martial tread sounding like the rushing of a mountain stream, and until the eye was weary of watching their (to me at least) inexplicable movements. A gentleman with whom my friends were acquainted, and who ought to know if anybody could do so, informed me that the Emperor was a very timid horseman, that he never mounted but mares of the gentlest and most docile temper, and that numbers intended for his use died ere they were sufficiently broken in. I do not now remember whether it was three or five years that he mentioned they were in training, but, to use his own expression, "les pauvres bêtes se brisaient le cœur ;" they died of grief, in fact, being wearied out with the trial.

An incident took place at one of these grand reviews in St. Petersburg which is greatly to the Emperor's honour. I will, therefore, relate it, especially as I had it from good authority ; indeed so much has been said against him of late, that a short anecdote in his favour will, I hope, prove an agreeable change. During the performance of some military evolution the Czar despatched a young aide-de-camp to an old general with a particular order. Whether the officer was confused, or timid, I do not know, but he gave an exactly contrary one to that which he had received. The astonishment of his Imperial Majesty may well be imagined when he perceived that the grandest movement of the day was entirely defeated by some unforseen stratagem of the general's. The Emperor is naturally *très emporté;* indeed I have heard that he is subject to fits of ungovernable rage, similar to those that Peter I. was so frequently attacked with, and, as may be supposed, his anger was unbounded on this occasion thus to be humiliated in the face of all the officers. He commanded the general to his presence, and before the crowd of military there present he called him "Durak!"* The venerable old warrior drew back; his grey hairs were insulted, and his veteran experience called in question; the angry flush mounted to his brow, but, remembering that it was the voice of the sovereign that had dared to utter such a term, he made a martial salute and was silent; but, complaining of sudden indisposition, he was allowed to retire. The review was nearly over, so the Emperor returned to the palace. Early the next morning the young aide-de-camp presented himself, and earnestly begged an audience of his Majesty. On its being accorded, he in the most frank and manly manner confessed the error of which he had been guilty, and, expressing sincere regret, entreated that he might be degraded from his rank, or suffer any punishment, rather than his venerated general should be thus disgraced. The Emperor heard his account in silence, and on its termination bade him return to his barracks and report himself under an arrest. What reparation could now be made by a Czar to the old man whom he had thus insulted? To the astonishment of the military, another review was ordered to take place, at which the same regiments were to attend; and when the whole were assembled, the Emperor, calling the veteran general to his side, made a public apology for his late conduct, embraced him, and, kissing him on each cheek, presented him with a star which he himself had worn. I heard some call this a theatrical representation; I do not believe it was so: why should the Autocrat of all the Russias not have the credit of possessing noble sentiments in common with any other gentleman, though he be the enemy of our country, and though his heart be proud and ambitious? The young aide-de-camp was not disgraced; indeed, the action redounded so much to his honour that he became an especial favourite.

* A fool, an ass.

After the grand review of which I have before spoken, the troops left the ground by different routes, and in half an hour the *Champ de Mars* was as silent as before; the only trace of the lately assembled host was the marks of the horses' hoofs by myriads in every direction deeply cut into the sand.

CHAPTER XX.

Foreigners in Russia—The Poles—The oath of allegiance—Disgraceful treatment—Want of cordiality—Polish exiles—Greek and Roman churches—Difference of creed—Saints—Christmas custom—Warsaw—Polish cottages—Peasants: their treatment—Germans in Russia: their customs: their mode of life—New-Year's eve—Pleasing custom—Character of the Germans—Variety of foreigners—The French—The Turkish renegade—Mixed society—Conclusion.

In writing about Russia, some notice of the foreign residents will not be out of place, as they form so great a proportion of the inhabitants of all the large towns. The most numerous among them are the Poles and the Germans: the former are dispersed all over the empire, being obliged to serve as *employés* and in the army. Centuries of warfare and mutual cruelties have caused these two great divisions of the same race to hate each other with an intensity that would have satisfied the great Dr. Johnson himself. Every Polish gentleman is forced to take the oath, in which he calls on Heaven to witness that he will shed the last drop of his blood for the Emperor's sake. It must be galling indeed to have to pronounce these words, with the recollection of the wrongs of his country weighing on his heart, and, perhaps, the remembrance of an outraged mother or sister who might have been publicly flogged for instilling sentiments of patriotism into his soul. Let it not be thought that these are merely idle words. Many a time have I been told of Polish *ladies* who have been sufferers from the executioner's lash, not many years ago, in the very capital of their country. A hundred instances have been told me, with the names of the unfortunate women who were the victims of such brutal treatment.

To them we may give our pity and compassion—the eternal shame and dishonour will fall on the head of those at whose command such acts were done.

Among my acquaintances abroad, I numbered a great many Poles, and I asked a noble one day how he could concientiously take the oath above-mentioned. "We wait patiently," replied he; "for the time is not yet come. As for the allegiance, we make a reservation to ourselves concerning it; but hope leads us still to expect that the hour for Poland's resurrection *will* arrive. What can *we* do at present?" Notwithstanding that the Poles are everywhere received in society, there is very little cordiality in regard to friendship: many have, it is true, intermarried with Russians, but they are not, for the most part, of the superior class of gentry, but are merely petty *employés*, or people of no "family," in the aristocratic sense of the word. In almost every part of Russia, Polish people may be met who have been banished from their native land for some political offence, either proved or suspected. Many have assured me that they were taken away in the middle of the night from their own house, and perhaps dragged from their bed, merely on suspicion of being disaffected. It was impossible to refute the accusation, because, according to the wise laws of despotism, they had never been confronted with their accusers, or even knew who they were: very probably, the information had been given by some government spy, the name of whom is "legion" in Poland. One of these victims was a gentleman who, with his wife, had been imprisoned four months, when they were hurried away from Vilna to the interior of Russia, and they assured me that they had not the remotest idea what the crime was of which they were accused. Added to the antipathy the Poles and Russians naturally feel for each other politically, the difference in religion contributes to their animosity; for, although the Greek Church and the Roman may appear in the eyes of Protestants to possess few points of difference, yet, perhaps for that very reason, their hatred to each other is the more intense. As far as I could learn, the chief differences between the Greek and Roman belief consist of a trivial distinction, scarcely more than verbal, in the doctrine of the quality of the three persons in the Trinity, of the denial by the Greeks of the necessity of their priests remaining unmarried, and of the substitution of pictures for images as objects of worship and reverence. It is true that, since the division of the Christian Church into the eastern and the western, a vast number of extra saints have been added to each, which may have caused considerable jealousy between them. If so, the Russians must triumph, for they have about twice as many as the Romanists; but, on the other hand, they are not quite so select.

I once went to dine with some Polish friends, on Christmas Day, and I remarked a quantity of straw scattered under the table. On my begging to know why this was done, I was informed that it was in commemoration of the Saviour having been born in a manger: the Russians have not this custom.

Warsaw is beautifully situated on the Vistula, and contains a great many buildings erected in former times; but it must be very vexing and grievous to the people to see the monument in their "grande place" supported by Russian eagles, publicly reminding them of their loss of nationality. The Vistula is so extremely shallow that the sand is everywhere visible through the water. As to the general aspect of the country, it much reminded me of some parts of England; even the whitewashed cottages with thatched roofs looked very like those we see at home, but the peasants bore no resemblance to our sturdy, independent-looking countrymen. *They*, poor people! with their sullen, downcast faces, too plainly showed, even more so than the Russian serfs, how hardly they fared, and how they were ground down by the oppression of their conquerors. It seemed to me that every Muscovite, dressed in a little brief authority, was at liberty to play the tyrant over them, and I used to feel quite indignant at the merciless manner in which the post-guards treated them. The blows they inflicted seemed almost enough to break the back of any human being, whilst the screams they elicited frequently broke the silence of the night, filling our party with horror and dismay, and made us sincerely pray for the time when retribution shall fall on the heads of their oppressors, and Poland shall be free again.

The Polish dishes are not at all according to the English taste ; they contain too much garlic and sour cream, and are much too coarse to be pleasant. In all the provinces of Poland through which I have travelled, the bread was extremely bad ; even in Warsaw, at the hotels, although the waiters presented us with what they called English loaves, they bore very little resemblance to the white bread of London. Perhaps the best bread in Europe is made in Moscow : it is perfectly delicious.

The Germans in Russia are extremely numerous ; they have spread themselves over the whole country and have monopolized a great deal of the trade. "There are only two patriotic nations in Europe," said a Russian admiral, "Russia and England ; the French are partisans of their party ; but as for those Germans, their country is where they find they can gain most money." In regard to his judgment on the French, it must be a false one, for in their history we see many proofs of real patriotism, which show that, in respect to *them*, he was in error ; but his assertion touching the German people, especially those in Russia, was probably the truth. They are not liked by the Russians, who look upon them with all the antipathy of race ; added to which, their penurious habits and desire for accumulating wealth, qualities so different from the national character of the people among whom they dwell, and their excessive severity as officers and overseers, cause them to be detested by the lower classes, while the upper classes look down upon them with disdain, and consider them as a sordid, money-getting nation, who possess no nobility of soul, so that with them the name German and "nobody" are synonymous, although, owing to the German predilections of the Emperor, many of the very highest places in every department are filled by people of that race. Among the lower classes they go by the name of sausage-eaters, from their love of that viand. The Germans in St. Petersburg are mostly from Livonia and Esthonia, countries long under the Russian rule: indeed the same may be said of those scattered over the empire; some of them are from Prussia, but, upon the whole, there are not many from the true Teutonic states. They live mostly in small colonies, mixing but little with the Russian society; indeed many of them, although they have been born and educated in the country, do not speak Russ at all well. They retain the manners and customs of their ancestors as well as their religion; they have their Christmas-tree on the eve of Christmas Day, their commemoration of Luther, and their festivities at the New Year in their own fashion. The Christmas-tree, with its gay decorations and hundred lights, the presents laid round it for the children and relations, and the croquemitaine, so formidable to baby offenders, are all now so well known in England that a description of them is not necessary. The Germans are a social people among themselves, and they enjoy life quietly—*mais ils mènent une vie ennuyante.* Their society, however agreeable, still wants that gay animation of the French, which makes even trifling subjects interesting in conversation.

A great many of the medical men in Russia are Germans, and people of that nation may be found in every town: I believe I may say, without exaggeration, that nearly all the bakers' shops, as well as those of chemists, are kept by them.

The ladies are exceedingly good housewives, but, as a French person of my acquaintance remarked, "Elles sont ou des heroïnes de Werter ou des ménagères." One of their greatest pleasures consists in going once a week to the Singanstalt, or singing-club, to which nearly all the young persons of both sexes belong : the evening is passed in singing German Lieder, and the choruses from operas and oratorios by national composers, which they perform in very agreeable style.

One of the most delightful New-Year's Eves I ever passed was at the house of a German friend. The family was a very large one, and all the members of it were assembled, even down to the third-cousins—grandmamma, grandpapa, all their married sons and daughters, with every one of the children, those of a few months old included, cousins, nephews, and nieces, not one was absent. After spending the evening in various social games, in which both great and small took part, the whole company took their seats round the room a little before midnight, and waited in silence until the clock struck twelve, announcing that another year had passed for ever, and that a new one had already commenced. All those who could sing stood in a group at one end of the hall, and the instant that the last stroke had solemnly sounded they burst into chorus of thanksgiving. Each then sang a verse in turn, the grandfather, although past sixty, commencing in a fine tenor ; after him sang the eldest son, and then the eldest daughter, and so on. The words, which are really beautiful, were partly composed by Voss ; other verses had been added by the singers themselves. They began by thanking God for the renewal of another great division of time, expressed delight that so many were thus joyously assembled, with hopes for the welfare of those far away : but in the midst of their rejoicings they affectingly referred to the dead, who were sleeping in solitude, wrapped in their cold and silent graves, and whose place on earth was no more seen ; and much emotion was excited by the following verses :—

"Wer weiss, wie mancher modert
Ums Jahr, gesenkt in's Grab!
Unangemeldet fodert
Der Tod die Menschen ab.
Trotz lauem Frühlingswetter
Wehn oft verwelkte Blätter.
Wer von uns nachbleibt, wünscht dem Freund
Im stillen Grabe Ruh, und weint." *

Tears fell fast from many an eye as each gazed round that circle of friends and relatives, and all seemed to dread that some beloved face would be missing ere another New-Year's Eve found them there assembled; they were scarcely dried ere the two concluding lines echoed cheerfully through the hall—

"Wohlauf, und: Gut seyn immerdar
Sey unser Wunsch zum neuen Jahr." †

And then the grand chorus of thanksgiving was sung in gratitude to Heaven for the hope of an eternal re-union hereafter.

As soon as the New-Year's hymn had been sung, the sons and daughters embraced the aged mother and father, and then the grandchildren came forward to do the same; after them the other relatives, according to their proximity of relationship, and finally the friends who had been invited. Champagne was then handed round; universal congratulations and affectionate embraces followed, after which a merry supper restored the gaiety and cheerfulness of the whole party.

* These lines may be thus translated:—

"Who knows how many wither
In a year sent to the tomb,
Summon'd unwarned thither
To meet their final doom,
In spite of th' warm breath of spring,
Which often faded blossoms bring?
Ah! which of us shall stay to mourn for those
That lie wrapp'd in the silent grave's repose?"

† "Cheer up! and good be ever there,
Shall be our wish at this new year."

Although I have mentioned the general character which the Germans bear among the Russians, it must not be concluded therefrom that they are not very frequently most estimable people; indeed many of them merit the utmost respect and admiration. It must be borne in mind that the lower class in Russia hold *all* foreigners in detestation, and the Germanic race more than any other. Until the present war broke out, all strangers to their country were designated by them "Germans,"* for the petty distinctions of French, English, and so on, were not known to the half-barbarous serfs; they only knew that they were not Russians, and concluded therefore that they came from Germany. *Now* all other nations of Europe are swallowed up in the designation of English, which at present is a word of hateful import to them, as our country-people are held up as the most to be feared and detested.

The French people, as well as the English, live in societies quite distinct from either the Germans or the Russians; but the French, being more liked in company, and considered more agreeable, from their gay and lively temperament, associate much more with the Russians, who take them as the established model for *bon genre* and politeness: their language also is as much used in society as it is in France, for everybody speaks it; so that, in making friends and acquaintances, our neighbours get on a great deal better than we do. Among the Russians the English *were* certainly greatly *respected* by the upper classes, and were perhaps (if it be possible for the lower classes to like *any* foreigner) preferred by them, especially in matters of business.

* German in Russ is *niemetz*, from *niemoe*, dumb. The Slaves always so designated those who could not speak their language. According to some authors, the name of Slaves is derived from *slovo*, a word, and *slovene*, *i. e.* men who speak. The letter *o* in Russian frequently takes the sound of *a*. Others say that the name is derived from *slava*, glory.

There are many Italians and Greeks established in the country; the latter visit a great deal at the houses of the nobility, their common religion being a bond of union between them. There are some renegade Mahometans also in the Russian service. I remember once dining at a friend's house where I met several; one of them was a general, who had previously served the Sultan, and was himself a Turk by birth. In throwing aside his nationality he seemed also to have thrown away his natural characteristics; for his laugh was the loudest, and his jest the merriest, in the whole party. He gave good proof of eschewing the doctrines of Mahomet, by drinking two bottles of champagne: and when one of his neighbours took the liberty of reminding him of the prohibition against wine, his reply was that the prophet had never tasted champagne, or he would have ordered the faithful to drink nothing else. There are of course a great number of Mahometans in the Russian army, as many of the tribes of the South of Asia profess that religion; also a vast number of Jews, and even gipsies, are to be found in the army, as no one in the empire is exempt from military service. I was told that all creeds are respected by the government. There are not many Englishmen in the imperial army; I believe the greater part of those so designated are Scotch or of Scotch extraction.

Perhaps in no country in the world does one meet so great a variety of foreigners; almost every nation has its representative in Russia; from the Norwegian and Swede to the Albanian and Turk, from the Spanish adventurer to the Moldavian and Wallachian, they are all to be encountered in society. At an evening party natives of perhaps ten or a dozen countries may be met, and that not by any remarkable accident, but merely in an invitation to one's general acquaintances. French is the medium by which all these people hold communication with each other, and interchange ideas; but it is necessary to understand German and Russian to enjoy a conversation, as it very often lapses into one or the other, according to the majority of people of either nation in the company. It is exceedingly disagreeable for those who speak only the French language, as very frequently, when some interesting anecdote is being recounted, a chance remark made by some one in German will cause the conversation to be continued in that tongue, to the great disappointment of the listener.

Having said thus much of Russia and the Russians, I have but few words to add. Of the character of the people I leave the reader to draw his own conclusions, from the anecdotes with which the preceding remarks are illustrated. That the Russians possess most excellent and amiable qualities of heart, no one can deny who has ever resided in their country, or had the pleasure of knowing them. Their virtues are their own, and many of their grave defects may be ascribed to the evil system of government under which they have so long suffered. Centuries of slavery and oppression are enough to change the characteristics of any people, and to infuse into the national mind all the meanness, cunning, and moral cowardice of a Helot. Wild though the country be, it is no inhospitable shore, and the warm-heartedness of the people richly compensates for the coldness of its clime. It is that which throws a kind of charm over the remembrance of Russia in the mind of one who has long resided on its snow-clad plains, and gives an interest to everything connected with them. There is much to love and little to esteem—much to admire and little to respect—in Russia and the Russians; and should these pages ever fall into the hands of my friends there, I entreat them not to consider what is herein written as ill meant. If I have remarked upon what is evil, I have not omitted to note that which is good. I have "nothing extenuated nor aught set down in malice;" and the greatest proof I can give of my attachment for them is the assurance of the sincere regret with which I bade adieu to the Russian shores forever, and of the anxious and earnest desire with which I look forward to the time when a change in their system of government shall free them from the withering thraldom under which they now suffer, and shall enable the many good qualities of their nation to expand and come to maturity under the fostering influence of free and enlightened institutions.

GENERAL REMARKS.

In examining the ancient mythology of the Slaves the reader will be particularly struck not only with the great resemblance it bears to that of the classic Greeks, but by the apparent engrafting of many of its superstitions and forms of worship on the Christian as professed in Russia and Greece. Perhaps this affinity between the ancient Pagan creeds of the two nations may be the cause why both have so easily embraced the same form of Christianity. The similitude which is so plainly seen between the Russo-Greek Church and the heathen system of former ages may also be the reason why mythology is forbidden to be studied in the schools throughout the empire. Paganism indeed seems not yet to have entirely disappeared from the land, and it is curious to remark how easy it is to trace some of the acts and ceremonies of the Russian Church to their heathen origin. Almost every god and goddess of antiquity has a corresponding saint in the calendar, and many of their high festivals are apparently merely those of their Pagan creed under another name; so difficult is it to eradicate the idolatrous superstitions of a nation, or to instil into the hearts of a people the sentiments of a pure religion. The extreme reverence with which the images of the Virgin and Child are regarded, and their rich settings, are most probably only the adoration of their former much-loved idol the Zolotaïa Baba, or the golden woman;

who, according to their mythology, was the mother of the gods. It was highly gilt, and held in its arms the figure of a child. In the Russian Church the Virgin is never, I believe, represented without the infant Christ.

The blessing of the waters, which is performed twice a year, although now regarded as a Christian ceremony, is one very likely to have been derived from the adoration of the great rivers by the Sclavonic races, especially the Bog, the Don, and the Danube. The first-named was, according to the historian, who quotes Procopius as his authority, held in the most estimation by them ; they never approached its shores without fear and trembling, and they drank of its waters with awe, as if by so doing they profaned the sacred stream. Lomonosof, the author, even asserts that the Russian name for God (Bog) is identical with its designation.

The great attachment of the people to the pictures of their saints, on which the rich, especially of the merchant class, lavish immense sums, may be traced to the domestic gods of their ancestors, which were called Domovi Doukhi, or house-protectors, the Lares and Penates of the Slaves.* In every wealthy shopkeeper's best apartment there is a place assigned for the patron saints of the family, generally in the corner, in which is fixed a closet with a glass door, entirely filled with them ; their settings are very costly, generally of silver, gold, and precious stones. Every shop possesses at least one image, and in the piazzas of the Gostinoi Dwor there are large portraits of the Virgin suspended, before which lamps are continually kept burning. In the nobility's houses the saints' images are usually placed in the sleeping-room.

The Russians say that on St. Elias's day it always thunders,

*I have myself seen in the remote villages grotesque figures painted on the wall outside of the cottages, or else a frightful demon on the apex of the roof in front, which the peasants called a domovoi or house-guardian.

which they religiously believe is caused by the rumbling of his chariot-wheels among the clouds ; as according to their account the saint takes a drive in heaven on his name's day. Undoubtedly this superstition must have been derived from the worship of Peroun, the Sclavonic Jupiter, which was formerly celebrated on the day now set apart for the above saint. The form of this idol was almost identical with that of the classic deity, and, like the Olympian Jove, he held lightning in his hand and announced his will in thunders. His statue had a silver head, moustaches and ears of gold, and feet of iron. Before it a sacred fire was ever burning, which if the priests neglected they would have been put to death. The profane representations of the Godhead remarked in a preceding chapter seem to be merely that of Peroun ; the only difference is, that in the former the figure holds a triangle in his hand instead of lightning. The heathenish rite mentioned in a preceding chapter, as being performed by the village women on Midsummer Eve, if it had not its origin in the worship of Baal, was probably derived from that of Koupalo, the god of the fruits of the earth, who was adored by the Slaves with a like ceremony. Perhaps indeed the Sclavonic races, in migrating from the East, brought with them the idols and traditions of their forefathers : in that case Koupalo and Baal may have been the same principle. I believe that the common people still call the rite by the name of Koupalnitza.

Many more instances could be cited, but the above will suffice to show that the remembrance of their Pagan creed still exists among the Russians.

When free access can be obtained to the various collections of ancient manuscripts that are preserved in the monasteries and cathedrals in Russia, much light will probably be thrown, not only on the belief of the Slaves, but on their social state, their laws and civilization, of which so little is at present known in Europe. A Russian gentleman assured me that he had seen and examined many of these collections, which he thought were well worthy of the notice of the learned.

There are not many readers of the ancient Muscovite history; indeed, I believe that few would deem the dry records of the Russian race very interesting, until the policy of Peter I. and Catherine II. forced the name of Russia upon the attention of Europe. It is a pity they have not been more generally studied, as perhaps they would have afforded a kind of key to the designs of the northern autocrats.

Probably nine out of every ten persons in England imagine that civilization was almost unknown to the Muscovites anterior to the reign of Peter the Great, and are not aware that the most powerful republic in Europe had for its capital the city of Novogorod; and that, until the ninth century of our era, its wealth and might caused it to be so respected among the neighbouring states, that the saying, "Who would dare to attack God and Novogorod the great?" is still a proverb in Russia. One would be apt to imagine that Peter's object in building St. Petersburg was to extend and strengthen his frontiers, and to forward more effectually the designs of his predecessors; yet perhaps he committed the greatest error in endeavouring to turn aside the slowly but surely advancing course of Muscovite civilization (which, although more Asiatic than ours, would probably have been more solid than it now is, because gradually acquired), by forcibly and prematurely introducing that of another race upon his people, teaching ideas that they could not understand, and making changes that they could not comprehend. The civilization of England and France was not certainly owing to the swords of the Romans, for the inundations of the barbarians swept away almost every vestige of it: the work had to be begun afresh, because it was not based on a solid foundation. Peter I. made the Russians *polished*, but not *civilized;* the heart of the nation was not prepared for the change; they therefore made more progress in learning that which is evil than that which is good; they were infinitely more apt at acquiring the vices than the virtues of those set over them as teachers, and from being simple they became corrupted.

Perhaps it would not be an error to assert that, excepting the nobility about the court, many of whom are not of Russian descent at all, but derived from foreign parvenus, and some of the upper classes, the nation still regrets the innovation of western civilization, and, if they could have a free choice, they would rather return to the good old times when Moscow was the capital of their country. The old Russian party, whose strength is centred in that ancient capital, are daily becoming more powerful, and may indeed be destined to cause a reaction against the artificial refinement which has polished a certain portion at the expense of the community at large. Perhaps it is possible to dam up the waters of the Volga for a time, but they would inevitably break their bounds, and find the way to the sea at last, through their own natural course.

The republic of Novogorod* must have existed for many ages, and had attained a considerable advance in commerce, and consequently civilization; for, towards the middle of the ninth century, we are told that it declined, and, being attacked by enemies from without, and weakened by dissensions within, the inhabitants, who could no longer defend themselves, were obliged to apply to Rurick, the chief of a race residing on the shores of the Baltic Sea, to become their general, and to assist them with his soldiers; and, just as we see in our own history that Hengist, Horsa, and Cerdic established themselves as princes on the shores of Britain, so did Rurick, and his two

* The city of Novogorod alone, it is said, contained four hundred thousand inhabitants.

brothers, Sinaf and Trouvor, become the sovereigns of Novogorod, and the immense territories belonging to the republic ; thus laying the foundation of the Russian empire, A.D. 862.

Rurick died in 879, and left a son only four years of age.

The best historians say that the Slaves are not the same race as the Russians, but that the former assumed the name of their conquerors ; the origin of both is so obscured by the mists of time, that the learned alone can decide upon the validity of their claims. According to Herbelot, who quotes the Tartar historian, Aboulgasi Baïadour, the Russians trace their descent through a long line of ancestors to Rouss, a son of Japhet, whilst the Slaves claim to be derived from Seklab, or Saklab, another son of the same remote progenitor.

I have heard the Russians frequently assert that they derived their name from the colour of their hair, which is of a peculiar yellow tint that I do not think is met with in other countries ; indeed, those of the true Russian race, in many of the villages, have hair of a light straw-colour.

Even so early as the ninth century, and probably long previous to that date, the Novogorodians had much commercial intercourse with the Greeks of Constantinople. We are told that, in their voyages thither, they descended the Dnieper ; that, on coming to rocks, they lightened the weight of their ships by discharging the cargoes, and carrying them on men's shoulders along the shores ; they re-embarked when the danger was passed. On reaching the mouth of the Dnieper, they waited for a fair wind, and then coasted along the western shores of the Black Sea, until they came to the Greek capital, which, in their language, was designated Tzargrad, or the City of the Cæsars.

Oleg, the guardian of Rurick's son, is said to have made a successful attack on Constantinople, and committed fearful ravages in its vicinity. Leo the Philosopher was then Emperor of the East, and, being too enervated to defend his capital by arms, he purchased the forbearance of the Russians by the payment of immense treasures and costly stuffs, the display of which, on their return home, struck their fellow-countrymen with astonishment. Perhaps that event was the origin of the restless longing and excessive desire of the Russian people to become the conquerors and possessors of Constantinople; for it is curious to remark how, ever since that time, they have, generation after generation, kept their eyes steadfastly fixed on the south, and have slowly advanced towards the attainment of their object. Treaties of peace and commerce are still, according to the historian, extant, which were made between some of the Greek emperors and the early princes of Novogorod.

Olga, who reigned as regent over the Russians from 945 to 955 A.D., was thought worthy of being canonized by the Russo-Greek Church, because she went to Constantinople and became baptised as a Christian; but religion does not appear to have been the sole object of her journey: like a true Muscovite, she had other designs hidden under its cloak, for we are expressly told that commercial views as well as pious ones induced her to go to the Greek capital. Constantine stood as sponsor at her baptism. The revenge this princess took on the Drevlians, a people who dwelt near the lake of Ilmen, was certainly anything but saintlike. Olga's husband, Igor, having invaded their country, was slain by them: the widow, after having caused the members of the two embassies, sent to her by their king, to be murdered, would not be appeased unless she took still greater vengeance on the nation: to do so, she dissimulated her hatred, spoke fairly to them, and expressed her willingness to forget what had passed, on condition that, for every house in their town, they should present her with three pigeons and three sparrows. The deceived Drevlians joyfully agreed to terms ; they brought the birds and then returned home ; but Olga caused lighted matches to be attached to them, and then let them go ; they naturally flew back to their nests, and thus set the city on fire. The inhabitants, in endeavouring to save themselves from the flames, were put to the sword. Yet, before the portrait of this cruel and wicked woman, the Russians of all classes bow and prostrate themselves to the earth, and beg her intercession for them at the throne of Heaven.

Alexander Nevski, the description of whose tomb has been given in these pages, reigned in Russia from about the year 1255 to 1264 A.D. The Russian Church has also thought proper to consider him as a saint, for no other quality, one would think, than that of his savage cruelty. His odious barbarities exercised on the inhabitants of Novogorod, after their struggle to resist their Tartar tyrants, must render his name hateful to any but Russian ears. He cut off the noses of some, the ears of others ; ordered their eyes to be pulled out, their feet and hands chopped off ; and committed all the actions of cruelty and wickedness he could think of in respect to them. Yet this wretch is revered and adored as if he had been a true benefactor to the human race.

In noticing the Nevsky monastery I forgot to mention that it was founded by Peter the Great near the spot where he had vanquished the Swedes, and he caused his relics to be transported thither: the costly tomb was erected by the Empress Elizabeth.

Perhaps Peter saw in Alexander Nevsky's conduct much resemblance to his own, and wished to increase his own power over his people by holding up to their adoration a Czar similar to himself in his actions.

Dmitri, surnamed by Russian historians "the False," was, according to them, the Perkin Warbeck of Muscovite history. They affirm that his real name was Jachko (or in English James) Otrepief; that he was brought up in a monastery, and assumed the habit of a novice at the age of fourteen. He himself asserted that he was son of Ivan the Terrible, or Cruel, and the legitimate heir to the crown. His history, which is perhaps the most interesting one in the Muscovite annals, is too long to be inserted here, but, after having obtained the protection of Sigismund and the Diet of Poland in 1603, he at last ascended the throne of Muscovy. There are many circumstances that would lead us to conclude that Dmitri V. was no impostor. Chuiski, his successor, aimed at the imperial crown, and, having murdered the Czar, it was to his interest, and to that of *his* successors, to proclaim that Dmitri was the false heir, lest he might have left one to inherit his title. Was it not also to the interest of Michael Romanof, the founder of the present dynasty, still to keep up the belief?

Michael Romanof, the ancestor of the present Czar, was the son of a Boyar, or Muscovite noble, named Phedor Nikititch. He was not a *prince*, or of *Russian* descent; but they say his forefather was a Prussian named Andrew, who emigrated to Russia towards the end of the fourteenth century. He was elected Czar in 1613.—*Levesque, from a MS. on the imperial family.*

Siberia was conquered by Yermak, an Ataman or Hetman of

the Don Cossacks, between the years 1577 and 1580, and by him secured to the Czar Ivan IV. Yermak was drowned in the Vagai, one of the tributary streams of the Irtish, 1583.

The Samoïdes, or Samoyedes, are a race of people inhabiting a wild marshy country in the extreme north of Siberia, its shores being washed by the Frozen Ocean. The word Samoïde, Samoïede, or Samoïade, means a cannibal according to most authors, but it does not appear that they merit such an appellation : they pay a tribute of skins yearly to the Czar, but, like most of the nomads of Siberia, they *govern* themselves.

The custom mentioned in the fourteenth chapter regarding the offering of bread, &c., made to the Church after a funeral, is apparently derived from Shamanism, for it is also a rite performed by those who profess that religion, and also on the fortieth day. Shamanism is still professed by immense numbers of the nomads, although its doctrines are now much corrupted : it was formerly an universal belief, even so far west of the Ural mountains as Jaroslaf.

The Russian language is one of the richest and most beautiful in the world : it is soft and agreeable in sound, and has not the defect of the Italian in being too effeminate ; it contains many words that express the same ideas. If ever a Sclavonic Milton or Shakspeare arise, he will find an inexhaustible treasure in his native tongue wherewith to express his thoughts, but at present there is scarcely any national literature, owing to the deadening influence of the government. The principal Russian authors are Poushkin the poet, Karamsin the historian, and

Kriloff the writer of fables. In the alphabet there are thirty-six letters, of which a great number are vowels : many of them are purely Greek characters. A friend who understood the classic tongues assured me that a great similitude existed between Russ and Greek ; the resemblance to Erse remarked by my Highland acquaintances has already been mentioned.

The words which appear to be spelled with so many consonants merely contain letters of which we have not the equivalent,—such as shtch, cz, tch, which are each expressed in Russian by a single character.

In the preceding pages, whenever Russian words occur, the true orthography has not been given, but they are written according to the sound as nearly as possible.

THE END

IX.

ORIGINAL WORK BY N. P. WILLIS.

LETTERS FROM IDLEWILD. 1 vol., 12mo., cloth, illustrated. $1 25.

X.

MELBOURNE AND THE CHINCHA ISLANDS. With Sketches of Lima, &c. By G. W. PECK. 1 vol., 12mo. $1.

XI.

CRYSTALLINE; OR, THE HEIRESS OF FALL DOWN CASTLE. A Romance. By F. W. SHELTON, A.M., author of "Salander," "Rector of St. Bardolph's," &c. 1 vol., 12mo. 88 cents.

XII.

MYRTLE WREATH; OR, STRAY LEAVES CALLED HOME. By MINNIE MYRTLE. 1 vol., 12mo., with illustrations. $1 25.

XIV.

LIFE OF ARCHIBALD ALEXANDER, D.D. By the Rev. J. W. ALEXANDER, D.D. 1 vol., 8vo., with portrait. $2 50; half calf $3 50; morocco extra $5 00.

XV.

ALEXANDER'S (Rev. J. W.) CONSOLATION. A new edition in one volume, 12mo. Price reduced to $1 25.

XVI.

SEVENTH THOUSAND.

A COMPLETE ANALYSIS OF THE HOLY BIBLE. Containining the whole of the Old and New Testaments, collected and arranged systematically in Thirty Books (based on the Work of the learned Talbot), together with an Introduction, setting forth the character of the work and the immense facility this method affords for understanding the Word of God. Also, three different Tables of Contents prefixed, and a General Index subjoined, so elaborated, and arranged in alphabetical order, as to direct at once to any subject required. By Rev. NATHANIEL WEST, D.D. 1 vol., royal 8vo., about 1,100 pages. $5 00; half calf $6 50; morocco extra $10 00.

XVII.

HISTORY OF THE APOSTOLIC CHURCH. By Rev. PHILIP SCHAFF, D.D. 1 vol., 8vo. $3 00.

NEW JUVENILES, ELEGANTLY ILLUSTRATED.

I.

OLD KARL THE COOPER, AND HIS WONDERFUL BOOK. By ELBERT PERCE. 1 vol., 16mo., with 9 engravings.

II.

BY MRS. L. C. TUTHILL.

BEAUTIFUL BERTHA. 1 vol., 16mo., uniform with "Tip-Top," &c.

III.

THE PLUM WOMAN: OR, THE CHILD WITH THREE MOTHERS. By GUSTAV NIERITZ. 1 vol., 16mo., illustrated. 50 cents.

IV.

THE RAT CATCHER. By GUSTAV NIERITZ. 1 vol., 16mo., illustrated. 50 cents.

THE CZAR, HIS COURT AND PEOPLE.

INCLUDING A TOUR IN NORWAY AND SWEDEN.

BY JOHN S. MAXWELL.

A new and revised edition. 1 vol., 12mo., cloth. Price $1.

This work presents a fair and candid exposition of the condition of the Russian people as well as of the personal character and government of the Czar. It was written before the breaking out of the present war, which has directed the attention of the world, with renewed eagerness, towards the mighty empire of the North. The exposition which the writer then gave of the designs and policy of the Czar has been abundantly confirmed by the developments that have since taken place.

"A volume of uncommon excellence upon a region of the earth hitherto not much treated by Americans. Mr. Maxwell's diplomatic position gave him remarkable opportunities for observing men and things in Russia. His scholarship and sound judgment have given to these observations a shape which must secure high esteem for the book. It is full of information and exempt from every suspicion of tediousness or egotism. The picture of the noble Scandinavian countries, with which this volume opens, is fascinating to a degree for which we confess we were unprepared."—*Princeton Review.*

"The whole is exceedingly well written, and contains a mass of valuable information difficult to be found in any other work. Its merits in every respect ought to secure to this volume a place in every library."—*N. Y. Home Journal.*

THE FALL OF POLAND.

CONTAINING AN ANALYTICAL AND A PHILOSOPHICAL ACCOUNT OF THE CAUSES WHICH CONSPIRED IN THE RUIN OF THAT NATION; TOGETHER WITH A HISTORY OF THE COUNTRY FROM ITS ORIGIN.

BY L. C. SAXTON.

2 vols., 12mo., cloth, $2 50; sheep $2 63.

"The entire work is no hasty utterance of crude opinions, for the author has evidently fitted himself for the task he has undertaken, by a study of history generally, and particularly by a careful collation of all those writers that bear upon the subject.

"In order to be more complete, the various topics are arranged under different heads, as Religion, Government, Great Men, Civilization, Society, etc., thus enabling the student to refer directly to the subject which he may desire to see, and fitting it, with its appropriate index, to make a valuable work for the library."—*Newark Daily Advertiser.*

"The work abounds with thrilling incidents and vivid, not to say gorgeous descriptions, as well as in valuable historic detail."—*Albany Argus.*

"It is the product of great thought and research, and presents a complete and accurate view of the History, Government, Laws, Religion, Popular Character, Literature, and, in short, everything connected with Poland that can have an interest for the scholar or the statesman. The author writes with great vigor and clearness, and his work is constructed throughout upon the best principles of historical science. It is a solid, symmetrical, and glowing incorporation of all the great points of interest of one of the most interesting nations of modern times, and deserves to be placed among the enduring ornaments of American literature."—*Courier & Enquirer.*

FUN JOTTINGS;

OR, LAUGHS I HAVE TAKEN A PEN TO.

BY N. P. WILLIS.

1 vol., 12mo., cloth. Price $1 25.

"As a cordial to the animal spirits when drooping with care or flagging with excess of labor, this volume of 'Fun Jottings' bears the palm."—*N. Y. Independent.*

"The character of this book is sufficiently indicated by its title. It is not purely fancy or fact, but a mixture of both. It bears throughout the stamp of the author's peculiar genius."—*Puritan Recorder.*

"This book contains some inimitable sketches."—*Boston Olive Branch.*

A HEALTH TRIP TO THE TROPICS, ETC.

BY N. P. WILLIS.

1 vol., 12mo., cloth. Price $1 25.

This book contains Mr. Willis's recent travels to the tropics.

"Mr. Willis has exceeded *himself* in his descriptions of his trip to the delightful tropical regions—a most delicious repose steals over you as you read. You cannot imagine that he is an invalid, and if one yourself he soon makes you think that you are one no longer. His pictures of the Bermuda Islands are perfect, and there are mingled through them the most valuable facts, lessons and suggestions."—*Albany Spectator.*

"The facility with which Mr. Willis describes, enables him almost to persuade his hearers that they are travelling with him—seeing with his eyes and hearing with his ears—those who would like a trip to the tropics during one of the long cold evenings of the approaching winter, may enjoy that luxury cheaply by taking passage in this volume."—*Christian Intelligencer.*

LETTERS FROM IDLEWILD.

BY N. P. WILLIS.

1 vol., 12mo., cloth. Price $1 25.

"A simple weaving into language of the every-day circumstances of an invalid retirement in the Highlands of the Hudson, written in letters to the *Home Journal*, and it was expected that they would owe their interest to being plainly truthful, and to picturing exactly the life that formed itself around the new-comer to one particular portion of our country—its climate, its conveniencies, its accessibilities, and its moral and social atmosphere. As it is a neighborhood to which the sick are often sent by the physicians of New York, for the nearest mountain air, which is completely separated from the seaboard, the author has thought it might add a utility to his book to give his invalid experience with the rest. In this feature of it he has aimed to serve his fellow-sufferers."—*Extract from Preface.*

HURRY-GRAPHS;

OR, SKETCHES FROM FRESH IMPRESSIONS OF SCENERY, CELEBRITIES, AND SOCIETY.

BY N. P. WILLIS.

1 vol., 12mo., cloth. (3d edition.) Price $1 25.

"This volume is filled with illustrations of his admirable skill. * * * We might look in vain for more just and felicitous portraitures, than those which are dashed off as 'Hurry-graphs' almost on every page of this living picture gallery."—*N. Y. Tribune.*

"As a light essayist and clever paragraphist, Willis has few superiors, and these 'Hurry-graphs' will be read with avidity by all."—*Detroit Free Press.*

PENCILLINGS BY THE WAY.

BY N. P. WILLIS.

A new and revised edition. 1 vol., 12mo., cloth. Price $1 25.

"One of the freshest and most sparkling ever written by its popular author."—*Philadelphia Evening Bulletin.*

"This work is too well known to need description. It contains graphic and spirited descriptions of society and scenes in the Old World, and has probably obtained a popularity second to no book of travels ever published in America."—*Boston Journal.*

"These graphic descriptions of foreign scenery, society, and manners, have never been equalled."—*Weekly Eclectic.*

A SUMMER CRUISE IN THE MEDITERRANEAN,

ON BOARD OF AN AMERICAN FRIGATE.

BY N. P. WILLIS.

1 vol. 12mo., cloth. Price $1 25.

This volume describes, in a pleasant and glowing manner, a visit to one of the most interesting portions of the globe—a region exceeding all others in the memorials of art, in historical and poetical associations.

"To read this book, one enjoys almost the pleasures of an actual ramble with him."—*Poughkeepsie Telegraph.*

"The public will give a hearty welcome to this beautiful volume, in which will be recognized an old friend, greatly improved since last met. It was written by Willis when a young man, and in his richest and most fascinating style."—*Cincinnati Gazette.*

N. P. Willis's Complete Prose Works.

RURAL LETTERS,

AND OTHER RECORDS OF THOUGHTS AT LEISURE.

BY N. P. WILLIS.

Embracing "Letters from under a Bridge," "Open-Air Musings in the City," "Invalid Rambles in Germany," "Letters from Watering Places," &c., &c. 1 vol., 12mo., cloth. Fourth edition. Price $1 25.

This volume has won for the author a reputation as one of the most agreeable writers of light and gossiping literature in our country.

"There is scarcely a page in it which the reader will not remember, and turn to again with a fresh sense of delight. It bears the imprint of Nature in her purest and most joyous forms, and under her most cheering and inspiring influences."—*N. Y. Tribune.*

"There is more than one passage, too, in the volume, whose deep, and true, and richly uttered pathos brings the heart into the throat with a spontaneous throb."—*New York Independent.*

PEOPLE I HAVE MET;

OR, PICTURES OF SOCIETY AND PEOPLE OF MARK—DRAWN UNDER A THIN VEIL OF FICTION.

BY N. P. WILLIS.

1 vol., 12mo. Third edition, cloth. Price $1 25.

"This book embraces a great variety of personal and social sketches in the old world, and concludes with some thrilling reminiscences of distinguished ladies—including the belles of New York."—*Buffalo Republic.*

"These stories and sketches are very amusing. One needs not the open avowal of the preface, or even the hint of the title-page, to teach him that Mr. Willis has drawn from actual life. It would be impossible to feign anything so perfectly life-like."—*Sartain's Magazine.*

LIFE HERE AND THERE;

OR, SKETCHES OF SOCIETY AND ADVENTURES AT FAR-APART TIMES AND PLACES.

BY N. P. WILLIS.

1 vol., 12mo., cloth. Price $1 25.

"And sketches they are, too. They are well worth perusing; for so spiritedly and so definedly are they drawn, that the reader can fill them up at his own leisure, or enjoy them just as they are."—*New York Albion.*

"The characters are all drawn from life, however, and several of them are portraits, done with studied faithfulness, of celebrated women whom he had the opportunity to know; while the scenes of the different stories are minutely true to the manners of the countries and the style of society in which they are laid."—*Merchant's Magazine.*

RURAL HOMES:

SKETCHES OF HOUSES SUITED TO AMERICAN COUNTRY LIFE.

BY G. WHEELER.

With Original Designs, Plans, Estimates, &c. 1 vol., 12mo., cloth. Price $1 25. (6th thousand.)

There is room for vast improvement in the construction of farm and village houses without adding to their expense. This work gives details upon every point which the builder needs to be informed about—the selection of a site, the choice and management of materials, and the best means of reconciling economy with comfort and taste. It is amply illustrated, and furnished with estimates carefully made.

"It is extremely practical, containing such simple and comprehensive directions for all wishing at any time to build, being, in fact, the sum of the author's study and experience as an architect for many years."—*Albany Spectator.*

"Mr. Wheeler's remarks convey much practical and useful information, evince much taste, and a proper appreciation of the beautiful, and no one should build a rural home without first hearing what he has to recommend."—*Philadelphia Presbyterian.*

THE FRUIT GARDEN.

BY P. BARRY.

OF THE MOUNT HOPE NURSERIES, ROCHESTER, NEW YORK.

A Treatise intended to Illustrate and Explain the Physiology of Fruit Trees; the Theory and Practice of all Operations connected with the Propagation, Transplanting, Pruning, and Training of Orchard and Garden Trees, as Standards, Dwarfs, Pyramids, Espaliers, &c.; the Laying Out and Arranging of different kinds of Orchards and Gardens; the Selection of Suitable Varieties for Different Purposes and Localities; Gathering and Preserving Fruits; Treatment of Disease; Destruction of Insects; Descriptions and uses of Implements, &c., Illustrated with upwards of 150 Figures, representing the Different Parts of Trees, all Practical Operations, Forms of Trees, Designs for Plantations, Implements, &c. 1 vol., 12mo., cloth. Price $1 25. (10th thousand.)

"It is one of the most thorough works of the kind we have ever seen, dealing in particulars as well as generalities, and imparting many valuable hints relative to soil, manures, pruning, and transplanting."—*Boston Gazette.*

"A mass of useful information is collected, which will give the work a value even to those who possess the best works on the cultivation of fruit yet published."—*Evening Post.*

"His work is one of the completest and, as we have every reason for believing, most accurate to be obtained on the subject."—*N. Y. Evangelist.*

Conybeare and Howson's St. Paul.

AMERICAN EDITION, UNABRIDGED.

THE LIFE AND EPISTLES OF ST. PAUL.

BY REV. W. J. CONYBEARE AND REV. J. S. HOWSON,

2 vols., 8vo., With Colored Maps and many Elegant Illustrations
Price $6 00.

The publisher, in presenting the "Life and Epistles of St. Paul," by the Rev. W. J. Conybeare and the Rev. J. S. Howson, needs no apology. During the short interval since its publication in England, it has commanded the admiration of scholars and intelligent readers of the Bible, both in this country and Europe, and has passed through the ordeal of criticism in the leading Quarterlies and journals of both countries, and received the highest commendation. The expense of the English edition, however, is such as necessarily to limit its circulation in this country, and the desire has been repeatedly expressed that the work should be published in a form and at a price which would bring it within the reach of ministers, students, and intelligent readers generally. The present edition, it is believed, will meet the existing want. Though offered at one-half of the cost of the London copy, the work has in no way suffered from abridgment, but has *been preserved complete in every respect.* The notes, coins, maps, plans, and wood engravings generally have been retained, and yet the size of the work has been reduced from the unwieldy quarto to a convenient octavo form.

The steel engravings, which appear in the English edition simply as embellishments, which are familiar to most readers, and which are in no way essential to the text or to the value of the work, have been omitted—since the expense of reproducing them here would be such as greatly to increase the cost of the work, and yet add nothing to its usefulness.

The *North British Review of February*, 1854, after a highly commendatory criticism of this work, makes the following remarks: "We commend the book to that numerous class, increasing every day, whose early culture has necessarily been defective, but whose intelligence and thirst for knowledge is continually sharpened by the general diffusion of thought and education. Such persons, if they are already Christians by conviction, are naturally more and more dissatisfied with the popular commentaries on the Bible; and if they are skeptical and irreligious, this great evil is probably caused by the undeniable existence of difficulties which such commentaries shrink from fairly meeting. They will find in the work before us a valuable help towards understanding the New Testament. The Greek and Latin quotations are almost entirely confined to the notes; any unlearned reader may study the text with ease and profit. And it is from a sense of the great value of the book in this respect, that we would earnestly entreat the publishers to supply it in a cheaper and more convenient form. In these days a quarto book except for reference, is a monster, *feræ naturæ*."

"We consider this republication by far the most important contribution which the press of our country has made for many years, to the cause of sacred learning. * * * We wish Mr. Scribner might *sell a copy to every clergyman and half the laymen in the land.*"—*The Congregationalist.*

www.ingramcontent.com/pod-product-compliance
Lightning Source LLC
LaVergne TN
LVHW020213110826
845151LV00003B/696

* 9 7 8 1 4 2 5 5 3 3 8 7 8 *